PHILADELPHIA BUILDS

PHILADELPHIA
BUILDS
Essays on Architecture

Michael J. Lewis

PAUL DRY BOOKS
Philadelphia   2021

On the cover: "Skyscrapers of Philadelphia," 1898. The numbered buildings are: 1. Real Estate Trust Co.; 2. Betz Building; 3. Drexel Building; 4. Provident Building; 5. Girard Trust Co.; 6. Hotel Walton; 7. Odd Fellows' Temple; 8. Aldine Hotel; 9. Independence Hall; 10. Masonic Temple; 11. Stephen Girard Building; 12. Penn Mutual Building; 13. Witherspoon Building; 14. Crozer Building; 15. Land Title and Trust Co.; 16. Fidelity Life Building; 17. Harrison Building; 18. Heed Building.

First Paul Dry Books Edition, 2021

Paul Dry Books, Inc.
Philadelphia, Pennsylvania
www.pauldrybooks.com

Printed in the United States of America

ISBN 978-1-58988-152-5

Library of Congress Control Number: 2021933125

Contents

For my dear friends Ralph & Valerie,
with thanks for 1001 Tuesdays

Author's Note

I have been writing about the architecture of Philadelphia for 35 years, intermittently rather than systematically, and as a pleasant distraction from whatever more pressing work was at hand. The essays and reviews in *Philadelphia Builds* first appeared in a variety of publications, some quite hard to find, including a Scottish newsletter and a French exhibition catalogue. I had no thought of collecting them until a friend of my publisher suggested that they would make for a readable anthology.

The prospect of publishing a new book that will require no work whatsoever is so tempting that authors always believe it is possible. It is not. Every piece in this collection needed substantial revision and updating; some I have rewritten beyond recognition. In part this is due to friendly correspondents who wrote to point out errors in the original publications and to contribute new information. But mostly it is due to newly digitized sources, especially historical American newspapers, which have brought forth information that a century in the archives would not have revealed. The essays on George Senneff and E. F. Durang, which are new here, could not have been written a few years ago.

A word about the tone of these essays. I write about my native city in a spirit of love, exasperation, and (if only for self-preservation) irony. I believe that architecture, like every human activity, is the stuff of tragedy and comedy—especially so in Philadelphia.

If her founding ideals were not so lofty, her failings would not be so woeful.

Philadelphia Builds is an episodic rather than a comprehensive history of Philadelphia architecture. Had I set out to produce a more complete account, I would have written about Wilson Eyre, Paul Cret, and George Howe, and not such one-hit wonders as Senneff and the unhappy P. A. Nicholson. But even if I had chosen a completely different set of architects and buildings to write about, the resulting portrait of Philadelphia would not differ significantly from that painted here.

Finally, these essays remain stand-alone pieces, which can be read independently and in any order. The author occasionally repeats himself, but then so does Philadelphia.

PHILADELPHIA BUILDS

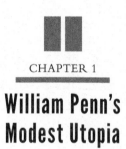

CHAPTER 1

William Penn's Modest Utopia

■ PHILADELPHIA, the only major city in the world founded and designed by Quakers, lies at the meeting point of the Italian Renaissance and the Protestant Reformation (fig. 1.1).[1] From the Renaissance comes its geometric regularity and its strictly gridded plan; from the Reformation comes its radical Protestantism and social egalitarianism. The result is a plan of extraordinary formal order but virtually without spatial hierarchy. Other American cities likewise modified Renaissance urbanism to serve Protestant colonies—New Haven or Savannah, for example— but never with the extreme, virtually Cartesian, egalitarianism of Philadelphia.[2]

Quakers (properly known as the Religious Society of Friends) originated in England during the 1640s as a dissenting Protestant denomination. Rejecting formal ritual and ceremony, they worship in silence, the better to hear God's "still small voice." But once inspired by that voice, they could stand up and speak to the gathering. They did this (and still do) in plain, sturdy meet-

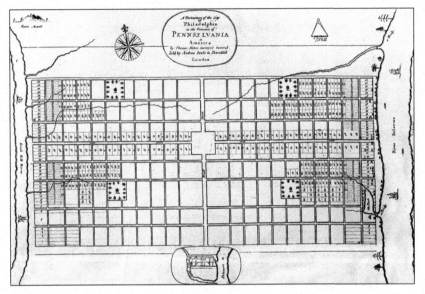

FIGURE 1.1 Philadelphia is invariably taken to be a regularly gridded city. In fact it is not a true grid at all; in his plan of 1683, Thomas Holme freely adjusted the spacing of streets and squares to make allowances for local topography.

ing houses with neither altar nor pulpit. The spatial character was communal rather than hierarchical, with rows of benches facing one another, so that attention might focus on whomever was speaking at the moment. This avoidance of hierarchy marks the architectural character of Philadelphia, as does the general Quaker disdain for pomp and display, and such vanities as wigs and jewelry.

England's civil authorities frowned on Quakers because of their moral scruples against military service, slavery, and paying tithes, and regularly persecuted them. When in 1681 King Charles II of England granted land in North America to William Penn, to settle debts he had contracted with Penn's father, the younger Penn seized the opportunity to make the colony of Pennsylvania a refuge for the persecuted Friends, a kind of Quaker Utopia.[3] Its capital would be the new settlement of Philadelphia, which in Greek means the "city of brotherly love."

The same Quaker disdain for spatial hierarchy in the meetinghouse distinguishes the layout of Philadelphia itself. In 1682, Penn's surveyor Thomas Holme (1624–95) surveyed the site, a flat swath of land between the Delaware and Schuylkill rivers.[4] Holme's plan showed a taut grid of nine by twenty-three streets, spanning from river to river. Its principal north-south and east-west streets were broader than the others, like the *cardo* and *decumanus* of ancient Roman towns, and intersected in the center at a large open square. Four smaller squares were evenly spaced through the rest of the plan, creating a strikingly open quality. Direct inspiration for the plan seems to have come from Richard Newcourt's proposal for rebuilding London after the catastrophic fire of 1666 that destroyed the historic core of the city. Newcourt envisioned a uniform grid relieved by open public squares, regularly distributed in much the same fashion as in Holme's plan for Philadelphia. Of course, there cannot be an absolutely regular plan without an absolutely regular topography, and the slight variations in the placement of Philadelphia's streets seem to accommodate problems of drainage and elevation.

Penn was haunted by the memory of the great London fire, as he knew his fellow colonists would be, and he stressed that Philadelphia's open layout and lack of density would make it incombustible: "Let every house be placed, if the person pleases, in the middle of its plot as to the breadthway of it, that so there may be ground on each side for gardens or orchards or fields, that it may be a greene Country Towne, which will never be burnt, and always be wholesome."[5] Here was a premonition of the garden city movement of the early twentieth century, which frequently invoked the example of Penn's enlightened plan, if not its unvarying rectilinearity.

Because they do not need priests or ministers, Quakers do not need theological seminaries to train them. Unlike the Massachusetts Bay Colony and the Connecticut Colony, which founded Harvard and Yale to supply them with Puritan ministers, Pennsylvania lagged in the founding of a great university. Like Quakers in general, Penn was suspicious of learning for its own sake, and of speculative or theoretical education. "Much reading," said Penn, "is an oppression of the mind, and extinguishes the natural candle, which is the reason of so many senseless scholars in the world." Instead, he expected his colonists to be useful, and urged them to devote themselves to the practical trades: "I recommend the useful parts of mathematics, as building houses, or ships, measuring, surveying, dialing, navigation; but agriculture especially is my eye. Let my children be husbandmen and housewives."[6]

It was thoroughly in this practical spirit that Benjamin Franklin (1705–90) wrote a pamphlet in 1749 recommending the creation of a Public Academy of Philadelphia. Students were to be "taught every Thing that is useful, and every Thing that is ornamental"; theology was conspicuously absent from the curriculum.[7] Even the objects in the library were to be chosen with an eye toward their usefulness: "Maps of all Countries, Globes, some mathematical Instruments, and Apparatus for Experiments in Natural Philosophy, and for Mechanics; Prints, of all Kinds, Prospects, Buildings, Machines, &c."[8] When the University of Pennsylvania was created a year later, it was the first major American university to be founded without a divinity school.[9] With this legacy, it is easy to understand why Philadelphia's educational legacy has been less theoretical than empirical and pragmatic (it quickly excelled in medical education, for example, in which field it remains a leader today).

Philadelphia prospered rapidly, the population within its municipal boundaries reaching about 13,000 in 1740 and 28,522 in 1790; many more lived in the adjoining settlements, or liberties, immediately outside the bounds of Penn's grid (where functions such as tanneries, forbidden in the town proper, were allowed to flourish). Philadelphia's two rivers contributed to this speedy growth: the broad Delaware was a superb harbor for international trade while the lowly Schuylkill connected the city to Pennsylvania's resource-rich hinterlands, and its abundant supplies of iron and coal. The city soon became a manufacturing center, and an early producer of textiles and paper. Its swift growth, however, did not occur equally as Penn had intended, and early devel-

FIGURE 1.2 Peter Cooper's *Southeast Prospect of the City of Philadelphia,* dating from about 1720, is one of the first painted views of a North American city. It is the last moment of the distinctively Quaker settlement, and not a church spire is in sight.

opment huddled with near-medieval density along the Delaware River, where the city's economic life was based (fig. 1.2). The Quaker meeting house that was optimistically placed on Center Square was demolished by 1700. Instead the city grew incrementally from east to west, and did not completely fill in Penn's grid until the middle of the nineteenth century. But it did not stop there; because Penn's plan was more in the nature of a flexible principle than a resolved aesthetic unity, its grid was soon extended to the north, west, and south.

The city did not long remain Quaker. Shortly after the beginning of the eighteenth century, the original population was diluted by an influx of English Anglicans and German Lutherans and Mennonites, and by the 1720s the Quakers were a shrinking minority. Nonetheless, the city retained its Quaker attitudes toward building and display, and a distinctive local vernacular emerged, distinguished by an emphatic plainness. Buildings were of red brick with white wood trim and marble steps; ornamental accents were held to a minimum, and were usually restricted to a classical frontispiece around the entrance.[10] Architectural monumentality was generally avoided, so that mansions for the wealthy and houses for the working class differed primarily through size.

The tiny scale forced Philadelphians to build long and narrow houses, and to exploit every possible square foot of space. The result was the Philadelphia rowhouse, that perfected machine of miniature living, honed by years of adaptation into a standardized type: a living room to the front and a dining room behind, lighted by a single corner window where the rear kitchen wing tucked in. Where possible, in houses over 16 feet, a narrow side hall granted access to these rooms; smaller houses had no separate stair hall, and a winder stair was tucked into a corner. The smallest of the house types was the "trinity," so-called because it consisted of but three small rooms, measuring perhaps 12 by 12 feet, one on top of the other. One eighteenth-century street survives largely intact, Elfreth's Alley, to give an idea of Philadelphia's early density.

Philadelphia's civic buildings were not particularly monumental, and little more than a wooden cupola indicated their public function. The most pretentious were artifacts of English rule: the Anglican church, Christ Church (1727–44), and the colonial State House (1732–48). But for Benjamin Franklin, writing in 1733, it was not the buildings and regular streets that distinguished the city, but its collective civic spirit, which he would soon mobilize to form a public fire brigade:

> This little City, but esteem'd great of its Age, owes not more at this Day for its long Streets and fair Stories, to Architects of any kind, than to those worthy inhabitants, who have always started at the first Warning, to oppose and vanquish the Rage of Fire.[11]

Philadelphia's true monuments were its philanthropic and civic institutions, in which Philadelphia—animated by the lively Quaker humanitarian tradition—abounded. Among other institutions, the city produced America's first hospital, first asylum for the mentally ill, first public library, first public water works, and first penitentiary. In establishing these institutions, Philadelphians showed great initiative and enterprise, and Franklin was often involved; it was his ingenious idea to raise "matching funds," whereby the colonial assembly would match those funds raised privately, an innovation that permitted the building of Pennsylvania Hospital and that has become a staple of modern fundraising. Although these institutions were rooted in Quaker humanitarianism, they were secular rather than sectarian in character, in acknowledgment of the city's religiously diverse population. In more religiously homogenous colonies, such as Boston or New Haven, these charitable functions were carried out by the church—or not at all. Thus, paradoxically, because Pennsylvania was among the first colonies actively to promote religious tolerance, and had the most variegated tapestry of religious beliefs, it also had the richest secular civic life.

Where possible, Philadelphia's philanthropic institutions built themselves large and spacious buildings on open, well-treed sites near the periphery of the developed town: the one aspect of Penn's garden city thinking to be realized. Among the most impressive were the Pennsylvania Hospital (begun 1754) and the House of Employment and Almshouse (1766–67), those favorite subjects for early views of Philadelphia (fig. 1.3).

This philanthropic tradition continued into the nineteenth century, when a number of progressive public institutions were built along the suburban fringes of the expanding city, including Girard

A View of the House of Employment, Almshouse, Pennsylvania Hospital, & part of the City of Philadelphia

FIGURE 1.3   Philadelphia created three enlightened public institutions before the Revolution and all appear in *A View of the House of Employment, Almshouse, Pennsylvania Hospital and Part of the City of Philadelphia* (c. 1767), made by Nicholas Garrison and James Hulett. Only the hospital, considerably enlarged, remains on its site at Ninth and Pine streets.

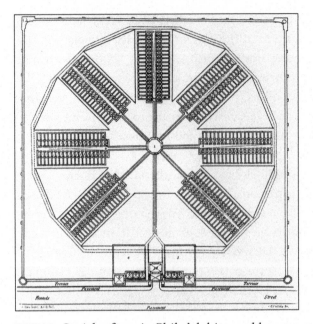

FIGURE 1.4 Social reform in Philadelphia would assume a crueler character—at least visually—in the utilitarian nineteenth century. John Haviland's Eastern State Penitentiary (1821–36), based on the panopticon principle, was the first American building to be widely studied in Europe.

College (1833–47),[12] Eastern State Penitentiary (1821–36),[13] and the Philadelphia Hospital for the Insane (1856–59).[14] All three had innovative, and explicitly rational, ground plans: a utilitarian grid of classrooms at the college, a panopticon at the penitentiary (fig. 1.4), and a series of staggered wings known as the Kirkbride Plan at the asylum. Such planning is schematic, the literal embodiment of an abstract mathematical principle in brick and stone. In all of these plans there is something of the Quaker meetinghouse itself, in which the architectural shell is incidental to the egalitarian communal space within. In early meetinghouses, the walls themselves were negotiable; partitions could be swung into place to divide the men's from the women's meeting, or to shrink the space for the small weekly meeting or expand it for the enormous yearly meeting (fig. 7.2).

This flexible spatial thinking lies behind Philadelphia's one distinctive contribution to the architecture of education: the school with moveable walls. In 1852 Samuel Sloan published the plans for a public schoolhouse (fig. 1.5) with sliding "glass partitions, which are so arranged . . . that the whole story may be thrown into one room, and thus the various divisions of the school may be taught separately or together, as desired."[15] One looks at Sloan's four-square plan, extending generously as needed, and sees the logic of the Quaker meetinghouse but also an image of Penn's plan for Philadelphia, an egalitarian and open-ended geometry of communal space.

With its culture of the meetinghouse, where anybody who heard the "small still voice" might rise and give voice, Philadelphia was the ideal neutral forum for the first great national debates, where the fervent Puritans of New England and Anglicans of Virginia could wrangle over the language of the Declaration of Independence and of the Constitution. Fittingly, for

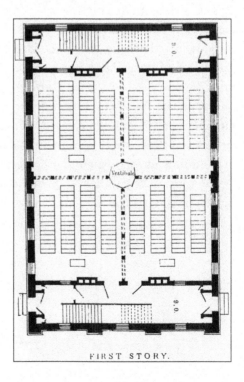

FIGURE 1.5 Samuel Sloan divided the classrooms of his Philadelphia schoolhouses with moveable partitions that could be folded away to create an assembly hall. He was inspired by the example of the Quaker meeting house, whose flexible space was free of both altar and pulpit, and could be expanded or contracted by partitions as needed.

a brief time in the 1790s, Philadelphia served as the capital of the United States but this was its last moment to command the national stage. Once the capital moved to Washington, D.C., in 1800, Philadelphia was overtaken in importance by other, more dynamic American cities. By the 1830s, New York was already richer and more populous. To some extent, Philadelphia's decline was ensured by the withdrawal of the city's Quaker minority from active involvement in public life, a process that occurred over the course of the eighteenth century. The key event was the French and Indian Wars in the 1750s: since participation in government meant involvement in military activities and raising taxes for the protection of the frontier, many Quakers chose a stance of quietism, permanently removing themselves from all political involvement. In the felicitous phrase of Franklin, they chose to pursue their principles rather than power.

Philadelphia presents a special case in the history of town planning. The grid plan thrived in the American colonies, as it has in all colonial societies since the time of the ancient Greeks, because it is a uniquely efficient and pragmatic way for measuring and partitioning the land. But Penn's egalitarian grid was a model of an ideal theological order even as it was part of a profit-making real estate venture—and these two motives cannot easily be separated. Such interlocking motives are not unique to Philadelphia but are characteristic of American culture in general, and are perhaps inevitable in a society whose roots lie simultaneously in religious utopianism and aggressive capitalist speculation. This is the tension at the heart of Philadelphia's poignant grid, which makes it one of the first and most eloquent creations of American culture.

CHAPTER 2

William Birch and the
Culture of Architecture
in Philadelphia

WHEN IN LATE 1798 William Birch began a set of engraved views provisionally called "Philadelphia Dissected: Or, the Metropolis of America," one of his first subjects was the Bank of the United States, the city's newest and most important public building (fig. 2.1).[1] He brought the project to a close two years later by once more drawing a bank, the Bank of Pennsylvania, that startling debut performance of Benjamin Henry Latrobe (fig. 2.2). This pair of financial bookends lent a pleasing symmetry to *The City of Philadelphia in 1800*, as Birch now called his book. Each was a stately rectangular block, prefaced by a colossal pedimented portico and, in what was a novelty in the city of brick, was faced with marble.

Yet considered purely as architecture, the two buildings could hardly be less alike. The Bank of the United States was a lovely paraphrase of the Maison Carrée at Nîmes but was affixed to a plain brick box as a frontispiece, a mask and not a face. Its ped-

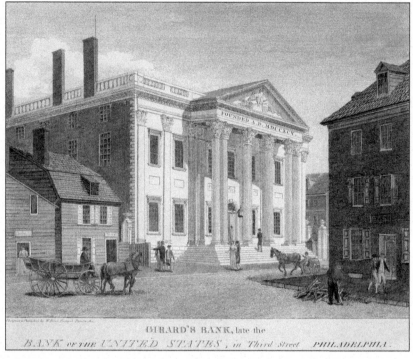

FIGURE 2.1   The First Bank of the United States, for all its monumental authority, shows the weakness of the bookish Palladian Revival. The "architecture" begins and ends with the marble facade, which is like a book illustration pasted on a brick cube.

iment had nothing to do with the actual roof of the building behind. The Bank of Pennsylvania, by contrast, was a resolved formal unity in which image, space, and construction were finely coordinated. Its central domed block performed three distinct functions with one shape that was simultaneously the building's principal space, principal structural unit, and principal visual element. And the pediment, far from being a frontispiece, was the extension of the roof itself. Only two years apart, these two banks represent two entirely different systems of thought, one advancing and one withdrawing. Birch may have set out to memorialize the architectural culture of eighteenth-century Philadelphia but he inadvertently wrote its eulogy.

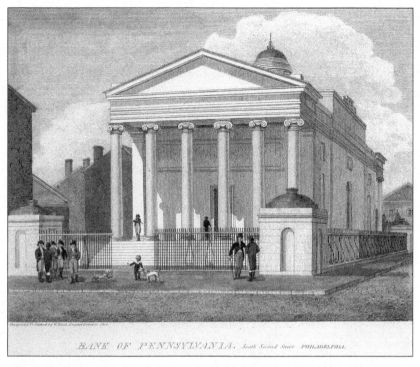

BANK OF PENNSYLVANIA, *South Second Street* *PHILADELPHIA.*

FIGURE 2.2 Latrobe, Philadelphia's first architect who could compose imaginatively in space, and his brilliant Bank of Pennsylvania.

The Philadelphia that Birch first saw in 1794 was in the process of swift and convulsive change, but especially in architecture. There arrived during the decade an entirely new cast of flitting nervous figures—architects and pseudo-architects hungry for public work—who crossed the stage so quickly that they scarcely left a trail. One cannot study their works; as with a hummingbird, we only know their velocity by the pitch of their movement. The few figures of consequence—Pierre Charles L'Enfant, William Thornton, James Hoban, Stephen Hallet—left their mark offstage, in Washington, and only a few morsels in Philadelphia, which has made them difficult to grasp. If the city of the eighteenth century has been studied in depth (one thinks of such pioneering studies as Charles E. Peterson's *Robert Smith* and George Tatum's *Philadelphia Georgian*), as has that of the early nineteenth (e.g., the indispensable *Papers of Benjamin Henry Latrobe*), the transitional decade in between has not yet received its illuminating study.[2] And yet this was the moment when Philadelphia, during its brief stint as the national capital, can be said to have discovered architecture.

To be sure, the public had always been concerned with architecture but in the utilitarian sense; it had a lively curiosity about individual buildings as commodities, or as markers of worldly achievement. But Philadelphia had shown little interest in architecture in the comprehensive sense, as a professional practice that joined art, science, and business. This changed around 1790 and the signs are everywhere: the sudden rise of private academies of architecture, the first exhibition of architects' drawings, the first signs of critical public discussion, a newfound demand for prints and views of buildings, but most of all an explosion in the variety and complexity of buildings that clients sought to build. In short, a city with a vigorous and durable building culture now developed an architectural culture.

Usually when we speak of culture, we mean the overall ambience and flavor of a particular historical social milieu. This ambience, as sociology tells us, has three constituent parts. First, there are regular patterns of meaningful behavior, which we call institutions. Second, there are values—the vocabularies, sentiments, images of self and others, and the worldviews that articulate those institutions. And, finally, there is the interlocking of those institutions to form social structures. We might summarize these components of culture as institutions, ideas, and behavior. All worthwhile social analysis begins with these components, and seeks to bring into common focus all the transactions and patterns of meaningful behavior—individual biographies, building histories, social forms, institutional history—that constitute culture. Translated into terms of architecture, the most important pattern of behavior is patronage, the process by which clients formulate their needs and select architects to realize them. The values expressed in those processes are variously social, mercantile, and intellectual, and run the gamut from good taste, respectability, and sophistication to the more restless values of ambition and swagger. And, finally, the social structures consist of all those formal and informal, organized or loosely affiliated, bodies involved in building, from building committees to builders' guilds (there would be no formal professional society of architects in Philadelphia until 1861).

Considered this way, every aspect of architectural culture displays a new sense of urgency and energy in the years after 1790. Traditionally, throughout the eighteenth century, Philadelphia's houses and public buildings were made according to vernacular building practice by builder-architects. It is perhaps surprising that in a city built of brick the leading builders should be carpenters. But carpenters found it easiest to coordinate the various building trades, including painters, plasterers, and glaziers. They were the ones responsible for the framing of the floor and raising of the roof truss, the decisive operations in the making of a house, while bricklayers might make their contributions in piecemeal fashion. Their principal institution was the Carpenters' Company, founded sometime in the early eighteenth century (its origins are unclear and we use the date 1724 out of convenience). A protective trade organization, like the medieval guilds from which it was descended, its purpose was to regulate prices, provide for indigent members and their families, and, like any cartel, to restrict entry into the trade.[3]

The members of the Carpenters' Company drew the plans for virtually all of the city's important buildings, but they did not design them in the modern sense, as an original artistic conception, either as a spatial essay or as the expression of a formal idea. Design was not a matter of free personal invention but of choosing a suitable model and adapting it to site and materials—as when Samuel Rhoads adapted the model of William Adam's Royal Infirmary in Edinburgh in 1754 for Pennsylvania Hospital. Palladio's *Four Books of Architecture* and the pattern books that followed in its wake offered a highly adaptable normative language that could be applied to buildings of any size or character. Robert Smith, the most successful of Philadelphia's builder-architects, was able to inflect the Palladian formula to serve his Zion Lutheran Church, his Walnut Street Jail, and his building for the

Carpenters' Company (which Birch did not engrave, a curious omission, perhaps because its crowded site was not suitable for the urban tableaux he favored).[4] Palladianism lent itself easily to use by gentlemen-amateur architects, such as William Thornton, who designed the Library Company after he "got some books and worked a few days," or Samuel Blodgett, to whom the Bank of the United States is traditionally assigned.[5] And so while the Palladian system was pliable enough to solve any building type or situation, it was also sufficiently of a piece to give the city a deep and satisfying sense of visual coherence.

Only for a building of a higher order of complexity would a European professional be summoned. English architects were responsible for the Chestnut Street Theater, a specialized building type in which acoustics figured, and the William Bingham House (1788), the finest house in the city (fig. 2.3).[6] In these cases, the English architect worked at a distance, sending his drawings—as John Plaw did for William Bingham—or in the case of the Chestnut Street Theater, a wooden model. But such long-distance design was a luxury in time and money, and so such stalwarts of the Carpenters' Company as Smith, Thomas Nevell, and William Williams divided up among themselves the plum commissions of the eighteenth-century city.

This is the building culture that began to change after 1790, largely as a consequence of Philadelphia's new status as the national capital. If the public became preoccupied by architecture, it was because the federal government was as well, one of its first duties being the design and construction of the District of Columbia. This was the country's first coordinated ensemble of public architecture and it was only natural that the public that was paying for it should be interested, and that its reverberations eventually made themselves felt in more humble buildings. All this increased the velocity of architectural ideas, as did the appearance of hopeful architects in Philadelphia, hungry (figuratively and literally) for work.

The modern definition holds that a professional architect is one formally trained who makes his living by the design of build-

View in *THIRD STREET*, *from Spruce Street* *PHILADELPHIA.*

FIGURE 2.3 When Bingham's house (1786–88) introduced stylish London neoclassicism to Philadelphia, its mid-Georgian neighbors began to look stiff and heavy. One was the house of Samuel Powel (the uncle of Bingham's wife), just to the right, and still standing on South Third Street.

ings, and not their construction. By this definition, Philadelphia had no true architects until the end of the eighteenth century. Although Benjamin Henry Latrobe is acknowledged as the first, strictly speaking he was merely the first to be successful, for every year seemed to bring one or two aspirants. Étienne Sulpice Hallet arrived in Philadelphia in 1790, having trained in Paris, and promptly anglicized his name as Stephen Hallet. In 1794 there arrived Joseph Bowes, who announced his intention to follow "the business of Architecture in all its departments."[7] In 1795 there followed Christopher Myers, offering "plans and elevations for houses from the simplest to the most suberb [sic]."[8] And in 1797, Christopher Minifee sailed into Philadelphia, where he offered plans for mansions and public buildings, rather alarmingly, "on the shortest notice possible."[9]

Others followed Hallet's lead, including Claudius Falize and Pierre Lacour, who billed themselves as "Architects from Paris."[10] If they were indeed from Paris, they came indirectly, cast off by the revolution in France or its sequel in Haiti. Lacour had been in New York, where he made the drawing for Pierre Charles L'Enfant's Federal Hall (fig. 2.4). And Falize seems to have been in Haiti, and evidently fled the slave uprising of 1791. No buildings are known by them, and they might not have had time to design any: they opened a drawing academy on South Third Street where they taught from nine until seven (with a two-hour lunch break). Despite their billing, they do not sound like architects. Falize seems to have been a surveyor, whose talent lay in drawing "the views of countries and gentlemen's estates, in water colours and thick kinds—takes copies of draughts, geographic, topographic and charts, and pastes them on linen."[11]

But William Birch himself showed that there was no need for professional architectural training if one had advanced technical expertise in a related field, such as painting and print-making. He belonged to that class of semi-professional architects who could make an intelligent and graceful plan for a house, as he showed with Springfield, his own country house, and Montebello, his house for General Samuel Smith just outside Baltimore. Besides art, one might come to architecture by way of surveying, landscape gardening, or military engineering, as L'Enfant did. Besides laying out the plan of the new city of Washington, D.C.—the kind of topographic study for which an engineer ought to be qualified—he was also capable of designing a building as complex as the Robert Morris house (fig. 2.5), a house of unusual voluptuousness and plastic richness. The failure of Morris that led to the abandonment of the house has unfairly suggested that the house was an aesthetic failure, a prejudice that Latrobe's abuse of the design did much to bolster—as did Birch's own view, which shows the building as a picturesque folly, veiled by trees and derided by gawkers.

View of the FEDERAL EDIFICE in NEW YORK.

FIGURE 2.4 Before he made the plan of Washington, D.C., Pierre Charles L'Enfant remodeled New York's Federal Hall where George Washington was inaugurated in 1798. And yet virtually nothing is known of his architectural work in Philadelphia, where he spent most of the 1790s, with the exception of the hapless Robert Morris house.

An UNFINISHED HOUSE, in Chesnut Street PHILADELPHIA.

FIGURE 2.5 Moreau de Saint-Méry, the French historian, was not impressed by the house of Robert Morris: "Never can marble columns . . . beautify the gloom of a brick structure." For Philadelphians proud of their humility, Morris's ill-fated house was a reassuring reminder that excessive pride is always punished.

THIS RAUCOUS JUMBLE of real architects and pseudo-architects, builder-architects and gentleman-architects, could align in surprising ways. Gentleman-amateurs happily made common cause with contractor-builders, with whom their relationship was benignly symbiotic. Having no intellectual pretensions to be creators of original form, builders worked freely with amateurs such as William Thornton or John Dorsey, the prolific designer of the original Pennsylvania Academy of the Fine Arts, built a few years too late, alas, to be included among Birch's views (fig. 7.4). Dorsey's builder was Owen Biddle, who was capable of designing a building as substantial as the Arch Street Meeting House, but who had no personal ambition to be regarded as a designer.

Together, these professionals and pseudo-professionals account for the new vibrancy that flared across the buildings of Philadelphia in the 1790s. They brought with them a living knowledge of the newest currents of architectural thought, particularly the new doctrine of the picturesque. This was the moment when the English landscape designer Humphrey Repton was winning fame with his doctrine of grasping the essence of a landscape intuitively, at the first encounter, after which he would immediately prepare his designs while the impression was still fresh. This seems to have been what Christopher Myers was getting at in his advertisement where he spoke of "producing decorative or picturesque effect in domains, pleasure grounds, and chases, sketching the ideas of gentlemen on the spot, so as to collect the aim of their intentions, and make them subservient to the rules of practice."[12]

Unfortunately, in no case can we definitely assign a building to Myers, or to any of his contemporaries. Such neoclassical gems as Henry Pratt's Lemon Hill (1800) or that prodigy of excess, Cooke's Building (1794), remain authorless (fig. 2.14). In only one instance does an immigrant appear to have been given a substantial job: Joseph Bowes may well have designed the octagonal workhouse that was added to the rear of the Walnut Street prison in 1795, for he made the drawing that was published in the *Philadelphia Monthly Magazine* (fig. 2.6).[13] Perhaps the unproven émigrés were not allowed a chance to prove themselves, the most lucrative buildings remaining in the hands of local builder-architects, as at Pennsylvania Hospital, where the crucial central block was assigned to Carpenters' Company elder David Evans in 1796.

The growing numbers of immigrant professionals put the city's carpenter-builders at a competitive disadvantage. At the same time, their newly arrived and friendless competitors had need of immediate employment. This convergence of interests must account for the rash of short-lived architectural academies that flourished in the 1790s.[14] Two opened in 1794 alone: Falize and Lacour's "academy of Drawing," and Joseph Bowes's evening class in "drawing in architecture, landscape &c."[15] In 1796/1797

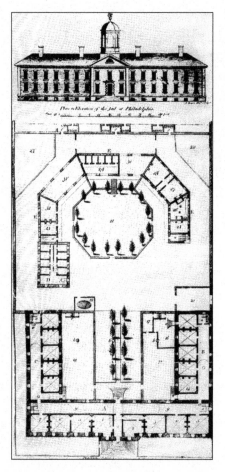

FIGURE 2.6   Philadelphia's new Penitentiary House of 1790 was a revolution in the treatment of prisoners, providing them with decent food, clean clothes, and productive paid labor. It was built directly behind Robert Smith's massive 1773 Walnut Street Jail (shown at bottom), with its brutalizing 20 by 18 foot group wards.

and again in 1797/1798, Stephen Hallet conducted an "Evening School of Architecture."[16] In 1797 there also opened Christopher Minifee's "architectural evening drawing school . . . in which will be taught, the rudiments of the art, on the most modern and improved system, as obtained under the first London masters."[17]

Most of these schools aspired to teach drawing—and not comprehensive programs in architecture—for accurate and expressive rendering was the primary skill that distinguished the professional architect from the builder.[18] Of course, the active practical builder could not attend class during the day, which is why most of these schools were conducted in the evening. From example,

Hallet taught from six to nine in the evening, Bowes from seven to nine (his advertisement explicitly read that "Tradesmen will be taught"). There was one curious late exception: John Hills insisted on drawing by daylight, "as drawing cannot be executed by candle light, which is so pernicious to the eyes."[19] He opened his school in 1807, offering "the theory of Civil Architecture in all its branches," with classes held Monday, Wednesday, and Friday from nine to noon, and again from two "until dark").[20]

The public was clearly interested in the fruit of these drawing schools. In May 1795 an exhibition was held at the short-lived American Academy of Painting, Sculpture, Architecture and Engraving, known popularly as the Columbianum, and among the 134 objects exhibited (the first nineteen listed in the catalogue were by William Birch) were a number of drawings by five architects or builders.[21] Only Joseph Bowes, who exhibited "Sundry pieces of Architecture," was a recent immigrant and the others were all native Philadelphians or immigrants of long standing: Robert Smith, William Williams, John Sproul, and Abraham Colladay. Their designs seem not to have been visionary but such practical subjects as "a dancing assembly" (Sproul) and a "draft of the wood-work of a Steeple built at Lancaster" (Colladay). Two of the exhibitors could not enjoy their fame for they were dead, Williams and Smith (his father-in-law, who had died eighteen years earlier). There can be no stronger sign that these drawings were no longer seen as means to an end, and therefore disposable, but were valuable secondary artifacts of the culture of architecture.[22]

Yet another sign of the public's growing literacy in things architectural was the new phenomenon of namedropping. An émigré would not boast of his connection to a prominent British architect unless he fully expected the public to recognize the name. Christopher Myers made a point of boasting that he had been "clerk to Sir William Chambers, architect, for some years."[23] (The namedropping did not help; soon he was in Washington, D.C., working for the Potowmac Company as engineer, and he died three years later.)[24] Likewise, the chief credential of

Joseph Bowes was that he was "Draftsman for several years past, to the celebrated Robert Adams [sic.], Esq. Architect in London."[25] So too, evidently, was Christopher Minifee, who called himself "architect from the Adams's, London."[26] Before the Revolution, such easygoing familiarity was not the case. A pupil of a prominent English architect might advertise his connection to "the great architect of the Adelphia Buildings at Ducham Yard"—as William Williams did in 1773—without ever giving his name as Robert Adam.[27]

These stray references to Adam and Chambers suggest that the literate public was speaking knowledgeably about architecture in the 1790s, and that there was an emerging culture of criticism. Certainly the five architectural competitions held in Philadelphia between 1789 and 1793 did much to advance that culture, for they demonstrated that architectural designs might be subjected to the comparative analysis that is the basis of all critical judgment.[28] Perhaps the earliest indication of lively public interest in architectural aesthetics came in 1786 with a letter in the *Pennsylvania Evening Herald*, entitled "To the gentlemen builders in Market-street."[29] An ingenious plea for the building of uniform houses, it marks the beginning of architectural criticism in Philadelphia.

Observing that the conclusion of the Revolution had brought a building boom to Philadelphia, the anonymous author argued for "the propriety of building your houses in some degree of uniformity with each other" by means of even cornices and story heights:

There perhaps never was, since the first settlement of the country, such an opportunity offered of ornamenting the city with a range of uniform buildings in so central a part. Should some of you incline to run your stories higher than the rest, and thus break the range of windows, faces, eves, &c. you would most certainly lose the effect intended to be produced: and, tho' separately considered as a detached building, such a house might every way be more admired—yet being intermixed with others, it would excite such a disagreeable mixed idea, as rather to disgust than please.

He went on to speak of the stirring effect that regularity has on the viewer, as when one sees matched teams of horses or the identical uniforms of Prussian soldiers. He distinguished landscape, where variety is desirable, from architecture, where uniformity was a virtue. Whoever the author was, he was well informed about modern garden theory, understanding that in "gardening and rural improvements, it is the fashion to pursue nature, and diversify the scene." He also knew the building history of Philadelphia, and well enough to speak knowledgeably about the work of Robert Smith, who we learn here was the godfather of the Philadelphia rowhouse:

> I do not mean by speaking of the market, to confine the idea of uniformity to the High-street fronts; for those on Third-street, being more in number, will have the finer effect, if order is observed. I would not wish to draw the public eye on the errors committed in many parts of the town by contiguous buildings of unequal height; but if you, gentlemen, who are now laying so many foundations at the same time, should cast your eyes around you, examples would soon present themselves of the faults I wish you to avoid—If you ask for a contrast, please to observe the three houses in Second-street, below Walnut-street, built some years ago by Smith, that ingenious architect. An attention to uniformity, at a very trifling additional expence, has produced the most pleasing effect.[30]

Besides referring to Smith, the author cited the example of Palladio and even the formal town plan of Bath, showing an ease with architectural points of reference that makes one curious to know who this first critic of architecture was.[31]

Whoever he was, his claim that uniformity would add "real additional value to your improvements" was persuasive, to judge by the evidence in *The City of Philadelphia*. In the fourteen years between the letter in the *Evening Herald* and the appearance of Birch's book, a number of prominent uniform rows were built. One handsome row of four houses was soon built on the north side of Arch Street, and Birch exploited its regularity to anchor his view of the Second Presbyterian Church (fig. 2.7). And "High Street, from Ninth Street" (1799) showed an even more ambitious row to the left, its sweeping continuity emphasized by the marble belt course above the second story windows (fig. 2.8). Once these experiments were prominently published, all that remained was to take the idea of regularity and apply it to an entire urban block, as was done around 1800 by Thomas Carstairs (fig. 2.9).[32] In terms of impact, the anonymous critic's essay must count as the most influential in Philadelphia history.

ARCH STREET, with the Second Presbyterian CHURCH.

FIGURE 2.7 In a gridded city with straight streets and uniform brick houses not lending itself to pictorial drama, William Birch was forced to generate his own. The marble belt courses of the houses in the right foreground plunge us deep into perspectival space, directing us straight to the spindly tower of the Second Presbyterian Church (1753).

FIGURE 2.8   By 1792, High Street had one of Philadelphia's earliest row of houses, Hunter's Row.
In the distance are the wooden market stalls that
would soon give it the name Market Street. The
lively procession is a squad of the First City Troop,
whose armory Frank Furness would one day build.

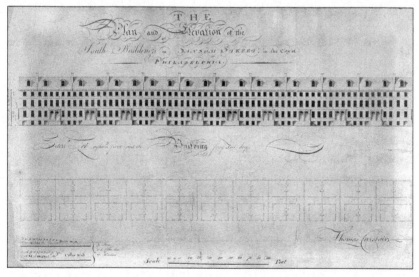

FIGURE 2.9.   On the 700 block of Sansom Street, builder Thomas Carstairs
and developer William Sansom created Philadelphia's first monumental
row of houses. Geometrical regularity was their watchword: windows
and doors align precisely (no easy feat in a rowhouse) while the front and
back rooms match in their proportions.

Nonetheless, implicit behind the letter are still the sturdy Palladian certainties that buildings are to be judged according to taste and uniformity; there was no sign yet of the coming neoclassical insistence on those Greek values of simplicity and chastity. A dozen years later, an anonymous reviewer praised Samuel Blodgett's Bank of the United Sates on just these criteria. He contrasted its "true taste and knowledge" with the work of earlier American builders who, not knowing

> on how solid a basis the antients established their principles, have vainly imagined themselves able to make improvements; but whose futile endeavours have only produced a multiplicity of incongruous parts, awkwardly huddled together, fatiguing the eye and distracting the attention. On viewing this building, the first impression is, one plain and beautifully proportioned whole. On a more [close] inspection, the eye searching for decoration, is richly gratified, finds every thing of its proper size and in its proper place, splended [sic] with neatness, nothing deficient, yet nothing crowded, sufficiently striking but not abruptly obtrusive, combining to form an elegant exhibition of simple grandeur and chaste magnificence.[33]

This, in a nutshell, was the central neoclassical insight, that nobility in architecture was a matter of restraint and sobriety, and that these qualities were best learned not in the works of Palladio but in the architecture of classical antiquity. The reviewer emphasized this by pointing out that the proportions of Blodgett's portico were close to those of the Maison Carrée at Nîmes (a building Blodgett had already paraphrased in his 1792 project for the United States capitol).[34] It did not matter that the Bank was praised as "a truly Grecian Edifice," since the essential distinction between Greek and Roman architecture was still imperfectly known. Again, one wonders who the unknown critic was (although there is always the possibility that the architect anonymously reviewed his own building).

BIRCH IS AN eloquent witness to Philadelphia's changing culture of building, but in one respect—the spatial art of architecture—he was silent. His chief interest in buildings lay in their expressive relationship to their setting, either in the city or in nature. Interior views are almost completely absent from his published work, a surprising omission at a time when such views were a well-developed genre. As a result, he missed the way that new spatial insights were radically transforming Philadelphia's interiors in the years he was establishing his practice. At the time of his arrival, architectural planning was still conducted according to Palladian practice. Rooms were generally squares and rectangles of simple numerical proportions, arranged in interlocking fashion so that a room measuring 1 by 1 might lead to another measuring 1 to 2, and in turn to another measuring 2 to 3. This practice gave an ordered and active rhythm to the interior but its expressive range was limited. It was not capable of much variety, surprise, or contrast—those picturesque values swept in by the neoclassical revolution, and which distinguish the brilliantly convoluted spatial sequences of Robert Adam, James Wyatt, and John Soane.

In a general sense Birch was aware of this. He knew that a fashionable country house required rooms of different shapes and sizes, but he was not able to thread them together to make a compact unity, as his cumbersome plan of Montebello proves.[35] And so his view of William Hamilton's Woodlands (fig. 2.10)—in his subsequent *Country Seats of the United States of North America* (1808)—presents landscape, building, and nature as a unified tree-occluded tableau, giving no indication that it boasts the most radical and furiously original planning in all of eighteenth-century Philadelphia.

Woodlands is the first building to explode the restricted spatial repertoire of Palladian planning, which was swept away in the years of Birch's activity although his exterior views give little sign of it. This is regrettable, since this was the most consequential change in Philadelphia architecture. In the case of Woodlands, it

FIGURE 2.10 William Hamilton's "noble mansion was for many years the resort of a very numerous circle of friends and acquaintances, attracted by the affability of his manners, and a frankness of hospitality, peculiar to himself . . . The study of botany was the principal amusement of his life."

seems to have been the act of a cosmopolitan gentleman-amateur. Hamilton inherited Woodlands in 1747, at the age of two, at which time the estate on the Schuylkill River comprised 356 acres. He doubled it in size by the end of the Revolution, when he sailed to England with the express purpose of transforming his estate to conform to English landscape practice. "The verdure of England," he wrote after his arrival there late in 1784,

> is its greatest beauty, and my endeavors shall not be wanting to give the Woodlands some resemblance of it. Having observed with attention the nature, variety, and extent of the plantations of shrubs, trees and fruits and consequently admired them, I shall (if God grants me a safe return to my own country) endeavor to make it smile in the same useful and beautiful manner.

And this he did. Upon his return from England in 1786, he placed at the front of his house a pleasure garden, "formed into walks, in every direction, with borders of flowering shrubs and trees. Between are lawns of green grass, frequently mowed to make them convenient for walking, and at different distances, numerous copse[s] of the native trees, interspersed with artificial groves, which are set with trees collected from all parts of the world."[36] But even more in line with English practice, he used screens of foliage "to prevent the entirety of estate being taken in at a glance, so that a spectator will be agreeably surprised to find that what terminated this prospect only served as an introduction to new beauties and varieties."[37]

Something like this delightful array of changing vistas recurred in Hamilton's transformed interior (fig. 2.11). The journey through the house took one from an octagonal vestibule to an apse-ended grand salon, thence to cubic corner rooms, and finally unequal parlors at either end (one an oval and the other a

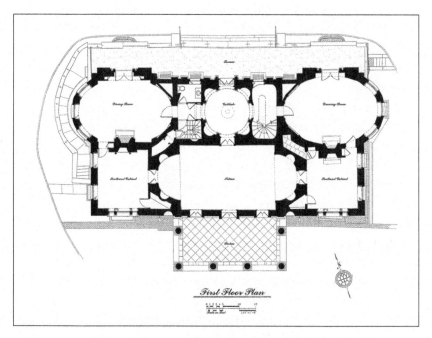

FIGURE 2.11 Woodlands offered the most spatially sophisticated plan of any American building in 1789, with rooms of oval, square, octagonal, and apse-ended form.

cube with a semi-circle at either end). It was an essay in spatial thought, and nothing like it existed in American architecture, let alone Philadelphia architecture. By comparison, the additions Hamilton made to the exterior—he doubled it in width and added a colossal portico—are tame.

The unusual sophistication of the Woodland interior has been ascribed to an unknown English designer, and John Plaw, John Soane, and Robert Adam have all been proposed as candidates.[38] An alternative model suggests that Hamilton designed the interior himself, inspired by his close inspection of English estates and the pattern books of Isaac Ware and William Watt, which he adapted with the assistance of his builder, John Child.[39] It is an attractive scenario, although only one of Hamilton's architectural books has been identified. This is James Paine's *Plans, Elevations and Sections of the Mansion House of Doncaster* (1751), and his copy, bearing Hamilton's signature, survives in the collection of the Wagner Free Institute of Science in Philadelphia. The Mansion House was an early work of Paine, who was born in 1717 and represented the generation previous to that of Adam and Soane, the mid-Georgian generation that achieved maturity around 1750.

To be sure, the Mansion House (fig. 2.12) looks nothing like the Woodlands, which is hardly surprising as it was built as a public entertainment facility for the mayor of Doncaster—a building type for which there was a brief vogue in the mid-eighteenth century, as mansion houses had recently been built in London, York, and Newcastle-on-Tyne. The real resemblance to Woodlands is not in elevation but the plan, which is a similar spatial configuration of an octagonal vestibule set between oval salons that represents precisely one half the plan of the Woodland (fig. 2.13). Here was all that Bingham needed by way of spatial inspiration to convert his Palladian house to something far grander and more monumental. It also has the great merit of explaining the mystery of Woodlands, which is the curious sense that it is not so much a house but rather a sublimated public building, with its festive array of salons and reception rooms.

FIGURE 2.12 At the center of his Doncaster Mansion House, James Paine set a Palladian window under a recessed blind arch; Hamilton repeated the motif to either side of his grand portico.

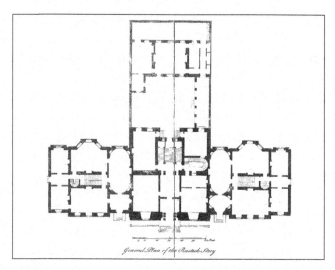

FIGURE 2.13 Hamilton owned Paine's monograph on the Mansion House, one possible source for the complex plan of his Woodlands.

The Woodlands sets the high-water mark of Philadelphia's older tradition of carpenter-builders and gentleman-architects. It shows that on the eve of the arrival of the national government in Philadelphia, there was already in Philadelphia the germ of a sophisticated architectural culture, which knew English and European architecture at first hand, could choose discerningly from among sources, and adapt them to make an architectural essay as thoroughly resolved as the Woodlands. But it marked the outer limits of what the partnership between gentleman-amateur and carpenter-builder, working together, could accomplish.

A fascinating instance of this marriage of convenience came in 1793 with the crisis over the building of the Capitol in Washington. In that year, William Thornton's design for the Capitol was not turned over for execution to a local builder, as had been the case with his 1789 Library Company design, but to a formally trained architect, Stephen Hallet. The choice of Hallet made sense, for the Capitol had a range of technical problems—such as the vaults that required some knowledge of spherical trigonometry—that would have challenged a seasoned carpenter-builder. But once Hallet began to take liberties with Thornton's design, introducing elements of his own project into it, there came the inevitable clash. The meeting that President Washington requested on July 15, 1793, to arbitrate between Hallet and Thornton, pitted two cultures against one another.

As in a duel, Thornton and Hallet each brought his seconds. Thornton brought William Williams and Thomas Carstairs, two of Philadelphia's most accomplished carpenters; Hallet brought a fellow architect, James Hoban (and also Samuel Blodgett, the superintendent of public buildings). Thomas Jefferson presided in his role as Secretary of State, making the meeting the first significant gathering of architects in American history.[40] At issue was the turning of Thornton's insufficiently studied plans into buildable three-dimensional construction. Williams offered a series of practical builder's improvisations, such as changing the height of the galleries so they would not block the windows, and spanning the intercolumniations with concealed brick arches. Jefferson was dismayed by these structural ad libs ("substituting one deformity for another"), and wearily adjudicated the dispute in piecemeal fashion, as the construction languished for another eight years until design authority and construction authority were united in the person of Latrobe.

The travails of the Capitol show the limits of the building culture of Philadelphia, as it was asked to perform tasks to which it was no longer the equal. Birch himself, with his competent but belabored architectural designs, was also part of this final act of the era of gentleman-amateurs and contractor-builders. We should not simplify this process. It is a mistake to believe that with Latrobe's arrival professional architects dislodged Philadelphia's builder-architects. On the contrary, it forced builders to elevate themselves to the status of professionals through self-study, travel, and private instruction in drawing. It is a conspicuous fact that most of the significant architects of nineteenth-century Philadelphia were former carpenters who had learned to render, and started winning architectural competitions with eye-catching renderings. Most would take classes at one of the public institutions that succeeded the ephemeral academies of the 1790s, especially the drawing school of the Franklin Institute.[41] Among them were the lions of the profession: Thomas U. Walter, John Notman, Stephen Button, Samuel Sloan, and John McArthur.

Birch's views depict this culture of ambitious builders at this moment of transition, just as they were starting to refashion themselves as architects. Cooke's Building shows the new sensibility, and prophesies the course of Philadelphia's nineteenth-century architecture (fig. 2.14). One can enjoy the frantic excess of its facade, with its stuttering repetitions of Palladian windows, while still noticing that its architecture goes no deeper than the epidermis. It is the solidly constructed brick box of the Philadelphia builder, and its whimsical Adamesque facade has the exact same relationship that a tablecloth has to a table. This was characteristic of the work of the builder-turned-architect, who thought instinctively and unconsciously in terms of construction, and quite self-consciously when it came to the making of a facade.

South East *CORNER of THIRD, and MARKET Streets.*
PHILADELPHIA.

FIGURE 2.14 Wallowing in Palladian windows and marble trim, Cooke's Building has an air of hectic amiability, as do the bustling shoppers below. It was built in 1794 and is Philadelphia's most ambitious interpretation of the recent work of the Adam Brothers in England.

And this would be the pattern for much of Philadelphia's architecture in the next century: empirical planning in the Palladian vernacular; solid construction in load-bearing masonry; and the addition of a respectable facade in one of the period styles, without which the building would be a sturdy but faceless warehouse.

Birch's images spread this process along. His arresting and memorable views, with their sheer graphic zest, helped bring about a new attitude toward buildings and their place in the city. Where owners once primarily considered the use, cost, and materials of a building—of which its external appearance was a byproduct—they now began to think of making visual prodigies, that would stand out in the street. No eighteenth-century Phila-

View of several Public Buildings, in Philadelphia.

FIGURE 2-15 The national government had just moved to Philadelphia by September 1790 when the *Columbian Magazine* published this view of Independence Hall, looking northeast. From left to right are the Episcopal Academy, Congress Hall, Independence Hall (or State House), the American Philosophical Society, and the Library Company of Philadelphia. By carefully choosing his view and by suppressing extraneous detail, the anonymous artist gave the loose jumble of buildings the character of a civic forum, a prophecy of a National Mall that was years in the future.

delphia renderings depict a building quite the way that Birch did, obliquely, palpable volumes described by light and shade, rising proudly over the tumult of the city. By contrast, previous views are correct but dry affairs of boxy shapes (fig. 2.15).

And having once seen Birch's views, subsequent patrons began to demand designs that would carry well graphically, and might earn a place in subsequent editions. For example, a building like Latrobe's Philadelphia Bank (1808) looks very sensational indeed, with a novel Gothic style and dramatic billboard of a facade—and Birch obligingly included it in his revised edition of 1828 (fig. 2.16).

As with all truly radical breakthroughs that permanently transform the way we see the world, Birch's success has made his achievement seem inevitable. He began his career by celebrating picturesque vignettes of Philadelphia, and Philadelphia returned

PHILADELPHIA BANK *in Fourth Street PHILADELPHIA.*

FIGURE 2-16 Latrobe's Philadelphia Bank (1807–8) was Gothic in name only, its pointed arches, finials, and rose window clipped to a planar neoclassical box. With Latrobe toiling in Washington on the United States Capitol, construction was supervised by Robert Mills.

the favor by giving him a great many more to celebrate. His *City of Philadelphia* is one of those precious historical objects that is both result and catalyst—it is the document of a historical process, even as it advanced and hastened that process, and in the most sumptuous fashion.

CHAPTER 3

The Author of
Fairmount Park

■ PHILADELPHIA'S Fairmount Park takes its name from the
Faire Mount shown on William Penn's plan of 1682, where the
Philadelphia Museum of Art now perches, and where the gridded Quaker city suddenly gives way to an undulating scenery of
2,100 acres of river and park (and, if the Wissahickon is included,
4,250 acres). It is one of the great urban parks of America yet the
man who created it remains unknown in his own city.[1]

The basic story is familiar: in 1812–15 a municipal waterworks was built on the banks of the Schuylkill, the site of which
soon became a popular resort location and a subject of picturesque paintings; in 1843 the city began to acquire tracts of land
along the river to safeguard the water supply; in 1859 the city
held a competition for the design of a picturesque park, which
was won by J. C. Sidney; after the Civil War, the Fairmount Park
Commission was established to oversee the creation of a much
larger park, whose layout was eventually entrusted to the German landscape architect Hermann J. Schwarzmann. This happened in 1867, the year that the park's official history begins.

In the files of the Fairmount Park Commission there is no reference to the plans made in 1859, before the commission was established. And so the best historians of Philadelphia could overlook the role of J. C. Sidney. George B. Tatum noted that an earlier series of "plans were prepared," although many of the specific proposals "were never carried out."[2] Richard Webster ascribed the winning design to Andrew Palles, whose design was "not executed, presumably because of the Civil War."[3] Theo B. White's monograph, *Fairmount: Philadelphia's Park*, does not even mention the 1859 competition, taking for granted that the history of the park only began with the act of the state legislature in 1867.[4] Among recent scholars, David Schuyler was the first to call attention to the 1859 plan, although he downplayed its importance, suggesting that "few of the improvements . . . were implemented."[5] The pattern of neglect goes all the way back to 1871, when the first history of the park was published.[6]

The truth is that Fairmount Park was indeed the creation of J. C. Sidney, an architect of sophistication and national significance. Although his original park measured only 130 acres, a fraction of the acreage of today's park, it was decisive for all its subsequent growth and development. He is as responsible for the creation of Fairmount Park, aesthetically and philosophically, as Calvert Vaux and Frederick Law Olmsted were for Central Park. That his name is unknown does not reflect his achievement so much as it expresses Philadelphia's characteristic reticence.

PHILADELPHIA in the early nineteenth century already had a ready-made park landscape, for along the banks of the Schuylkill were situated some of the city's most stately aristocratic country seats. Just as English aristocrats commuted to their seats upriver along the Thames, so did Philadelphia's colonial elite take to their riverside estates each summer (and probably a little more hastily, since they were also fleeing outbreaks of yellow fever). The story of Fairmount Park is the tale of the gradual democratization of these picturesque aristocratic seats—unlike the story of Central Park, which is that of a single heroic civic building enterprise.

By the 1840s Philadelphia's Schuylkill River estates were no longer fashionable: the water was becoming unclean, tainted by industry from the upriver mill town of Manayunk. Meanwhile, the railroad and the steamboat were extending the reach of the convenient commute, at first to Germantown and Chestnut Hill and later to Riverton, New Jersey. The lovely estates just to the north of the waterworks, Sedgeley and Lemon Hill, fell prey to commercial development. Sedgeley, which had been owned by William Crammond, was purchased in 1836 by Isaac S. Lloyd, who ruthlessly scalped its splendid trees; the fine Gothic villa, built by Benjamin Latrobe, moldered until it was demolished in 1857. Meanwhile Lemon Hill, that authoritative Federal villa built by Philadelphia merchant Henry Pratt, was reduced to peddling ice cream; in 1843 it was sold to the city. The outlook grew brighter in 1851 when Frederick Graff, Jr., made a design for landscaping Lemon Hill and integrating it into the grounds of the waterworks, where he served as chief engineer.[7] This paved the way for City Council to pass a resolution in 1855 opening the estate, already called Fairmount Park, to the public. The formation of New York's Central Park in 1857 and the adoption of the plans of Calvert Vaux and F. L. Olmsted spurred the city. In that same year the city acquired Sedgeley, the adjoining estate, by public subscription.[8]

In late 1858 the Committee on Public Property (later renamed City Property) of Philadelphia's city councils (select and common councils) invited "Plans for the Improvement of Fair Mount Park." The goal was to fuse the newly acquired upriver estates, along with a few other slivers of land, about 130 acres all together, into a unified park on the New York model. The committee announced a deadline of February 15, 1859 and dangled a hefty $500 premium before the competitors.[9]

Eight firms contended, of which only four names survive: William Saunders, Andrew Palles, Edwin F. Durang, and Sidney & Adams. Landscape architecture was still in its infancy—the term itself not yet coined by Olmsted—and the competitors embraced a range of professions. Saunders was a landscape gardener, Palles a civil engineer, and Durang a prolific architect (as can be seen later in this book). Saunders was the clear favorite; he had designed Philadelphia's Hunting Park a few years earlier and enjoyed close personal connections to the proponents of the Fairmount scheme.[10] But the prize, and the privilege of executing their design, went to Sidney and his firm. The second prize of $250 went to Palles while Saunders and Durang were voted a bonus of $100 "as an expression of approval of the labor, skill and taste which they display in a very high degree."[11]

James Clark Sidney (ca. 1819–81), an English-born surveyor and cartographer, had come to architecture obliquely.[12] He was the protégé of John J. Smith, the director of the Library Company of Philadelphia, who engaged Sidney as a surveyor. Smith's son was Robert Pearsall Smith, a prominent map publisher, who in the late 1840s and early 1850s made a series of maps with Sidney, first of Philadelphia, then of New York, and then all the way up the Hudson River to Albany.[13] These maps were based on Sidney's own measurements and were highly successful, helping to establish Philadelphia's preeminence as a center of map publishing. With the surveying came private commissions for landscape projects, beginning in 1849 with the design of South Laurel Hill Cemetery in Philadelphia, followed by Oakland Cemetery in Troy, New York, then one of America's fastest growing cities. A premonition of what was to come at Fairmount, these were picturesquely wooded landscapes, with rambling paths and juxtapositions of cultivated meadows and wild sections, in the romantic landscape tradition of the original Laurel Hill Cemetery.[14]

The chance to design Fairmount Park seems to have lured Sidney back to Philadelphia from New York, where he had been working in 1858. A practical plan for the park required more than a few picturesque squiggles on a map; it needed considerable work on-site. To that end he established a partnership with Andrew Adams (ca. 1800–1860), an architect about whom we know nothing, presumably to assist with the surveying and preparation of drawings. Perhaps, like Andrew Jackson Downing and

F. L. Olmsted, those other great landscape architects, he needed a technically proficient architect to complement his expertise in landscape.[15] And like Downing, Sidney served a suburban clientele, often working on the rural outskirts of Philadelphia, where he practiced in a picturesque Gothic mode, and he too published a volume of villa designs.[16] But he also built churches and public schools, one of which pioneered a radically innovative system of ventilation.[17] An early member of the Philadelphia chapter of the American Institute of Architects, he is also noteworthy as the first architect in the city—perhaps in America—to employ women in his office, not as secretaries but "as designers."[18] But all this is secondary in importance to Fairmount Park, the central achievement of his career.

Sidney's plan proposed a few eye-catching elements, a Grand Avenue and carriage drive, an open parade ground, and a terraced garden, which were to be interlaced by a network of serpentine paths (fig. 3.1). Much of this was inspired by the example

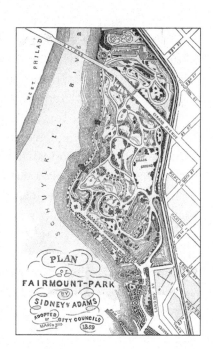

FIGURE 3.1 Fairmount Park had one advantage that New York's Central Park did not have, a readymade picturesque landscape of hills, craggy cliffs, and a scenic riverbank.

of Olmsted's work in New York. Like Central Park, it too was to "present the greatest possible contrast to the artificiality of the city." Toward this end, Sidney proposed to plant "a thick screen of deciduous trees on the outside boundaries of the Park . . . to shut out as much as possible the view from within the Park, of buildings now existing or likely to be put up around its borders."

Sidney believed, as did Olmsted, that "once in the Park one should not be reminded of the city."[19] And like Olmsted, he laid out underpasses and bridges to screen the major road that bisected his park, Girard Avenue.

Also from Central Park came the idea of a formal carriage drive, which Sidney made the great entry of the park, and which formed the transition from the geometric regularity of the city to the irregular landscape beyond. It commenced at the southern entrance to the park in a graceful sweeping curve, and then straightened into a grand avenue ninety-six feet in width lined with American lindens; strips of grass separated the carriage drive, sixty feet in width, from the pedestrian paths on either side. This promenade led toward the river, where it terminated in a roundel beyond which it turned into a meandering romantic drive along the river. In length the Grand Avenue extended half a mile. Other carriage drives measured thirty to forty feet in width, and meandered more picturesquely through the wilder sections of the park. Together the whole park encompassed over three miles of carriage drives and three miles of walks.[20]

Sidney also proposed various park pavilions as well as a series of riverfront boathouses to serve the sport of sculling, which was then undergoing its first flush of popularity. Rather than simply inserting useful buildings into his schemes, he insisted that the architecture served to "aid materially in giving effect to picturesque scenery, thus showing the strong relationship which always exists between landscape gardening and architecture."[21] He even wanted thatch, calling for park buildings to "have as little of the saw and plane about them as possible."[22] Here again he was following the lead of Vaux, who was responsible for the rustic architecture of Central Park, with its bark-covered logs and self-consciously primitive carpentry.

In some respects, however, Sidney's plan differed from that of Vaux and Olmsted. At Central Park a massive and artful reconfiguration of the landscape took place, while Sidney worked to augment the existing features of the landscape. As much as possible he treated the terrain as it was, or—in the case of the clear-cut fields at Sedgeley—as it had once been. He delighted in the rugged rock outcroppings along the banks of the Schuylkill, which were dramatically excavated for the winding course of the riverside drive.[23]

But above all, Sidney avoided the moralistic tone of Olmsted's program. Fairmount Park was to be a democratic institution, but its central feature, the carriage drive, was emphatically an aristocratic one. Even the sport of sculling, with its boathouses, was a rather restricted pursuit. And although there was the open field of the Parade Ground, this was not exactly a sweeping expanse of turf, the great hallmark of Olmstedian planning. Sidney concerned himself with the tactile and the useful, rather than the moral. While he carefully arranged for a screen of evergreen trees alongside the river to shield the glare from the water, he gave no sermon about the mixing of different social classes on the neutral fields of the park.[24]

FOLLOWING the acceptance of their plan, Sidney and Adams were appointed architects to the park, for which they received a fee of 5 percent of construction costs.[25] They threw themselves into their work and in the process committed a public relations blunder of the first order. It is strange, given Sidney's formative experience in making and publishing maps, that he did not prepare a large and attractive engraving of his winning design. All he showed the public was a crude woodcut in the *Gardener's Monthly* and Philadelphia newspapers, copied from the printed pamphlet that accompanied his entry.[26] This left an opening and it was swiftly filled by Palles, the second-place winner. Andrew

Palles (1829–1900) was an Irish civil engineer who designed most of Philadelphia's street railways between 1856 and 1860 before returning to his native Dublin.[27] Palles now made a dazzling chromolithograph of the *Plan of Fairmount Park*, measuring over 28 by 20 inches, and published by Louis N. Rosenthal, Philadelphia's brilliant pioneer of chromolithography (fig. 3.2).

Of course the whole thing was misrepresentation of the most presumptuous sort. The full title reads: *Plan of Fairmount Park, as adopted by City Councils, with the proposed Addition of the West Bank of the River Schuylkill, by Andrew Palles, Civil Engineer, 1859.* Any reasonable person reading that would conclude that Palles had designed the whole thing. In fact, he only designed the proposed extension to the park across the river, which takes up the upper left corner of the print. And even here the landscaping of the

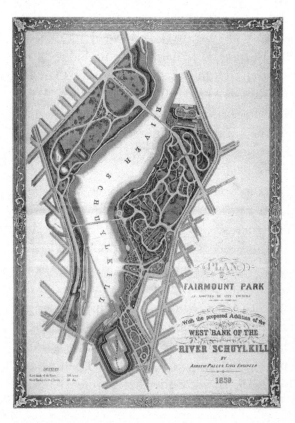

FIGURE 3.2 Andrew Palles, an Irish railroad engineer, designed only the section of the park in the upper left corner, but the wily labeling of his chromolithograph implied that he was responsible for the entire park.

railway engineer is much simpler and more schematic than that of Sidney, who was by now a practiced hand at shaping terrain. Yet the crafty title fooled everyone, not only the general public but even modern historians, who took it to mean that the city "adopted the plan of Andrew Palles."[28]

Palles's stunning image cast Sidney's drab woodcut into the shadow. Had Sidney depicted his winning plan in a chromolithograph, or at least a first-rate engraving, this essay would not have been necessary.

To BE SURE, Sidney's hands were already full. Construction began immediately that summer with an appropriation of $8,500. In that first year a third of the carriage drives were graded, the first American linden trees planted along the Grand Avenue, and "walls winding about the hillsides at the south end have been cut out, affording varied and beautiful views of the city."[29] By the second year the deciduous and evergreen trees at the perimeter were planted, the principal walks laid out, and the carriage drive was completed "in the most durable manner, gravel on a stone bedding with chains at the sides." *Gardener's Monthly* praised it as "beautifully undulating with easy grades, now skirting along the margin of the beautiful Schuylkill and then winding up on the high ground, affording most exquisite views up and down the river."[30]

Sidney's work at the park is an extraordinary example of what might now be called public-private partnerships. While private building might still occur in the city's park, Sidney acted as a one-man architectural review committee. When the Skaters' Club sought to build a new boathouse in January 1860, the Committee on Public Property selected the site (Sidney & Adams had designated an area for boathouses, indicating three sites in a symmetrical arrangement, with room to insert other boathouses subsequently). In March Sidney & Adams made the preliminary plan, which was turned over to the architect William S. Andrews for development. Finally, before the contract could be let, Andrews had to present the drawings to Sidney for approval.[31] Thus architecture in the park would be coordinated with the character and scale of Sidney's design.

The Civil War broke out in April 1861, the third year of construction, but enough of the park had been laid out to accommodate visitors in their carriages. Already $22,500 had been disbursed, and about a third of the work envisioned by Sidney had been completed.[32] The curmudgeonly Philadelphia diarist Sidney George Fisher paid a visit on November 21 and found it disappointing. "Not much work appears to have been done at the park," he complained, "except to make some winding drives. A few clumps of trees, most of them evergreens, have been planted, but seem neglected."[33] Of course, the war had paralyzed work on the park, and only a token $500 was spent during the year, as an anxious city huddled for invasion.[34]

Meanwhile, Sidney's firm underwent change. Adams died and was replaced by Frederick Merry, although responsibility for the park seems to have remained with Sidney. By the start of 1862 the city had rebounded, and it allocated $10,000 for the park.[35] Now Sidney hit his stride: he supervised the addition of many new roads, including a "beautiful drive" along the east or urban side of the park, a new approach to Girard Avenue, and a series of serpentine walks along the river shore of the park. Sidney even remodeled Frederick Graff's old engine house at the waterworks to serve as the park's chief restaurant.[36]

Allocations for the park fluctuated in response to the war. In 1863 the Committee on City Property requested only $8,000, noting that "under other than the present circumstances of the city, the committee would ask a larger appropriation."[37] The request, although it came in the same month as the battle of Gettysburg, was granted. This seems a piddling amount, and it is certainly negligible compared with the cost per acre of landscaping Central Park. But the estate of Lemon Hill and Sedgeley had already been landscaped and, as Sidney & Adams pointed out, the "natural features of the ground are, happily, so park-like already, that little more art is necessary than to complete what is already so perfect in outline."[38] A year later, the end of the Civil War in sight, the city granted $20,000 for the park.[39] Work was largely complete by 1866, and Sidney turned to the task of building a river wall to form an embankment along the Schuylkill.[40] This marked the end of his official connection with the enterprise. What had been built was a 130-acre park, complete with its apparatus of drives and paths, its planting scheme, and landscaping. Contrary to the conventional account that the designs "were never carried out," Sidney's plan was in large measure realized.

EVEN AS THE PARK was being completed Philadelphia citizens took steps to expand it dramatically. The city acquired new parcels to the north and also to the west, across the Schuylkill. With this much larger municipal park came a more formal arrangement for its control. During the course of the war the city experienced a great wave of municipal activism, culminating in the Sanitary Fair of 1864, a vast exhibition that was held on Logan Square. The success of the fair suggested that future municipal undertakings might be coordinated with the actions of spirited public groups. And no longer would the park be under the charge of the Committee on City Property, which also handled the city's market halls and wharves. Instead it would be governed by its own municipal commission. Accordingly the city formed the Fairmount Park Commission in 1867.[41]

The newly established commission evidently had no interest in Sidney. At any rate, the man who was Philadelphia's preeminent landscape architect was not invited to work again at the park. And the Committee on Public Property seems to have had enough of him; when it requested four rustic pavilions in 1866, it pointedly ignored the man who had advocated thatched construction and turned instead to young architect Frank Furness, just back from the war.[42]

If the city had imitated Olmsted in the first campaign at Fairmount Park, now it summoned the real thing. One of the first acts of the new commission was to invite Olmsted to make a study.[43] He was to review the existing work in the park and make proposals for its expansion, and perhaps even to superintend it himself.

Olmsted glided in, sniffing over Sidney's work, not mentioning him by name in his report, perhaps not wanting to give undue credit to his colleague. Likely he smelled a commission. But at the same time Olmsted was not about to criticize either; Sidney's work was too close in spirit to his own, and too sensitive to the spirit of the landscape. Instead he laid out his own philosophical program and proposed, in effect, that the new precincts of the park be treated like the old.

What Olmsted did contribute, and what Sidney could not, was a theoretical statement of the purpose of the park. Olmsted drew on a different intellectual tradition than Sidney, who was decidedly a product of the rather empirical culture of Philadelphia.[44] For Olmsted the park had a higher moral dimension: it was a place where class stratification was overcome.

> It may be considered one of the great advantages of a public domain of this kind that it gives occasion for the coming together of the poor and the rich on the ground which is common possession and that it produces a feeling which to the poor is a relief from the sense of the restriction, which they generally experience elsewhere in comparing their limits of activity with the apparent freedom of those whose cares and duties have a wider scope.[45]

In other words, a sense of mental freedom was to be conveyed by suggesting the possibility of physical freedom in space. This was an imaginative stroke, quite unlike Philadelphia's more utilitarian recreational space, which still spoke the early nineteenth-century vocabulary of pleasant vistas and charming views. Here was high moral seriousness, and here also was a direct translation of Olmsted's particular conception of mental freedom into a specific program for the landscape, and one in which the meadow loomed large:

As art deals with the manners and morals of men through the imagination; this is one of the many reasons why the expression of amplitude and free sweep in the scenery of a park which can only be produced by broad meadow-like surfaces with shadowy and certain limits, is an artistic requirement of the first importance.[46]

The whole mental furniture of this debate—the appeal to social mixing, the use of a moral as opposed to utilitarian vocabulary, and above all the transcendentalism—was all foreign to Philadelphia tradition. While some of the park commissioners might have appreciated Olmsted's ideals, they were also practical industrialists and engineers who shared the Quaker habit of viewing the world in prosy terms.

In January 1871, the commission asked Olmsted and Vaux to submit a formal proposal for the completion of the park. As payment they were to receive a maximum of fifteen dollars per acre, as opposed to the 5 percent architectural fee that Sidney had claimed. In August of that year Olmsted submitted his plans, fully expecting to be named park architect.[47]

Philadelphia may have been envious of Central Park, but this envy did not go so far as to hire its designer. At the last minute the park commission turned instead to an ambition-streaked young German architect, Hermann J. Schwarzmann, who had made his own plan.[48] In 1869 Schwarzmann had been appointed park engineer, charged with the ongoing work of park maintenance. In this capacity he had ample leisure to study the Olmsted reports and to devise his critique of them. Apparently, he had been waiting at the periphery of negotiations, planning his move from the curtains. (This was an old technique of his, and he used it like a dagger: he would do the same thing in 1874 when he stole the commission for the Centennial buildings from Collins & Autenrieth.) On January 25, 1872, the Olmsted plan and the Schwarzmann plan were considered by the park commission. The local man was hired; evidently Olmsted's lofty theorizing about the social role of the park was too abstract for its pragmatic commissioners, who after all had begun their undertaking with the goal of safeguarding the city's drinking water.[49] Or perhaps they simply felt that Olmsted was too uppity, a constant, nagging reminder of that park in Manhattan that they would prefer not to recall.

FAIRMOUNT PARK is the culmination of a particular Philadelphia tradition of public gardens and parks that extends back to the city's founding in the seventeenth century. William Penn himself was a botanist of note, who from the beginning placed public squares in his "greene country towne." For the sober Quaker temperament, which avoided the sensual arts, horticulture offered an acceptable outlet in which the aesthetic impulse and the utilitarian might meet without contradiction. Philadelphia, by the eighteenth century, boasted John Bartram's internationally known gardens and was the center of American botany.

Bartram's gardens, accessible to the public, had created a tradition of public gardens in the city. Among others, Philadelphians soon enjoyed the stately formal garden behind Independence Hall and the festive fountain and garden adjoining Benjamin Latrobe's waterworks in Penn Square. The success of Philadelphia's romantic landscapes (Laurel Hill Cemetery, Fairmount Park, and Hunting Park) was prepared by the public gardens of the eighteenth century. Another hallmark that was passed on from the scientific gardens of Bartram's day was a high degree of sophistication in the selection of individual species for particular settings.[50]

Any effort to praise Philadelphia must turn in the end to a comparison with New York City, and so the effort must always fail. The comparison itself is an admission of defeat. Since the 1840s, when New York emerged as the nation's financial leader, Philadelphians have reflexively looked upon it as the arbiter of all that is stylish and fashionable. On the other hand, such a comparison is not wrong. In their way, each park is the faithful mirror of its city. Central Park is the product of a single heroic act of civic energy; Fairmount Park is the cumulative product of decades of compromise and incremental growth. Central Park is the abrupt and satisfying departure from New York's grimly utilitarian real estate grid; Fairmount Park is the culmination of Penn's "greene countrie towne," which had open squares from the beginning. And, finally, Central Park is an international treasure today, its designer the subject of biographies and television documentaries; Fairmount Park has become dowdy, neglected, and bisected cruelly by an expressway permitted by the park's own stewards, even as the name of its original designer was allowed to drop into oblivion.

"Had he lived in ancient Rome," Tobias Smollett wrote of a character in his *Humphry Clinker*, "he would have been honoured with a statue at the public expence." The same can be said of J. C. Sidney. His great accomplishment was to translate the ideas of New York's new Central Park into the conventions of scale and character familiar to Philadelphia, which had its own vigorous and longstanding tradition of landscape architecture. The park that he helped shape is Philadelphia's finest man-made object. Naturally, he is forgotten today, which says nothing against his artistic gifts, only that they did not include the gift of self-promotion.

CHAPTER 4

"Facts and Things, Not Words and Signs"

The Idea of Girard College

■ A FEW YEARS before his death Stephen Girard (1750–1831), the Philadelphia financier and America's richest citizen, turned his mind to one of the burning social problems of his day, that of the orphan. The childless Girard now become preoccupied with the fatherless child, and conceived the idea of founding a school for orphans. That was not a novel idea but what was new was the precision with which he expressed his ideas, and the fortune that stood behind him. In his will he detailed not only the precise educational philosophy but also gave meticulous architectural directions, extending from materials and plan down to the thickness of the wall and location of doors.

Girard was not himself a Quaker but his school embodied two of the chief Quaker traits, the impulse to philanthropy and the rejection of pomp. Philadelphia built the country's most enlightened public institutions, and the least monumental buildings. Girard was certainly public-spirited: during the deadly summer of 1793, when a Yellow Fever epidemic devastated Philadelphia, he remained in the city to tend the sick at a time when those who could afford it fled to the country. His own architecture was solid and simple, in the Quaker way, even his speculatively built houses. Thomas P. Cope, a Quaker with great experience in building, noted that Girard's houses "were built with more judgment, being of the best materials . . . and calculated for posterity, differing in these respects from those . . . who built for present income."[1]

In 1811 Girard shifted from mercantile operations to banking. In that year Congress refused to renew the charter of the first United States Bank, and Girard deftly purchased the building and retained most of its staff, which opened early the following year as the Bank of Stephen Girard. As with so many of his decisions, the timing was impeccable. By the end of the year the War of 1812 was in progress, and Girard became the principal financier of the American side. His later years were disagreeable and—after the death of his infant daughter and confinement of his young wife for insanity—lonely. He seems to have brooded over his own youth, when he left home at the age of thirteen to sail. On February 16, 1830, Girard devised his will, in which the vast bulk of his fortune, upwards of two million dollars, was to be devoted to a charitable institution for "poor, white, male orphans."

Girard was struck by Benjamin Franklin's role in founding Pennsylvania Hospital, and his peculiar genius for action. With his will he determined to follow Franklin's model: to identify a social problem and to establish a formal institution to address it. There mixed in with this a heady dose of Quaker pragmatism, even utilitarianism of the Gradgrind sort we know from Dickens. Defiantly anti-theoretical, it imbibed the Quaker suspicion of higher education and of theory. Instead, Girard's College was to teach "Arithmetic, Geography, Navigation, Surveying, Practical Mathematics," and so forth. Language was to be taught as well, but chiefly French and Spanish: "I do not forbid, but I do not recommend the Greek and Latin languages." And then, to make doubly sure that the sternly pragmatic character of his curriculum not be missed, Girard added portentously: "I would have them taught facts and things, rather than words and signs." Here was the tersest statement of Quaker pragmatism ever uttered, Franklin included—and by a Voltaire-reading French Catholic!

If only facts and things were to be taught in the college, likewise the building was to have nothing in it of "words and signs," that is, the program uttered not a word about style, symbolism or history. Throughout his life Girard took no special note of architectural fashion, or fashion of any sort. To the end he dressed in eighteenth-century fashion, with a full-skirted coat, a white neckcloth, and a long pigtail down his back. Likewise his will centered on practical rather than aesthetic matters. The college was to be "constructed with the most durable materials, and in the most permanent manner, avoiding needless ornament, and attending chiefly to the strength, convenience, and neatness of the whole." Its main building was to be oriented precisely north south, at the center of an ensemble of four out-buildings, whose location was to be "consistent with the symmetry of the whole establishment," each of which "devoted to a distinct purpose" (one being the maintenance of Girard's collection of plate and furniture).

In the three-storied main building were to be four classrooms to a floor, four rooms, "each not less than fifty feet square in the clear," arranged in a square. This was schematic design, a philosophic program translated into abstract geometry. But what looks rational as a rectilinear diagram does not always work in reality (or our own blood vessels would be laid out on a grid plan). By insisting on four box-sized rooms, fifty by fifty, and arranging them in a larger box of at least one hundred by one hundred, and fronting them with stair halls, Girard made certain that each classroom could only be lighted from one side, the other three being buried in the mass of the building. This did not seem to trouble him. He only cared for the solidity of construction. In all he showed he was far more concerned about fire than he was about light and air. In this he was a man of the eighteenth century, building an institution for the nineteenth.

Girard made a fetish of solid construction, and he banned any use of wood, "except for doors, windows, and shutters . . ." Each classroom was to be fifteen feet high, and groin-vaulted. A stair hall containing two stairs was to be placed at either end of the building, running across the entire front of the building. The outer walls were to be three feet thick at the base, and built of marble or granite, in blocks of at least two feet thickness. He even gave advice for the strengthening of the walls of the stair hall, advocating the use of iron chains in the wall.

In June 1831, Girard added a codicil to his will that changed the site of the college. Recognizing that the lot at Twelfth and Market streets would soon be surrounded by the growing city, he purchased the old Peel Hall Estate. Here were farms and orchards, built on higher land with better air, which is why Eastern State Penitentiary was built nearby. Soon thereafter, on December 26, 1831, Girard died and the mighty machinery of his will was set in motion.

CHARGED WITH EXECUTING Girard's will, Philadelphia's City Councils (then composed of two branches) formed a building committee. On June 14, 1832 the committee decided to hold an architectural competition to choose a design for the college; the best three would win premiums of $400, $200, and $150—hefty sums in those years.[2] It is normally the practice to engage an architectural advisor to draw up the program for such a competition, but in this instance Girard's obsessively precise will seemed sufficient. It was not.

By the December 31, 1832 deadline, at least 17 architects or firms had submitted; four late entries trickled in during the following weeks.[3] The principal fact of the entries is their startling quality. Only once before had there been a national competition—for the capitol in Washington, D.C., in 1793—and that was a hodgepodge of gentleman-amateurs and ambitious carpenters. Forty years later the competitors were professionals, the leading architects of Philadelphia, New York, and Boston. They ranged in age from 21 to at least 48.[4] Nobody over fifty competed: competitions are a young man's game (which accounts for the absence of such mature professionals as Robert Mills, Charles Bulfinch, and Alexander Parris).

Thrilled with the quality of the projects, the building committee decided that they should become the property of the City Councils and not be returned.[5] To make this agreeable to the competitors, additional premiums were authorized beyond the original three. Fourteen additional sets of drawings were purchased in this way, the premiums ranging from $100 to $25. The committee was princely in its generosity, paying out an additional $825 for their trophies; after all, it was not their money. It must have been a jolly meeting: the accounts show a receipt for ten dollars on June 14, 1833, "cash paid A. Walker, for a box of Spanish segars for the use of the building committee of the Girard college."[6]

NOT ALL OF THE designs were taken seriously. Marshal Tufts (1802–55), a graduate of Harvard's divinity school living in Lexington, Massachusetts, apologized that he was "no artist or professional architect," enclosing a careless scribble of a plan to prove it. His sketch was politely ignored, as was the brainstorm of "Mr. Jenks, Germantown" (presumably Theodore Russell Jenks, headmaster of the Germantown Academy), which no one saw fit to preserve. Most bizarre was the proposal by Charles F. Egelmann, a Fraktur artist from Hagerstown, Maryland, who made his living drafting illuminated certificates in medieval German script.[7] (In good German practice he wrote his specifications directly onto the drawing.) If he read Girard's will at all, it is not clear that he understood it, since he proposed to cap his building with a heavy—and categorically forbidden—timber roof. His design, both in architecture and draftsmanship, was a charmingly preposterous anachronism, which gives the impression that he knew no architecture more recent than the communal buildings of the Pennsylvania-German Moravians from the 1760s.

One should consider the seventeen premiated designs in order, from worst to best, according to how the building committee

ranked them. Five competitors received the lowest premium of
$25: Robert Waln Israel, William W. Mather, William R. Crisp,
John Skirving, and Thomas Somerville Stewart. The committee
correctly recognized them as amateurs and carpenter-builders,
perhaps by their supporting letters but certainly by the quality
of their designs. That of Lt. William W. Mather (1805–59), professor of "Geology, Chemistry, and Mineralogy" at West Point,
does not survive but we do have the grim project of Robert Waln
Israel, a builder in Lowell, Massachusetts, the vast and progressive mill town whose new works were the most sophisticated in
America.[8] Of all the competitors, he is the only one who took
Girard's insistence on a plain building absolutely seriously. He
turned in a proposal of real ingenuity, thought out to the last
bolt and joint, but the facade itself was as gaunt and brutal as a
Dickensian workhouse—or a textile mill, which was after all,
the world he knew (fig. 4.1).

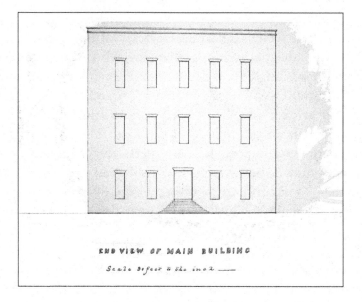

FIGURE 4.1 Most of the 22 entrants in the competition for Girard College
winked at the requirement that they should avoid "needless ornament."
Only Robert Waln Israel took it seriously, submitting perhaps the only
project that Stephen Girard might have approved.

As a practical man, Israel was bothered by Girard's specifications, which prescribed walls too thin for the lateral thrust of the masonry vaults. Girard's remedy—the insertion of iron tie rods into the vaults—seems to have struck him as inadequate. Instead Israel recommended that the vaults be made of cast iron: panels four feet square were to be cast in iron, with flanges extending back nine inches along each side. These flanges were to be either one or two inches in thickness, according to their relationship to the chord of the arch and the amount of stress they were subjected to. These panels would be coffered and painted in imitation of stone. Israel also proposed that the vaults carry a set of piers which, in turn, would support a system of iron rails upon which would be laid the marble slabs of the next story. All was worked out with the same obsessive precision as Girard's own will. The building committee was properly horrified, and it disposed of Israel with the minimal premium.

Curiously, those in the building trades were typically more practical than their professional rivals. William R. Crisp, a carpenter-builder, seems to have never heard of the Greek Revival but he was nonetheless one of the few who made thoughtful provisions for drainage and ventilation. He refused to be intimidated by Girard's will: ignoring the requirement for a cumbersome stair at each end, he devised a more sensible central stair hall, entered from the middle of the long side and marked on the exterior by a cupola. It was a perfectly intelligent design, quite well-drawn, but it looked more like an oversized Federal house than an institutional building. Crisp, like Israel, never had a chance. (Happily for him he had other things on his mind in 1833; he spent the year designing and building a new Catholic church for Philadelphia.)[9]

Another builder made the mistake of thinking that the building committee would take Girard's directions literally, and appreciate "a simple building, as described by the will, without pretentions to any order of architecture."[10] This was Thomas Somerville Stewart (1806–80), a Scots-Irish immigrant who arrived in Philadelphia in 1818 and apprenticed from 1822 to 1827 with Carpen-

South Elevation

FIGURE 4.2 Thomas Somerville Stewart, an ambitious builder, opted for plainness although he took the liberty of a semicircular portico (perhaps to demonstrate his prowess at drawing the shadows made by curved shapes).

ters' Company member John Guilder. Like Crisp, his project was domestic in character: the main building he treated as an unarticulated mass of masonry with "no needless and useless ornaments"; the only feature not required by the will was the semicircular portico, which he defended as "an excrescence to the building to protect the steps." To the rear he tucked the residence wings, essentially the same as the central block, only smaller (fig. 4.2).

Eventually Stewart succeeded in transforming himself into a successful architect.[11] It must have given him pleasure when Girard College, desperately needing alterations and ventilation for Founder's Hall, turned to him, the same man that they had earlier fobbed off with the minimal $25 premium of the carpenter builder.[12]

Far more accomplished was the project of John Skirving (1804–65), so much so that it seems unjust to call him a master bricklayer, which was his trade when he sailed from Liverpool to Philadelphia in 1827. He was a designer of the first class, who like his friend T. U. Walter used the Girard competition to establish himself as a professional architect. With its rusticated base, graceful blind panels, and arcaded central block, his design evokes Regency London, and comes closer to the lighthearted picturesque classicism of John Nash's Regent Street than any other of his competitors. There is even a dash of whimsy in the delicate carved ships over the dormitory entrances; they recall Girard's mariner days with what is virtually the only allegorical sculpture in the entire competition.

Skirving struggled valiantly against Girard's rigidly utilitarian will. He could do nothing about the requirement that all three stories needed to be at least fifteen feet high, which made it difficult to diminish the height of each successive story, as classical principles dictated. And so he ran a cast iron balcony across the length of the second story, suggesting the fashionable *piano nobile* of a townhouse, when it was nothing of the sort. But one of Girard's strictures he thought madness: instead of the identical stair hall at either end, he placed a single elegant stair in the center and marked it with a pleasantly proportioned shallow dome.

Where had Skirving learned to render so effectively? His monochrome perspective is a marvel of atmosphere: a passing cloud casts a shadow over the dormitory to the right while the main building bursts into bright sunlight (fig. 4.3). Proud of his

FIGURE 4.3 John Skirving moved Girard's two stair halls to the center, a violation of the will but a happy one, which gave his design the character of a gracious civic building.

artistic ability, he exhibited his genre paintings and architectural drawings at the Pennsylvania Academy of the Fine Arts and the Artists' Fund Society. Here was genuine talent but Skirving's career was thrown off course by the Panic of 1837. He moved to Washington, D.C., where he worked on modernizing the heating and ventilation of the U. S. Capitol and other public buildings.[13] He was that characteristic American type, the inventor–artist who recognized no distinction between aesthetic and technical imagination, a category that included Charles Willson Peale and Samuel F. B. Morse. Perhaps it was to justify himself that Skirving's last great project was to initiate Christian Schussele's nineteen-figure group portrait "Men of Progress—American Inventors."[14]

THE FOUR WINNERS of fifty dollar premiums, at first glance, do not seem to have performed significantly better than those who won twenty-five dollars. The only substantial difference is that George Strickland, Edward Shaw, William Rodrigue, and Michel de Chaumer were all architects, not builders, and were treated accordingly as gentlemen. Yet each of their designs show certain deficiencies, suggesting why they were placed at the bottom rung of the architects.

George Strickland (1797–1851), the brother of William and his clerk of works, received a fifty-dollar premium, which is surprising, since his plan was not all that different from Skirving's. In good Regency fashion, which always paid attention to the edges and divisions of things, he surmounted his schoolhouse with a balustrade and banded it with delicate iron balconies, marking its corners with paired pilasters; it might have been a London club or townhouse (fig. 4.4). Clearly Strickland had been pouring over images of John Nash's recent work, perhaps in prints brought from London during William's visit there in the 1820s. And like a Nash work, the design could have as easily been carried out in brick and stucco, with cheap plaster ornament, rather than the slabs or marble or granite that Girard prescribed. But a London club was hardly the centerpiece for an ambitious modern college.

FIGURE 4.4 George Strickland apparently resolved to submit a design as different as possible from that of his older brother. While William proposed a classical temple on a podium, George offered up a contemporary London townhouse.

It was all facade and no building, a two-dimensional conception that divulged his education as a painter and engraver. In early 1833 he advertised an ambitious school of architectural drawing that would meet daily in his brother's office and use his "valuable library of classical works."[15] The requisite "seven or eight scholars" he needed did not materialize, and the lesser Strickland moved to Washington a few years later to take a position in the patent office.

One would expect a higher placement for Edward Shaw (1784–1859), for the Boston architect was one of the most prominent of the competitors.[16] He had just published *Civil Architecture* (1831), one of those odd American treatises that went from the Greek orders to practical stair-building, with little in between. But Shaw had begun life as a carpenter-joiner in New Hampshire, and never quite shook off the habits of a rural house-builder.[17] His facade for the college was a neat composition articulated in Ionic pilasters and recessed panels, but it looks like a frame townhouse in the Federal style, enlarged and translated into stone. And not sufficiently enlarged, the portico still scaled to the townhouse that Shaw was unconsciously recreating (fig. 4.5). The liberties with the orders are also awkward: the pilasters have no bases and the entablature is strangely bulky. In every

FIGURE 4.5 The Ionic order was "the emblem of the dignified simplicity and elegance of Diana," Edward Shaw claimed in his *Civil Architecture*, and his design implies that Girard's motherless orphans needed a feminine presence, if only architectural.

respect it is a polite but stilted essay, like someone speaking with unaccustomed formal diction.

As a practiced house-builder, Shaw did better with his dormitory designs, which were much freer and more interesting. He devised luxurious suites for the pupils, with two bedrooms opening off of a living room—something far more generous than Girard could ever have envisioned. Apparently he forgot he was designing for eight-year-olds. Shaw, however, did not hold a grudge and his 1854 *Modern Architect* proclaimed Girard College "a magnificent specimen of the Corinthian order."[18]

The five bays + pilaster theme is handled with much more aplomb by Michel de Chaumer. Another of those hapless French architects that revolution periodically tosses, bewildered and hungry, into the streets of Philadelphia, he wrote a cover letter that oozes self-pity:

> Thrown upon this Country by unexpected misfortunes & forced to apply myself to occupations below my former station for the maintenance of a large family, a stranger without protection, I appear before you under unfavorable auspices: but I hope that giving a due & impartial attention to my Plans you will permit me to contend for the Premiums offered.

Without offering any names, Chaumer boasted that he had worked under "the most imminent [!] architect in the City of Paris." Perhaps he worked on the new Paris Bourse, which had just been completed in 1826; his letter cites it approvingly. There he would have learned his competence in masonry construction, which was of a high order, to judge by the drawings in his competition portfolio with their boldly curved stone stairs and precise stereotomy of the cut stone vaults (fig. 4.6). He spoke knowl-

FIGURE 4.6 The awkward central window on the second story of Michel de Chaumer's entry betrays him as a novice architect whose background was in stone masonry. He pelted the building committee with irritable letters.

edgeably about the quality of American freestone and his drawings of the ashlar construction carefully distinguished between
supporting members and the infill.

No graceful Ionic order for Chaumer but only the sober
Doric: "the architecture of a palace ought to find no place in a
House of Charity." This was in the spirit of Girard's will which
Chaumer otherwise ignored. He cut down the width of the classrooms from 50 to 38 feet, lowered their height, and increased
their number from four to six. In this and his submission letter
(and in the subsequent letters with which he pestered the building committee), Chaumer showed a striking presumptuousness,
which might help explain those "unexpected misfortunes" that
he complained about.[19] In any event, whatever he had to say was
full of comic bombast, with a cascade of flourishes and bows, and
compliments to the building committee:

> Gentlemen, with the incorruptible materials abounding in
> this happy country, the buildings ought to last, I might say,
> as long as the world, were they constructed according to the
> strict rules of art; because they would be able to resist the
> scourges that would annihilate the human species; unless a
> total subversion of the order established by the Deity should
> occur. To substantiate this I appeal to the antique monuments
> of Rome & Athens &c.

All this affectation and garrulousness seems to have annoyed
the committee, which ranked Chaumer, for all his prowess in
masonry, at the bottom of the architects (which only brought
forth more complaints).

The other Frenchman among the competitors, William Rodrigue (ca. 1798–1867), was more tractable. The son of refugees
from French San Domingo who fled to Philadelphia during the
slave uprisings of 1793, he traveled to France and spent three
years studying architecture, after which he returned to Philadelphia to work in the office of William Strickland. With Strickland
he worked on the design of the Pennsylvania canal system during
the 1820s.[20]

FIGURE 4.7 William Rodrigue was stymied by Girard's program and, fearing to carry any feature beyond the plane of the wall, he turned in the flattest composition of the entire competition.

Rodrigue followed Girard's will inconsistently. His boxy building was suitably plain, with no columns or porticos, only delicate pilaster strips, as slender as straws, that indicated on the exterior the location of the classrooms. But he placed his stair hall directly in the center, a clear violation of Girard's will (fig. 4.7). The result was not terribly distinguished, but this seems to be the consequence of Rodrigue trying to give the building the plainness that Girard mandated. He could certainly do better; his design for the Wills Eye Hospital, submitted a year earlier, was a bundle of robust forms and expressive energies, qualities that were suppressed in the Girard project.[21]

WITH THE $100 winners there is a sudden leap in quality, but also a change in character. John Kutts, Higham & Wetherill, Town & Davis, John Haviland, and Isaac Holden were all designers of imagination, and they knew how to give their designs expressive character. In general, if your design looked like a house, you won $50, and if it looked like a tomb you won $100.

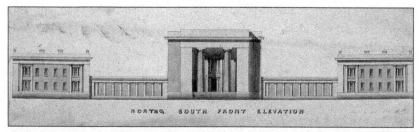

NORTH   SOUTH   FRONT   ELEVATION

FIGURE 4.8 To judge from the general air of gloominess, one might think that John Kutts thought he was designing Girard's tomb and not his school.

John Kutts, a Boston architect, had just won second prize in the design for the Albany State Capitol, and turned to Philadelphia in a hopeful mood.[22] Not only did he prepare an unusually large submission (twelve drawings survive) but he also arranged to spend a week in Philadelphia in order to consult with the building committee. He might have saved his time. He believed that an orphanage should frighten children, or so his sepulcher of a design suggests. It was nominally in the Greek style but the use of absolutely monolithic pediments, single slabs of uncut stone, gave the pile an Egyptian severity about them, better suited to the gatehouse of a cemetery. Five porticos, built at three disconcertingly different scales, stretched across the lengthy wall of the college, striking a note of morbid solemnity (fig. 4.8).

Kutts worked hard to make Girard's plans workable, augmenting the staircases at either end with a grand central hall and an axial corridor. The surgery to the plan was excessive, however, resulting in a building that had as much circulation as classroom space. He also submitted an alternative plan, which in character was scarcely different, a transposition from one minor key to another. All this suggests an active restless architectural mind, although Kutts does not seem to have fulfilled his early promise.[23]

Even grimmer was the windowless temple proposed by Higham & Wetherill. Cyrus Wetherill, an English émigré, had practiced in upstate New York since 1814; together with Albany architect Robert Higham, he opened a short-lived office in New York City. This is their only known work.[24] Their main facade

FIGURE 4.9 Most competitors realized that they could aim higher than the plain masonry box that Girard's will seemed to imply, but none aimed higher than Higham & Wetherill, whose neoclassical monument would have made an agreeable French supreme court building.

was a prodigy out of Revolutionary France, monumentality at its chilliest, and utterly unlike anything else in the competition (fig. 4.9). Like Kutts, the architects seem to have regarded it as their principal duty to terrify orphans. But they also offer a thoughtful amenity in the covered walkways that connect the main building to the dormitories. (A number of competitors thought to do this, perhaps thinking of Thomas Jefferson's newly built University of Virginia.)

For designers seeking to give architectural character to Girard's dry box of a building, neoclassical severity was not the only possible approach; there was also Greek elegance. This was the approach of the New York firm of Town, Davis & Dakin, America's first consequential architectural partnership. Their talents complimented one another, the elder Ithiel Town (1784–1844) serving as the monumental classicist and Alexander Jackson Davis (1803–92) as the romantic artist.[25] Davis's rendering is a tour-de-force, making the unavoidable squat mass glisten like a marble jewel box (fig. 4.10). They offered two variants, a flat-roofed version with Ionic pilasters, and one with a low pedimented roof and no pilasters. (The offering of alternatives is always a useful marketing device; it suggests to the client an eagerness to please.)

By far the most ravishing of the renderings, if not the finest design, was the moody bird's eye view presented by John Haviland (1792–1852), the celebrated architect of Eastern State Penitentiary (fig. 4.11). Haviland trained in London with James

FIGURE 4.10 Town, Davis & Dakin calculated that a plain marble box under a Greek pediment would fulfill the demands of both fashion and Stephen Girard's will. They were wrong.

FIGURE 4.11 John Haviland's bird's-eye perspective recalls similar views of his Eastern State Penitentiary; in each case, an intricate array of interlocking buildings and wings gains in authority by being shown as a compact unity.

Elmes, who taught him how to plan buildings, and then spent six months with John Nash, who taught him how to plan a career. This involved real estate speculation, with hearty investment by the architect himself, clever planning to maximize income, and striking eclectic facades to attract attention. In 1826 Haviland built a pair of Arcades, one in New York, near Broadway, and the other on Chestnut Street in Philadelphia. But he was now under a cloud, having been exposed diverting funds for a naval hospital in Virginia, and forced into bankruptcy. Victory in the Girard College competition would have reestablished his reputation.

Haviland had lived for a time in St. Petersburg, home to some of Europe's most monumental neoclassical architecture, and perhaps it is there that he acquired his feeling for the poetry of architectural masses. His design certainly exploited the expressive potential of geometry: four cubic dormitories mark the four corners of the ensemble, connected by low wings to the central building, a pedimented Greek temple with octastyle porticos and baseless Doric columns. He left the outer walls of his dormitories absolutely blank, adding to the sense that this was a sacred temple precinct, turned inward on itself. It was a stupendous design, entirely in accordance with Girard's will, but it left the judges cold. (Haviland's financial escapades cannot have helped.)

The final $100 winner was a veteran of Haviland's office, Isaac Holden (1803–84), and a fellow English émigré. But unlike Haviland, he saw no use for a Greek temple and explained the thinking behind his Regency design in a rather cheeky cover letter. (Among other things, he complained that "Mr. Girard in his will has so nearly described what he intended the college to be as to leave little for the Architect to do except in Arrangement and Embellishment.") Holden saw the architectural challenge as to make a building as inexpensive as possible without sinking into monotony:

The External decoration of the Accompanying designs You will perceive are as plain as would be consistent with the Magnitude of the Building, yet are sufficient to destroy the

Monotony of the Front and Maintain its Respectability. As all Edifices are in a great measure Judged by comparison and as the Buildings in the Neighborhood are of necessity so far removed from it both in distance & Size that in Magnitude alone it becomes sufficient Important, an Elaborate application of Ornament would be useless and consequently Extravagant. A more Formidable reason however presents itself to the consideration of the Architect namely The Enormous Expense necessary to Embellish this Edifice with Porticoes and their accompanying decoration.[26]

Holden came from a family of bricklayers and as he read Girard's will he grew alarmed at the weight of the vaults, which he calculated at over two hundred tons, a load that would overstress the walls. And so he violated the will, placing two columns in each of the classrooms, dividing the ceiling into six groined sections. The building committee seems to have appreciated the technical advice, for he was the only architect to receive a $100 premium who had not submitted a temple. (Holden later prospered, building Philadelphia's Hospital for the Insane before later returning home to establish a prominent practice in Manchester.[27])

SUCH WAS THE grab-bag of projects that received special premiums. The three winners, on the other hand, have enough of a family resemblance to show us that the architectural preferences of the building committee were neither neoclassical nor Regency but strictly Greek. The third-place prize of $150 went to the Boston architect Isaiah Rogers (1800–1869), a Greek Revival enthusiast and a planner of rare imagination (his Tremont House in Boston nimbly fitted a complicated array of spaces onto a triangular shard of space). His Girard College project was similarly unshackled. He took liberties with the plan of the main building, making it more serviceable, and arranged six separate dormitory and dining hall buildings around it (fig. 4.12). These he fronted with low Doric porticos of stringent character, hinting

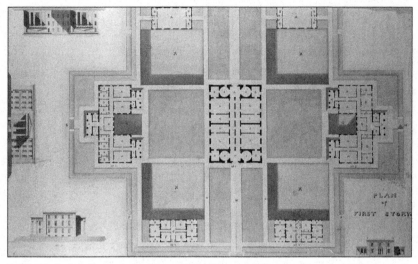

FIGURE 4.12 Isaiah Rogers had just built Boston's elegant Tremont House, which may be why his design had nothing of Girard's utilitarianism but rather the intelligent planning and comfort of a well-ordered hotel.

that Rogers' formative years were spent in Boston, where massive construction meant granite. His whole sprawling ensemble suggested a modern Acropolis, a community of Greek buildings drawn tightly together behind Girard's ten-foot walls.

Beyond question the favorite in the competition was William Strickland.[28] His Second Bank of the United States (1818–24) was the most sophisticated Greek Revival building yet built in the country, a brilliant arrangement of interlocking vaulted spaces, all carefully poured behind a scrupulous copy of the Parthenon. And surely it was the ambitious masonry vaulting of that building which prompted Stephen Girard to demand the same for his college. Strickland must have expected to win the competition. To come in second with a $200 premium clearly infuriated him, to judge by his subsequent actions.

As at the Second Bank, Strickland placed a pedimented temple front at each end building; this time it was not Doric but Corinthian, lifted onto a Roman podium. At the sides the various internal rooms burst through the wall in agitated rhythm, a lively semaphore that expressed the welter of classrooms, cor-

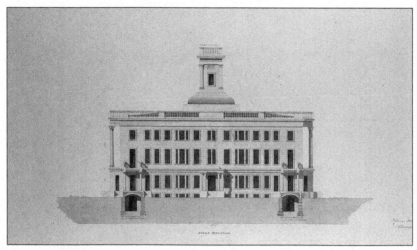

FIGURE 4.13 William Strickland made an eminently buildable design on the reasonable assumption that the competition was his to lose. But the more he tinkered with Girard's program, the more complicated became the plan, and on the side elevations all hell broke loose.

ridors, stairs, and offices (fig. 4.13). This was quintessential nineteenth-century design: a historical show facade to the front, and a functional facade to the side. At the top was an astronomical observatory, treated as a cupola to indicate that this was a public building.

Strickland also knew the walls were too thin for the vaults. He modified Girard's plan by placing a curious square vestibule in each of the four corners of each classroom. The vestibules were built of slabs of solid stone, around which straps of iron were threaded to tie the vaults. The result was a plan of concentric rectilinearity: square within square within square. Since the corner vestibules would make the rooms smaller than Girard mandated, Strickland expanded the classrooms so that they measured sixty feet across their extremities. Even as they sacrificed space in the corners, his classrooms had considerably more clear space than Girard's rooms. Few of the other competitors had approached the technical side of their designs so brilliantly, and none had bothered to provide an interior perspective of the classrooms (fig.

FIGURE 4.14 Strickland balked at Girard's spartan grid of fifty-by-fifty-foot rooms. In response he placed vestibules in each of the corners to carry the groin vault, giving the classrooms spatial interest as well as letting him flaunt the concealed iron straps and solid stone slabs that buttressed the vaults.

4.14). But Strickland went to the additional trouble and expense because he was confident he would win easily.

He did not, of course, and the $400 first prize went to Thomas Ustick Walter (1804–87), his erstwhile pupil. Walter was an unknown quantity. Only twenty-eight years old, he had enjoyed what he called a "liberal but not collegiate" education. After serving an apprenticeship with his father, a bricklayer, he turned to architecture, studying with Strickland and also, briefly, with John Haviland. In addition, he had taken lessons with the landscape artist William Mason, whose influence is apparent in the capable water color drawings of his submission. Walter's practice was in its infancy, having been launched when he won the 1831 competition for Moyamensing Prison with a castellated Gothic design cribbed from Haviland. But he must have thought he had a good shot at the competition because he prepared for it with great thoroughness.

Walter undertook a study tour "through the Eastern States," visiting Thomas Jefferson's campus for the University of Virginia

FIGURE 4.15 Thomas U. Walter won the competition with a temple mounted on a podium, pleasingly balanced between two dormitory wings with colossal orders. No other competitor had dared to sling so many columns (38 in all) across so long a front.

and probably Harvard and Yale as well.[29] Evidently he found American academic models unsatisfactory, for he took his design from the Place Louis XV (Place de la Concorde) in Paris, with its twin buildings by Ange-Jacques Gabriel, graced by that favorite French device of a second-story colonnade enframed at either end by pavilions. Shouldered between these monumental dormitories was the school itself, lofted above an impossibly high podium, making the whole thing a kind of Parisian ensemble, the church of the Madeleine thrust into the Place Louis XV (fig. 4.15).

Here Walter revealed an extravagant, almost Baroque taste that is out of keeping with the austere Greek Revival; if anything, it looks forward to his florid U.S. Capitol dome. It was not a perfect design, and suffered from its excessive frontality. A short stroll to the rear of the building would expose it as a carefully contrived frontispiece. All the same, it proclaimed a thrilling grandeur and confidence that matched the magnitude of Girard's extraordinary gift.

THE SELECTION OF Walter was not a political choice but it was regarded as such. Philadelphia's City Councils were controlled by a newly elected Whig majority, of which Nicholas Biddle was the champion. Biddle was the director of the Second Bank and a passionate believer in the Greek Revival, who claimed there were only "two truths in this world, the Bible and Grecian architecture." This line is often cited without attribution; in fact it was originally quoted by William Strickland in his testimony against Walter.[30]

Biddle swiftly gathered power in his hands; he was declared a trustee of Girard College on February 4, 1833, college president on the 11th, and on March 27th chairman of the building committee. This quick spate of promotions was not welcomed with universal approbation, and both Biddle and Walter found they had abundant enemies. During these weeks, until Walter's official appointment as college architect on March 28, a rogue's gallery of disappointed architects and disgruntled Democrats gathered around the competition, forming alliances and fomenting intrigues.

For a time it was hoped that Girard's will could be broken. One of its provisions suggested extreme hostility to religion: "no ecclesiastic, missionary, or minister of any sect whatsoever, shall ever . . . be admitted for any purpose . . . within the premises." In fact, it was persuasively argued in a case that reached the Supreme Court that Girard did not want to shelter his pupils from religion but from religious strife. But for a moment it seemed that Walter's grandiloquent project could be dislodged by a more modest design. Biddle's foes commissioned an alternative design from twenty-two-year-old John Trautwine, yet another pupil of Strickland, and displayed it at public meetings.[31] Done in a rush, it was a vast stone block animated only by the window hoods and a Doric porch that could be omitted, "if in conflict with the will." Other architects waded into the fray. Michel de Chaumer waged a one-man battle for the commission, critiquing the prize-winning projects, damning them all as unbuildable, and resolutely defending his own project. (He continued to write angry letters well after the buildings were under construction.)

Strickland made the most determined effort to wrest the project from Walter. Knowing that it was now Biddle's taste that mattered, he jettisoned his Roman design to make a Greek temple that was even more Greek than Walter's.[32] While Walter's temple

FIGURE 4.16 Strickland may have heard that Walter was revising his design to make it more Greek and less Roman, for his hasty revised project did just that. And like Walter he continued his colonnade all the way around the building, a full peristyle, but to no avail.

had only Greek porticos, Strickland gave his a full peristyle (fig. 4.16). In the process, he realized he could not maintain his system of corner vestibules and so he jogged the grid of classrooms so that the transverse walls on one side of the building came to rest against the middle of the classrooms on the other side. In this way, the opposing wall acted like a buttress, supporting the lateral thrust of their vaults.

We do not know how the building committee reacted to Strickland's last minute desperate ploy, only that it was not considered. By April 23, 1833, Walter's revised design had been definitely approved, rendering futile all further architectural intrigue.

PERHAPS IT WAS the knowledge that Strickland was preparing a design for a temple with a full peristyle that helped persuade Biddle and Walter to redesign the winning design to make it even more purely Greek (fig. 4.17). At any rate, Walter reshaped his design to make it the most fully realized Greek Revival object in all of North America, something that almost certainly would have horrified Stephen Girard. In the process he turned an impractical building into an unworkable one. The acoustics were already calamitous and the peristyle wrapping around all four sides badly reduced light; in the third story classrooms, light entered only from above through skylights or at the pupils' ankles.

FIGURE 4.17 By making his dormitories simpler, Walter was able to make his main building grander, America's most fully realized monument of the Greek Revival. It would not be complete until 1847.

And for all that, the architectural competition for Girard College is surely the most important architectural competition in nineteenth-century America. No other competition brought together so many celebrated architects; nor dangled so tantalizing a prize. Its painfully restrictive terms, giving the tiniest scope for invention and originality, fettered all competitors equally, making it a contest of uncommon challenge. That the result was unhappy does not detract from that. Girard wanted to build a plain school where orphans were taught "facts and things," not an abstract classical monument. But a monument is what he got, and perhaps the most satisfying monument to philanthropic idealism that America will ever know.

CHAPTER 5

The Strange Germanness of
the Academy of Music

■ THE ACADEMY OF MUSIC has perplexed Philadelphians since it opened in 1857 (fig. 5.1).[1] The interior rewards both eyes and ears, a splendidly festive auditorium whose brilliant acoustics were exploited by Leopold Stokowski to produce a sound that was "the sleekest vehicle of musical expression ever created."[2] But the exterior is another matter, and it has given rise to all sorts of urban legends—that the building committee had the funds for either an attractive interior or exterior, and decided to skimp on the facade; or that the plain brick exterior was only provisional, and that a beautiful facade was to be installed in better days. Neither story is true—the building was at the height of fashion when it opened—but they contain a garbled memory of the competition that produced the Academy, an uncommonly peculiar episode in the architectural history of Philadelphia.

Like so much in Philadelphia, and not only in architecture, the Academy of Music was saturated with feelings of inferiority toward New York. No sooner had construction begun on

FIGURE 5.1 The Academy of Music (1854–57) is Philadelphia's most visible memorial to the enormous German immigration in the wake of the revolution of 1848.

the New York Academy of Music (1852–54) than Philadelphia hatched a plan for a similar building. On May 24, 1852, the public was invited to subscribe to an *American* Academy of Music, a carefully devised name that recalled the time when Philadelphia's culture was American culture. (The name did not stick.) It took more than two years to raise sufficient capital and on September 22, 1854 the building committee announced an architectural competition for its building, which was to stand on a lot at Broad and Locust Streets, measuring 238 × 150 feet.

Only one architect served on the building committee, Frederick Graff, Jr. (1817–90), engineer of the Philadelphia Water Works and son of its designer. He would have drafted the competition program, which required room for 4,000 spectators, arranged in three tiers of boxes, a balcony, and a parquet. It was to serve both as an orchestra hall and opera house, and Graff insisted on the strictest measures for safety, fire-proofing, and ventilation. The building was to be "of simple but imposing style" and built of brick with "dressings . . . of granite, brownstone or cast iron."

Submissions were originally due December 1, 1854—a short time for preparing all the necessary plans and elevations—and local architects insisted on, and received, a two-week extension. By the new deadline seventeen projects had arrived, most by Philadelphians, with a smattering from Boston, New York, and Baltimore.[3] Proposals came from the architects of the new academy of music in New York (Alexander Saeltzer) and of the Boston Athenaeum (Edward Clarke Cabot), hoping to repeat their triumphs. Typically, unsuccessful competition designs are returned and vanish into history. And understandably so, as they can only bring chagrin to their unhappy authors. But five Philadelphia architects saw fit to preserve their unbuilt projects for the Academy of Music, and they form the subject of this essay.

Poverty and Magnificence

The hopeful competitors for the Academy were not on an equal footing, and included seasoned professionals and ambitious fledglings. When examined in order of the age of the designer, the drawings reveal conspicuous differences in ability and education. Their authors comprise John Notman, a 44-year-old Scottish émigré with a lucrative practice; Stephen Button, 41, a carpenter-builder from New England; the partnership of Napoleon LeBrun, 33, and Gustav Runge, 32, an American architect and a German émigré, respectively; Edward Collins, another German, also 32; and E. F. Durang, a 25-year-old draftsman with architectural aspirations.

John Notman (1810–65) was the oldest architect whose drawings survive. He was a native of Edinburgh, then in the process of being reshaped along neoclassical lines by William Henry Playfair, who was Notman's architectural mentor. Before emigrating in 1831 Notman also spent some time in London in the school of Michael Angelo Nicholson. This early training is apparent in his Academy project, which does not use the classical orders but nonetheless has all the discipline of Greek classicism. He treated it as an arcaded palazzo, well-balanced and graceful, but its entire aesthetic interest was restricted to its abstract qualities of rhythm and proportion (fig. 5.2). These he handled with consummate control, although one senses Notman working diligently to keep within the budget. In the end, restraint and Scottish sobriety were not the qualities needed to rival New York. Notman's project went unrecognized as the committee looked elsewhere for something more eye-catching.

They found it in the work of Stephen Decatur Button (1813–95), an equally successful but far less talented Philadelphia architect.

FIGURE 5.2 John Notman was one of Philadelphia's most gifted architects but his oddly monotonous project for the Academy of Music was no more musical than a metronome.

Button had trained as a carpenter in Connecticut and he experienced classical architecture in its wooden American version. He thought in terms of framing and joinery, even when working in brick, and his designs had the conceptual flatness of carpentry, of planes on which intricate details might be glued but without any sense of masonry masses. Neither his training nor his reference books had prepared him for a project as monumental as the Academy, and he handled it in additive fashion (fig. 5.3). He fastened architectural elements—pilasters, arches, pediments, a rudimentary dome—on what was effectively a crate. But while his porticos and dome proclaimed magnificence, the factory-made cast iron window hoods and the frugal stuccoed walls suggested poverty. And his sculpture sat uneasily in his pediment, betraying his lack of experience of integrating architecture and sculpture. In good eighteenth-century fashion he simply attached it to his cornice. The effect was appropriately theatrical, as thin as stage scenery, but it captivated the jury enough to earn Button second prize.

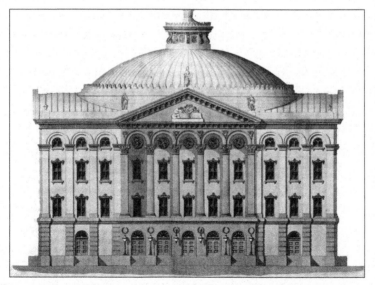

FIGURE 5.3 Despite its flimsy portico and bulbous dome (which would have been invisible from the street) Stephen Button's design would place second.

FIGURE 5.4 Edwin Forrest Durang was still a rookie architect but evidently hoped that his distinguished theatrical and musical family might tip the balance in his favor.

The design of E. F. Durang (1829–1911) suffered from similar weaknesses. A member of a picturesque family of actors and singers, and a devout Catholic as well, Durang divided his career between building opera houses and Catholic churches, which resembled each other a bit more than they should. Given his family's musical background and connection, he may have thought he had a chance with the Academy. His design was acceptably competent, an arcaded base in brownstone surmounted by two stories in stucco with elaborate brownstone window surrounds (fig. 5.4). And his decision to bring the end bays forward and cap the cornice with a segmental pediment show a commendable desire to mark the ends and center. But the whole composition is small-minded; not only are the individual parts small-membered and fussy, but they do not relate to one another. Read Notman's design from top to bottom, or from left to right, and each opening clicks precisely into place. But Durang squirts his little inventions across the walls without caring whether or not they align. (They don't.) Nor could he figure out how to adjust the rhythm of his bays so as to put an opening in the center, for which his bizarre central pediment serves as a half-hearted apology.

It is curious that neither Durang nor Button were interested in modeling their designs sculpturally. Their buildings swelled to fill the property line, the artistic impulse yielding to that of the real estate developer. But this was in the nature of American design, where such buildings were private affairs, seeking to maximize income and rental space, and not to glorify the state or express civic pride. In this respect, the work of the German competitors differed. They belonged to a different world, one in which such cultural buildings were royal projects, where formal expression counted for more. Of them, the most daring design was produced by a recent German émigré, Edward Collins (1823–1902).

Despite his English name, Collins was born in Königsberg, the son of a Prussian state judge. He trained at the Berlin Bauakademie, later transferring to the prestigious Polytechnical School in Karlsruhe. These were at that time the most influential and sophisticated schools of architecture in the German world, and perhaps in Europe; Collins was easily better trained than any architect in Philadelphia. It is easy to see why John McArthur, Jr., engaged him as junior partner in 1851, following his immigration. And it is just as easy to see why Collins, a year later, thought he might do better alone.

Needing help to make the elaborate drawings for the Academy, Collins engaged a pair of assistants from Württemberg, Charles Autenrieth (1828–1906) and Charles Herman (1827–91). Autenrieth was a spectacularly gifted renderer whom Collins plucked from Samuel Sloan's architectural sweatshop. Thus was born the partnership of Collins & Autenrieth, which thrived into the twentieth century, and would become one of Philadelphia's most successful firms. (Herman would end up working for the federal government.)

Collins's design shows the planning intelligence he had developed in Berlin. He recognized at once that the demanding program would push his building to the full dimensions of the tight lot. Such a building, with only its front and the Locust

FIGURE 5.5 Edward Collins and Charles Autenrieth submitted a superb and up-to-the-minute essay in modern German classicism, forgetting that Philadelphia was not Berlin.

Street flank visible, would simply read as two perpendicular walls and not as a sculptural solid. Nor could any porticos or porte-cocheres project in front of the building to relieve its insistent rectangularity. But if the building could not be extended outwards it was nonetheless possible to carve and model *into* it. Here was the genesis of Collins's solution (fig. 5.5).

Collins realized that less space was needed on the upper stories than the ground floor, where the auditorium required a bulky entrance vestibule before it. By sacrificing a certain amount of space in the middle of the building's front, he created a recessed loggia on the second story. Notman had done something similar, but he neglected to take advantage of the recession and projection. But Collins projected a handsome screen of Corinthian columns across the void in the upper stories, itself a kind of proscenium through which the recessed auditorium might be glimpsed. This was a rich neoclassical gesture, full of originality and grace, easily the most poetic idea in the entire competition—and also the finest drawings. It had all the sophistication of contemporary Berlin; unfortunately, it was to be judged by the industrialists and merchants of Philadelphia.

One firm united European theoretical sophistication with American practicality, that of Napoleon LeBrun (1821–1901) and Gustav Runge (1822–1900). LeBrun was something of a prodigy; a pupil of T. U. Walter, he won the commission for Philadelphia's Catholic Cathedral when he was only 25. He had also built Philadelphia's most important auditorium, the rebuilt Music Fund Society (1847). For all that, LeBrun was a provincial in comparison to Runge. A member of a highly musical Bremen family, Runge turned to architecture in his youth and studied in Berlin and Karlsruhe, where Collins was his classmate. There he learned modern German classicism in its highly academic and theoretical form. But like LeBrun, his personal taste inclined to the florid, and he built a number of highly mannered storefronts in Philadelphia in the 1850s.[4] A "superb cellist," perhaps the only serious musician among the competitors, Runge took acoustics seriously.[5]

Runge was no humorless German. Something of a character, he enjoyed performing:

> Among friends, Runge was an accomplished humorist. From time to time, when prompted, he would delight us by singing a lecture, accompanying himself on the guitar, in which he impersonated an itinerant virtuoso with a mile-long Italian name. When his comically pompous lecture ended in applause, he would turn red in embarrassment as he announced that his servant was ready to show a collection of relics for sale at cheap prices, such as torn off buttons, cuffs and collars that had become somewhat antique through wear, and other similar items.[6]

The partnership of LeBrun & Runge was one of convenience, and given their very different backgrounds it could hardly have been otherwise. Runge seems to have done the work while LeBrun (at least in the newspapers) got the credit. But LeBrun and

FIGURE 5.6 Philadelphia architect Napoleon LeBrun and Gustav Runge, a recent émigré from Berlin, easily carried the day with their ravishing Venetian essay.

Runge evidently worked amiably together. They produced an opulent Venetian design, drawn variously from Andrea Palladio, Michele Sanmicheli, and their sixteenth-century contemporaries (fig. 5.6). It consisted of an arcaded entrance capped by a colossal Corinthian colonnade, between whose columns were set round arches carried on Ionic columns, forming a loggia with open balconies.[7] Here the exterior precisely described the interior, for these same Ionic columns were repeated in the "grand saloon" behind the loggia, an opulent mirrored space to be used for receptions or for smaller recitals. Statues at the summit celebrated the arts that would commingle within: Poetry, Music, and Dance. Festooned with festive ornament and garlands, it was a genial daydream, recalling the Venetian origins of the modern opera. The Baroque theme that had befuddled Button was developed here with confidence and bravura. Of all the entries of which we have evidence, it was clearly the most musical.

Bait and Switch

On December 16, the drawings were laid out and the building committee went to work under the direction of the distinguished attorney George S. Pepper. He handled the deliberations with quiet efficiency: each of the local architects was invited to present the "merits and peculiarities" of his designs, while the recent opera houses of New York and Boston were visited and inspected. The entries themselves were then compared against the plans of Europe's important opera houses. Two months later, on February 12, 1855, judgment fell. Collins & Autenrieth's sumptuous project, sublime though it was, seems to have alarmed the jury and was dismissed without a prize; likewise Notman's sober design. On the other hand, Button's domed auditorium-temple captivated the jury. Although an inferior piece of architecture, it was drenched in theatricality, and theater, after all, was the order of the day. Button pocketed the second prize of $200.

But there was no question that LeBrun and Runge deserved the first prize and it was awarded unanimously. Their Venetian style was "a novelty in this country" (thus the *Public Ledger*) that "admits of powerful and striking effects." But they offered more than Venetian theatricality. As an engineer, Graff could assure the jury of its inner workings. The architects had arrived at a simple, effective ventilation system with an eight-foot wide shaft above the hall for expelling noxious fumes. They also proposed a sunken pit beneath the stage, forming a sound box for the vibrating wooden floor above, which would give the Academy one of the richest aural signatures of any concert hall.

Behind the scenes the celebration was muted. It was clear that the ultimate form of the building depended on the amount of money that could be raised, and receipts continued to lag behind

New York levels. The acceptance of the LeBrun and Runge design was only provisional, so long as "certain alterations and modifications" were made. Here George Pepper stepped in and the sumptuous Venetian facade was the first casualty.

Pepper was a forty-seven-year-old lawyer who was a protégé of the legendary Philadelphia lawyer Horace Binney. Of considerable wealth, he was a connoisseur of the arts (and later a director of the Pennsylvania Academy of Fine Arts), and had a strong interest in architecture. In particular, during the course of his interviews with the competing architects, he developed a predilection for the sober, austere lines of the modern German round-arched style. After all, New York's Academy of Music, by the German architect Alexander Saeltzer, was in that style. Taking pen to paper, Pepper now made his own amateurish drawing for the facade of the building, which survives in the archives of the Philadelphia Orchestra. He proposed that LeBrun and Runge strip their facade of its applied columns, leaving a simple pattern of round arches outlined with brick moldings. He must have done this in February or March, when he first asked his architects to revise their design. It is unclear exactly what happened. In the pertinent board minutes, the reports of the building committee are missing, and are listed as having been "removed by Mr. Pepper."[8]

But LeBrun and Runge were perfectly content to be conducted by Pepper. They promptly prepared a frugal round-arch facade based on his drawing, stripped of all applied columns and entablatures, to be built of brick (fig. 5.7). LeBrun and Runge had allowed the committee to dream fantastically but now they had to act responsibly; it was a classic example of bait and switch. Only a few florid vestiges of the original Venetian fantasia survived the purge, and only on the interior. The elaborate proscenium, flanked by pairs of Corinthian columns, made it, as did the second story salon, although its strong Ionic order no longer continued in the facade. A model of the revised design was unveiled on April 20, 1855 at the Merchants' Exchange, where LeBrun and Runge had their offices.[9]

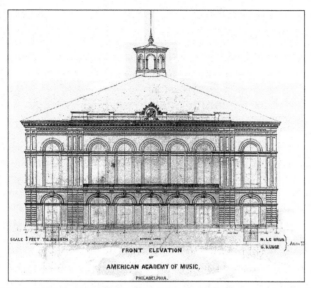

FIGURE 5.7 Runge's revised facade was a highly literate essay in the modern German *Rundbogenstil* but it baffled Philadelphians and gave rise to the urban legend that it was only a temporary facade, meant to serve until there was enough money to clad it in marble.

The revised facade was clearly the work of Runge. He was from northern Germany, where brick construction had been the rule since the Middle Ages. He had studied in Schinkel's own *Bauakademie*, itself a monumental building in strident red brick, boldly girded with pilaster strips and arcades. Here he had been taught the most modern and progressive of German architectural styles, the *Rundbogenstil*, or "round-arched style." This was the radical architectural doctrine that insisted that architectural form should be derived from the facts of construction and materials, not from historical precedent; ornament and decoration should be left to the "free invention of the artist." The result was an "objective" architecture—the first time in history that that word was applied to architecture—which one could appreciate without any prior knowledge of history of archaeology. This theory was formulated by Heinrich Hübsch, Runge's professor of design in Karlsruhe.

The revised academy, therefore, was a first rate piece of modern German architecture, directly imported by a product of the

German university system. And yet its sophisticated German pedigree was lost on its American audience. Even the official program at the Academy's dedication mangled the source of the style, describing the building as being

> in the Italian Byzantine school, such as is frequently to be met with in the northern parts of Italy. Its character is massive and imposing, although exceedingly plain, with window frames shaped in a manner approaching the Gothic, which is peculiarly calculated to produce a pretty effect in the evenings when the interior of the building is illuminated.

To be sure, German architects had been diligently mining medieval Italian architecture during the 1840s but the specific ways that Runge detailed brick—from the articulation of the walls and entrance arcade to the details of the frieze and cornice to the delicately profiled window surrounds—all derive from the round-arched architecture of Berlin, Hamburg and Karlsruhe.

Runge had high expectations for his workmen. "The carvings and enrichments are to be executed in the best style, with spirit, boldness, and sharpness." *Spirit, boldness, and sharpness* were exactly the features that cast iron trim, with its flattening out of edges and folds, could not hope to achieve. Such triumphant enthusiasm was usually absent from technical documents.

With Runge's version now approved, construction moved swiftly. After detailed drawings were made and bids tendered, the cornerstone was laid on July 26, 1855. The contractor was John D. Jones, an old friend of LeBrun and a fellow architect, who had also trained with Walter before turning to the more reliable business of building. Supporting Jones was an excellent team of decorative artists, including the decorative painter Russell Smith, who created the rich backdrops, and Joseph A. Bailly, the French sculptor. It was Bailly who carved the five heads of the entrance keystone: Tragedy and Comedy at either end, Music and Dance within, and at the center Poetry, represented by a head of Apollo—now sadly marred by recent painting. The allegorical paintings atop the ceiling of the auditorium were by

Carl H. Schmolze. But even as these artists worked, subscriptions continued to lag, and the building continued to suffer as it was scaled back. Even the lavish ornament of the entrance lobby, which was to be articulated with pilasters and a bold cornice, was sacrificed. Instead of being executed in plaster and gilding, they were merely painted on the wall in a flat *trompe l'oeil.* In a perverse but fitting gesture, the ornament of the building was now as insubstantial as that on stage.

"Lebe Wohl, Lebe Wohl"

The Academy opened with its first opera on February 25, 1857, a lavish performance of *Il Trovatore.* In attendance was the city's most bellicose social critic, Sidney George Fisher, who had rarely had a kind word for any Philadelphia social event since the 1830s. He praised the building for its "4 tiers of boxes, an immense parquette, wide corridors, with saloons, dressing rooms for ladies . . . The woodwork is white & gold, the seats all covered with crimson velvet and the walls with crimson paper. It is thoroughly heated and brilliantly lighted." He also marveled at the great chandelier, "a fairy fabric of gleaming crystal & diamonds." Fisher repeatedly visited the new building, commenting on it in his diary, but also stepping down from praise to express that peculiarly Victorian hope that the building could "exert a beneficial influence on taste and manners."[10]

Fisher praised the Academy according to the lights of 1850s taste, finding it "admirable, solid, massy, spacious and rich but simple and in good taste." These terms, *solid and massy,* were precisely the faults that would be held against the building by later generations of Philadelphians, who nostalgically wished that the committee had built the classical variant of the facade intended for brownstone. But for the moment, solid and massy ruled, and American buildings of the 1850s continued to embrace German architectural taste, the round-arched style of the Academy enjoying a prestige that would not wane until the Second Empire mania of the late 1860s.

The architects themselves were soon dispersed. LeBrun failed to succeed in Philadelphia, perhaps because of his too narrowly Catholic patronage, and perhaps also because of some shabby intrigues in other competitions. During the Civil War he moved to New York, where he established a family architectural dynasty. Runge had it worse. Although he managed to work for the wealthy Drexel clan (the German banking family), he was mortified to be bested again and again by half-educated builder-architects, while his sophisticated Berlin training counted for nothing. In 1859 he returned to his native Bremen to test the waters for a permanent return. Before he sailed, his German friends in Philadelphia honored him with a testimonial dinner and Schmolze, who painted the Academy ceiling, wrote a parody of Goethe's *Faust* for the occasion. It can be taken as a lament for any professional European architect trying to start a practice in America. Stephen Button, it should be noted, is singled out for special abuse:

> But what's the point of mental and physical power,
> Of knowledge and artistic self-respect,
> When here it's carpenters, stone cutters,
> And engineers who play the architect?

> Why waste my taste on the Hottentotten,
> Who prefer the cabbage salad of Mr. Button,
> Who's twisted the festive pretzel of Lent
> Into fitting artistic ornament?[11]

Before he set sail, Runge was serenaded triumphantly in his own Academy. "*Lebe wohl*," he was admonished, as the Germania choir sang Mendelssohn—"live well." Runge took the advice: after a brief return to Philadelphia he settled permanently in Bremen, where he soon became chief municipal architect. His first act upon his homecoming was to publish the Academy of Music as a portfolio of drawings, one of the first American buildings to be published in Germany—although, in fact, it was in most respects a German building.

The Academy of Music is an odd episode in the history of taste where German architectural theory, in its most rarefied academic form, was embraced by untheoretical Philadelphia. But this is perhaps not surprising. The perpetual dilemma of Philadelphia architecture has always been to be fashionable while still being Quaker. Philadelphia architects followed the changing pageant of stylistic fashion, but they also served clients who were steeped in the Quaker plain style of the eighteenth century. Often the two were irreconcilable, but whenever modern taste and the Quaker plain style were brought into alignment, a quintessentially Philadelphian building emerged. From Frank Furness to George Howe to Louis Kahn, the city's great architects learned to do this, taking the standard ingredients of Quaker eighteenth-century architecture—brick construction, minimal ornament, and anti-monumentality—and interpreting them in the light of changing fashion. In this sense the Academy of Music is a characteristic piece of Philadelphia art, where cosmopolitan Venetian opulence was defeated by progressive German theory—to produce something that even Quaker Philadelphia could admire and comprehend.

CHAPTER 6

"Silent, Weird, Beautiful"

The Making of Philadelphia City Hall

■ EDMUND BACON, legendary director of Philadelphia's City
Planning Commission, dealt curtly with developers who wished
to build higher than Philadelphia City Hall—or more precisely,
higher than the brim of the hat of Alexander M. Calder's bronze
statue of William Penn, which since 1894 has crowned the 547-
foot tower of City Hall (fig. 6.1). Bacon, who was tall, patrician, and extraordinarily handsome, would say, "You understand
that the rule that no building in Philadelphia can be higher
than City Hall is not written down anywhere; it's what we call
a gentleman's agreement. Now my question for you is,"—and
here he would lean in alarmingly over the developer—"*Are you
a gentleman?*"

The gambit worked all through Bacon's long tenure as planning director (1949–70) and beyond, right up until 1987 when a
mayor who wanted to be known for bringing construction jobs
to Philadelphia authorized One Liberty Place. It topped out at
945 feet, although it too was soon surpassed; today eleven build-

FIGURE 6.1 When City Hall's cornerstone was laid in 1874, its Second Empire architecture was already fading from fashion. But it was not completed until about 1901, by which time it was a curious anachronism, although a glorious one.

ings tower above City Hall, the tallest more than doubling its height. Were their creators gentlemen? Bacon died in 2005 and is not around to give us his answer, but one can guess.

It is curious that the building has become associated with its spectacular tower, which is by no means its most significant feature. For Philadelphia City Hall is itself a replica of Philadelphia at the center of Philadelphia. Like the gridded city it presides over, it is a symbol of equality—a square building with four entrances equally spaced, with a great square in the middle, offering infinite views in the four cardinal directions. The whole has a diagrammatic rightness that seems obvious—the capitol of a city of squares should be a square, just as the capitol of the tic-tac-toe board should be a miniature tic-tac-toe-board—and yet the building began very differently and only assumed its present form after years of false starts, controversies, and lawsuits, during which three different sites were considered. No one set out to make a city hall that looked like its host city; collective forces, acting incrementally, shaped something as succinct and authoritative as any conscious design.

"Woe to the Taxpayers"

On February 2, 1854, the Act of Consolidation expanded the boundaries of Philadelphia to the county limits, and in an instant Philadelphia was 75 times larger. Germantown, Frankford, and other outlying towns were gobbled up as William Penn's compact unity of 1,200 acres sprawled to take in 90,690 acres. Water, police, and fire departments now had to serve a city that had grown by almost two orders of magnitude. Its public offices, grouped in a complex of eighteenth-century buildings around Independence Hall, had become inadequate overnight.

The first impulse was simply to enlarge the space for public business by placing "plain and unadorned buildings" around Independence Hall. In January 1858 the Committee on Public Property issued a report, calling for two fireproof buildings, one on Fifth and the other on Sixth Street, designed to "harmonize

PLAN OF THE PROPOSED ALTERATIONS OF THE COUNTY BUILDINGS.

FIGURE 6.2 Samuel Sloan's 1859 project for a low-budget city hall building enveloping Independence Hall would have set new standards for municipal cheapness.

in taste with the State-House building." They were to be built of pressed brick with brownstone trim, each costing no more than $200,000.[1] Tentative plans were drawn up by Samuel Sloan, that brilliant but overworked hustler, whose design achieved the feat of looking both ambitious and cheap (fig. 6.2). Sloan would have effectively enclosed Independence Square within a wall of continuous building, each of its four corners treated as quasi-independent pavilions. To unify the complex, Sloan capped each pavilion with a lofty cupola that echoed the form of Independence Hall's steeple. The intention was to make it the centerpiece of the complex, a Colonial gemstone in an Italianate setting. But the flagrant cheapness frustrated the intention. The architecture, instead of harmonizing with Independence Hall, just looked dated, the four corner buildings looking like nothing so much as a convention of geriatric provincial courthouses.

Nonetheless, in October 1859 the project was approved by Select Council (in those years Philadelphia had both a common council and a select council), but before anything could be done, events moved forward. On April 2, 1860, the Pennsylvania State Legislature passed the Public Building Act, authorizing Philadelphia to build not one but two public buildings, a city hall and a county courthouse. A seven-man building committee was formed, comprising Mayor Henry Alexander, two city councilmen, and four judges.[2] There was no architect or architectural advisor—a mistake.[3]

Before the buildings could be designed, a site was needed. Only two were considered, Independence Square and Penn Square, and each was rich with symbolism. Independence Square had the prestige of Independence Hall, the cradle of American democracy, where the Constitution was forged. But Penn Square stood at the intersection of Broad and Market streets, the epicenter of Penn's "greene country towne," where he had intended its public buildings to stand. Such were the high-minded terms of the site debate, at least superficially, but beneath the surface everything pivoted on self-interest. Those with addresses in the older city naturally preferred Independence Square and those with a stake in a growing city, especially real estate developers and traction magnates, just as naturally preferred Penn Square. Neither faction was inherently wrong, for the question was ultimately a philosophical one: should the public building serve the city of the present, or the city of the future?

The fiercest, and by far the most intelligent, champion for Independence Square was Henry Charles Lea (1825–1909), the internationally known historian. The Lea family were prominent publishers of medical textbooks, with large real estate holdings around Independence Hall. But his self-interest was also that of a tax payer. He feared that the enormous open site of Penn Square would encourage a far more palatial building than was needed, diverting money from the real problems of the expanded city, such as roads, water, sewers, and gas works. An extravagant set of buildings would bankrupt the city and be nothing more than "a laced coat on the back of a beggar." So he wrote in a public letter to the mayor on June 15, 1860, signed by hundreds of Philadelphia's most prominent citizens.[4]

A subsequent letter, published in the *Public Ledger* on July 31, made the case for a modest building on Independence Square. A personal survey of seventy leading businesses, Lea claimed, showed that they agreed with him by a factor of two to one. But it was already too late: at a meeting on July 6, the building committee chose Penn Square.[5] Knowing that public feeling was running high, they claimed that their hands were tied. Independence Square had just been designated the site of an ambitious monument to the Signers of the Declaration of Independence. New public buildings on the site would "obstruct the view and mar the effect" of the monument. Although it would never be built (the Civil War took care of that) it provided a convenient excuse.

Falsely believing that they had settled that matter, the committee set about finding a design. In mid-July, they placed advertisements in the *North American* and the *Philadelphia Press*, inviting plans and specifications for the two buildings, a courthouse on the northwest corner of Penn Square and a city hall on the northeast. They were due September 1, an impossibly short time to design beautiful, attractive buildings, and to make the necessary drawings. Each building required three plans, two elevations, a section, and a perspective—a total of at least fourteen large-scale drawings. Only three architects went to the trouble, and those that did had all drunk deep from the municipal trough. Samuel Sloan, having made the plans for the $400,000 addition, was well connected. So was John McArthur, Jr., who had designed Philadelphia's enormous House of Refuge. And George S. Bethell was a straightforward municipal jobber, a hack with good friends in City Council. The city's other architects, doubtless smelling a rat, sat out the contest.

The projects of Sloan and Bethell are lost, and all we have are brief newspaper accounts. Bethell turned in a hodge-podge, "a mixed style of architecture, in which the Norman seems to predominate." Sloan went for extravagance this time, and his buildings were "very elaborate and appear to partake more of the Byzantine style. . . . there is a centre building with columns and wings, less ornamented. There is a steeple on the municipal building." It sounds as if Sloan had simply enlarged his Lycoming County Courthouse, designed earlier that year. Given his frenetic pace of work, he could hardly have done more. His chief assistant, Addison Hutton, was in Natchez, Mississippi for the summer and the office was so short-handed that Sloan did not even write the specifications for his entry.

McArthur's project, by contrast, shows that he had thought profoundly about the nature of the project. Recalling that Philadelphia had once been the nation's capital, he celebrated that history (figs. 6.3 and 6.4). His courthouse was a miniature version of the United States Capitol, as it was then being enlarged by T. U. Walter, right down to the form of the dome (although McArthur substituted a female figure of *Justice* for the *Liberty* of the Capitol). The competition of patriotic symbolism and characteristically intelligent planning was irresistible. The committee voted for McArthur unanimously.

The next order of business was choosing a contractor and the committee acted swiftly. On September 10 they advertised for bids and by September 18 they had six.[6] Choosing the low bidder was no easy matter: the committee had requested three different bids for three different materials (blue Pennsylvania Marble, white marble from Lee, Massachusetts, and "good sandstone"). The low bidder in one material was not necessarily the low bidder for the other two.[7] In the end, the committee voted to award the construction contract—astonishingly—to McArthur himself, letting the architect build his own design. Unfortunately, he was not the low bidder. His bid of $1,487,600 for a building in Lee Marble was undercut by John Ketcham's bid of $1,225,600. (The committee insisted that Ketcham's bid was so unrealistically low that it would result in "defective work.")

This was too much for Henry Charles Lea, who published

FIGURES 6.3 AND 6.4 John McArthur, Jr.'s project of 1860 would have expressed that Philadelphia was both a city and a county. The clock tower was the mark of a town hall (top) while a stately dome signaled the county courthouse (bottom). Had the Civil War not intervened, the two buildings might well be facing each other across Penn Square today.

several anonymous newspaper articles on September 27. In the *Public Ledger* he complained that the building committee, by allowing McArthur to interpret his own plans and specifications, had removed every restriction to his financial profit but his own sense of moderation. The version in the *Philadelphia Inquirer* was angrier: "We now have the remarkable spectacle of architect, builder and contractor all in one person. How is Mr. McArthur, as the city's architect, to watch over Mr. McArthur, as the city's contractor? Who shall guard the guardians? . . . Woe to the taxpayers!"

McArthur's contract was scheduled to be ratified that day but the public scrutiny unnerved Select Council, which decided to delay the vote for two weeks and study the matter. The issue was a technical one but one of great sensitivity: the accountability of the contractor for following the specifications and drawings prepared by the architect. Normally these two offices policed one another: the architect carefully supervised the workmanship and quality of materials used by the contractor, while the bidding process presented an impartial evaluation of the cost of building an architect's design. But with these offices united in one person, this safeguard was removed. Furthermore, the competition drawings were scaled too small to permit dependable measurements. "A difference of six inches more or less in the thickness of the walls," Henry Charles Lea pointed out, "would make a vast variation both in solidity and expense, and yet this is dependent on the thirty-second part of an inch in the plan."[8]

Ketcham promptly brought a lawsuit against the city, bolstered by affidavits by leading Philadelphia architects (Samuel Sloan, John Stewart, and John Fraser) who confirmed that he was a builder of skill and probity.[9] But so was McArthur. As a young man he had superintended the construction of John Notman's Athenaeum and William Strickland's Officer's Building at Philadelphia's Naval Asylum, and he had even invented a new and improved girder.[10] There was no reason to doubt his competence, and yet some did, and Philadelphia's architects were at each other's throats.[11]

By October, the building committee had lost all control of the process and City Council intervened. Lea's warnings seemed to be coming true: the building committee and their architect-contractor would now be free to build as extravagant a building as they wished, with no accountability to the taxpayers of Philadelphia. But there was no consensus over the remedy. One faction wanted McArthur's contract revoked and given to Ketcham; another remembered Sloan's low-budget project, which suddenly seemed more appealing; and still another defended McArthur, saying that his plans and specifications had been approved by the city's engineer, building inspectors, and "a number of the best architects of the city."[12]

Contributing to the chaos was a vacuum of leadership. Alexander Henry, the mayor of Philadelphia and head of the building committee, might have made the case but he was too weak to do so (or thought he was, which is much the same thing). He had been elected by a coalition between the American Party and the recently founded Republican Party, and he was unpopular with the city's newspapers, most of which were Democratic (this would change after the Civil War). Aware of his weakness, and aware of the generally pro-Southern public mood of Philadelphia, he refused to support Abolition, the great cause of the Republican Party. He supported McArthur, nominally, but without the energy or savage wit of Lea.

McArthur's designs were now seen as a nefarious scheme to loot the public legislature.[13] But what was the alternative? When a few councilmen proposed a new competition for cheaper buildings on Independence Square, it fell flat. Low-budget prudence is not the stuff of passion. A few months later, when the Civil War put a stop to all building projects, the sense among the exhausted participants, including the taxpayers of Philadelphia, was one of relief.

"I have no fear of being compromised"

Until 1865 Philadelphia was preoccupied with far more urgent matters. As soon as the war was over, a prosaic brick courthouse was built to the south of Independence Hall, on South Fifth Street. The architect was George Bethell, the municipal jobber who won third place in the original competition.[14] It made no one happy and three years later City Council tried again; on the last day of 1868 it passed an ordinance "to provide for the erection of city buildings." This time it was to sit on Independence Square. An impossibly large building committee was formed, including the mayor, building and road inspectors, and seventeen members of the city's Common and Select councils. But this time there was an architect on the committee, T. U. Walter, who had just retired to Philadelphia after completing the enlargement of the U. S. Capitol with its sublime dome. There could scarcely be a more qualified judge.

Walter wrote a thoughtful and thoroughly professional program for a competition with attractively hefty premiums: the winner would receive $2,000, and the next three finalists $1,500, $1,000, and $500. Competitors were to submit a complete set of plans, elevations, and sections, "finished without color," and perspective drawings to be "colored and embellished at the discretion of the designer." Some councilmen wanted to limit the competition to "five or six of the most eminent architects," thereby eliminating the inevitable novices and tyros, but in the end five hundred pamphlets were printed and distributed; two hundred architects across the country received copies.[15] On April 16 the doors were thrown open.

To prepare drawings for an architectural competition is extraordinarily time-consuming. Simply to study the number of spaces needed, to arrange them sensibly and conveniently, and to give them a pleasing exterior was the work of several weeks; the preparation of a dozen or so plans, elevations, sections, and perspectives. In the end, it might amount to a month of work, costing perhaps $120 in wages (the amount John McArthur paid his assistants during the Civil War), making competition a costly gamble. Only two types of architects competed: those who thought they had a good chance of winning, and those were just starting out and whose time was not that valuable in the first place. Both types figured among the ten submissions that arrived on September 3.

It is customary in professional competitions that the designs are identified only by cryptic mottoes, the authors' names kept secret in sealed envelopes. In Philadelphia the names were public knowledge from the outset. Six were nobodies: Samuel Rumer was a draftsman, Benjamin D. Price was just starting out, and Isaac Hobbs had done nothing more substantial than contributing fanciful houses to *Godey's Lady's Book*. About Maximilian Schroff, Duncan Macrae, and a certain C. Wanner (or Warner), we know nothing. Only four firms were serious contenders, and each of them imagined it held a trump card.[16]

When it came to colossal government buildings, no one was more experienced than Thomas Fuller, who won the competitions for the Canadian Houses of Parliament (1864) and the New York State Capitol (1867). He put together a team consisting of another Canadian, Augustus Laver, and—in order to overcome any qualms the building committee might have about hiring a foreign architect—a Philadelphian. This was Henry A. Sims, which gave them a man on site to supervise the building should Fuller, Laver & Sims win the commission.

Napoleon LeBrun's trump card was to have built two of Philadelphia's most visible monuments, the Academy of Music and the Catholic Cathedral of Saints Peter and Paul. To bolster his chances he recruited two German professionals of exceptional competence, Paul Schulze and Paul Schoen (among other things, Schulze had just built two major buildings at Harvard).[17] LeBrun was a former pupil of T. U. Walter and perhaps he imagined this might help him. It would not; he could not know that Walter was disgusted by his behind-the-scenes intrigues during the 1860 competition and that he regarded LeBrun as a "bad man."[18]

Samuel Sloan's strong suit was a genius for self-promotion, and a volubility and hustling energy worthy of a character out of Charles Dickens. His *Model Architect* (1851–52) and a torrent of subsequent books had made him the best-known architect in the United States. He found architectural competitions irresistible and distance was no object (he won third prize in the 1857 competition for an opera house in Rio de Janeiro). Determined to win the Philadelphia commission, he decided to ingratiate himself with the key juror. He visited Walter and invited him to write an article on his U.S. Capitol dome for the *Architectural Review and American Builders' Journal,* a journal that Sloan had just founded. While not technically a bribe, it would ensure that Walter would feel warmly toward Sloan when it came time to judging Sloan's drawings.

But of all the participants, McArthur was the clear favorite. Yet having already won the commission, only to see it pried away from him at the last minute, he decided to take no chances. He wrote Walter at his Germantown villa to ask if they might meet. Walter's response on April 27 was blunt: "I want you to make designs for the P[ublic] Buildings and I earnestly desire that you may be the successful competitor." Although he claimed that "I have no fear of being compromised," Walter knew that such a meeting could raise eyebrows, and so he proposed that instead of meeting in McArthur's office they meet "in the other place you mentioned."

The next morning Walter trained to Philadelphia to lunch with McArthur. This was the prelude to one very sociable spring and summer: Walter visited McArthur on May 5, 7, 10, 12, and 22, and dined with him in Germantown on May 11; all is recorded in Walter's diary. The two architects had barely seen one another in the previous year; now they maintained a schedule of two to three visits a week throughout the summer. According to modern standards, this was a flagrant conflict of interest. Yet Walter would not have viewed it that way. The Baptist Sunday School preacher, the man who returned the checks for his church commissions uncashed, the man who refused to send his friends copies of articles praising him because it would be "indecorous"—this was not the man to fix a competition. Walter evidently believed he could separate the two lobes of his architectural mind. He would help his friend and pupil perfect his design, and then he would step back and assume his other role, that of impartial judge.

Ten sets of drawings arrived by the September 3 deadline. Unfortunately none survives, although newspaper descriptions suggest that it was a carnival of mansards and pavilions: "every plan submitted, with one single exception, has an outcropping of the French roof mania, in various degrees of horridness."[19] (What was the exception? Did Fuller try something Gothic, like his Houses of Parliament in Ottawa?)

ON SEPTEMBER 10 Walter rode into the city to supervise the hanging of the ten sets of drawings for public display in the hall above the Department of Surveys. The following week he spent every day studying the drawings, reading the architects' specifications, writing a detailed memo about each project. No one else on the committee spent so much time with the drawings; clearly they deferred to Walter's judgment. After a week of studying the competitors and their ideas, he relaxed on Sunday, the 19th. That evening, perhaps thinking of the competitors who had been ceaselessly importuning him, he addressed his Sunday School class on "the brazen serpent."

On September 28 the winners were announced. Walter seems to have recognized and eliminated the second-tier designers early in the game. The four premiated prizes seemed to show that those with large offices, or with collaborative projects, had the best chances. (It was also smart to pay Walter a call. The three architects who visited Walter during the competition were the three highest ranked.) Schulze, LeBrun, and Schoen won fourth place while the team of Fuller, Laver & Sims placed third, winning $500 and $1,000 respectively. Such was the state of American public architecture at this juncture that Anglophile Canadian or Germanic architecture could do so well. Most astonishingly, the first two places exactly repeated the results of the 1860 competition: Sloan again in second, with a $1,500 premium, and McArthur the victor. Walter's "earnest desire" that McArthur win was fulfilled.

McArthur's project showed a U-shaped block, its open arms embracing the State House. It was a difficult siting problem, to create a building of monumental power and presence, while at the same time not overpowering the relatively small, domestically-scaled block of the State House. This McArthur did by sensitively modulating the scale of the building between its Chestnut and Walnut street fronts. On Walnut Street the building presented a continuous unbroken front, anchored by corner pavilions between which it grew progressively in scale to culminate at the central towered block. But the Chestnut Street facade simply presented two end pavilions, gauged to the size of the State House, and themselves looking more like Second Empire houses, rather than the end blocks of a mighty civic building several hundred feet in length. McArthur worked with considerable tact, although in the end he could not eliminate the jarring stylistic contrast between the mansarded pavilions and the Palladian State House. In this respect, Sloan's disingenuous 1860 proposal to simply extend the existing buildings to Walnut Street was far less overpowering. But overpowering architecture was the order of the day, across the city at large.

It was precisely on these grounds, though, that the building was now criticized. As in 1860, those with vested interests used the architectural issues to mask their own motives about the choice of site. Those committed to a site in the old commercial district argued ingeniously in 1860 for a unified building, claiming that the extended Walnut Street front offered the chance for a more monumental structure. In 1869, the proponents of a central site, towards the new districts opened by the railroad, argued exactly the opposite: the Walnut Street design crowded the old historic site, and ruined its character. Walter angrily spoke out against this line of thinking: "It is said the new buildings will *desecrate* the sacred enclosure. On the contrary—What about the present buildings? Do they embellish it?" It was rather weak tea to argue that McArthur's buildings were less offensive than the later additions around the State House, but Walter insisted on the point: "The new buildings will be a fine setting for Independence Hall [which] ought to stand alone [and] free . . ."

Alarmed by the criticism, Walter proposed in early October that McArthur make a number of changes to his design in order to better harmonize the new with the old. Painfully aware of the stylistic contrast between Strickland's delicate cupola and

FIGURE 6.5 McArthur easily won the second competition for City Hall because of the superb quality of his design. It cannot have hurt that he frequently met the judge of the competition, his old mentor Thomas U. Walter.

McArthur's jagged needle-like spire, Walter appears to have proposed something more complimentary to the existing building.

Along with these changes, Walter mandated a whole range of other changes which transformed McArthur's design (fig. 6.5). He made McArthur overhaul the massing of the Walnut Street facade, which rose and fell in pavilions and intermediate wings, but without much sense of power and vigor. In fact, McArthur's original design had the lackluster massing of his Civil War–era hospitals, such as his Laning Hall (1868) at the United States Naval Home—drawn into wings and pavilions for visual variety, but without really suggesting the grouping of powerful sculptural masses. Based on Walter's criticism, McArthur now drew the shoulders of the central pavilion towards the center, gave them more emphatic rooflines, and more clearly presented a hierarchy of parts culminating in the center.

At the same time Walter suggested a more plastic treatment of the wall surfaces. In the original design the wings were little more than massive masonry walls that were regularly pierced by segmental windows, with little modeling of the surfaces in depth. McArthur now rethought his walls to make them more sculptural, applying a screening order of engaged columns and pilasters around the perimeter of the building. These changes were reflected on the wooden model that was prepared by Allen Bard in November and December to express the spatial qualities of the revised design (fig. 6.6). The model cost over $700 and along with the revised drawings was submitted to the building committee on December 27, 1869.

The final change mandated by Walter was the introduction of architectural sculpture into the tower. Here was the beginning of what ultimately became the building's lavish and ingenious program of allegorical sculpture. There was little hint of this before, other than the lone figure of Liberty on its dome. Perhaps Walter had warned McArthur that the designs would be evaluated according to their cost early on; if so, it was a case of bait and switch. Having overcome the initial hurdle, they were now free to start exceeding their original, artificially low estimates.

In the 1869 wood model the building suddenly came alive with sculpture, particularly in the modified tower which once more had the figure of Liberty from the 1860 design. The corners were beveled and marked by free-standing heroic figures, representing allegorical virtues of the city. At first confined to the tower, these statues would soon spread to the most remote

FIGURE 6.6 The wooden model of the 1869 City Hall design was intended to show the relationship to eighteenth-century Independence Hall, but anybody looking at the photograph in a stereopticon viewer would instantly see how Independence Hall would be dwarfed into insignificance.

corners of the building. In part this was the consequence of preparing drawings at smaller scale; there were simply many more
details that suggested embellishment. At this time the sculpture
seems to have increased through simple accretion, without any
notion of unifying the parts through an allegorical program.

Walter was delighted with the revised City Hall design, and
he spent the first day of 1870 writing a glowing description for
the *Philadelphia Press*.[20] He had reason to be pleased: much of the
building—its new plasticity of surface, its muscular massing into
pavilions, its striking cupola, and the beginnings of a rich program of allegorical statuary—reflected his criticism. The design
was conspicuously better for it, more vigorous, more imposing,
and more disciplined artistically. The country was given an advance look at Philadelphia's new city hall early in 1870, when
the *American Architect and Builders' Monthly* published his drawing,
which was much more detailed than the wood model. And yet
McArthur had little opportunity to enjoy the triumph, for during the frantic early months of 1870 the commission was again
pried from him.

IN APRIL 1870 a bill was brought forward in the state legislature to establish a Commission for the Erection of the Public Buildings. This body would have the authority to procure
plans, advertise for bids, and oversee the construction of the new
public buildings. The crucial figure was James McManes (died
1899), the political boss who controlled the Gas Trust. McManes
shepherded the bill forming a building commission through both
houses of the state legislature, so swiftly that the bill was never
printed.[21]

The most vexing question was still the site. To many of the
city's newspapers, the Independence Square site was a foolishly
backward move, not in keeping with the city's progressive character. The *Philadelphia Post*, the *Evening Telegraph*, and the *Sunday
Dispatch* all saw the progressive meaning of the Penn Square site.
On the other hand, Independence Square had powerful friends,
especially the Lea family. Matthew Carey Lea conducted a one-

man campaign to declare the Independence Square site legally binding.[22] On February 28, 1870 he submitted a petition to the legislature arguing that the site was twice authorized by Acts of Assembly.[23]

McManes's bill resolved the site issue with Solomonic wisdom: the decision would be made by the citizens of Philadelphia, who would vote in a public referendum to be held in October. But this time, they would not be offered the difficult choice of Independence Square or Penn Square, which confused matters by raising the distracting issue of historic preservation. Now the alternatives would be Washington Square or Penn Square. It was now a clear referendum between a site in the older city of the colonial era and one in the growing city to the west, without anxiety about "desecrating the sacred shrine."

There was a curious codicil to the Public Building Act, as it came to be called. If the public chose the Washington Square site, Penn Square would be donated to the city's cultural institutions. The Franklin Institute, the Academy of Natural Sciences, the Pennsylvania Academy of Fine Arts, and a future Philadelphia library would each be given one of the square's four quadrants, on which they would erect new monumental buildings. This ensemble would constitute a grand cultural forum, much like that built by the Prussian kings in central Berlin. In this way, the Pennsylvania legislature cleverly mollified Philadelphia's pro-growth faction: even if municipal government remained in the colonial city, these new civic monuments to the west would serve as an attractive lure to real estate development. (Of course, such a decision would have robbed the crowded city at one stroke of two of its principal open spaces, but in a decade where Fairmount Park was vastly expanded, this seemed not to matter.)

The idea that Penn Square might form a civic ensemble did not originate with McManes. Ultimately, it dated back to Penn's original plan, which showed a cluster of buildings there, but this remained purely hypothetical until the city's pace of development reached the site, as it did by the time of the Civil War. At this point, the city's cultural and civic organizations began agitating to build there. The most adamant was the Academy of Natural Sciences, which organized a building committee in 1867 that was to negotiate with the city over a site at Penn Square.[24] When the attempt failed, the Academy instead held a competition in the summer of 1868 for a different site. Nonetheless, when the second project for City Hall began to falter, the Academy grew hopeful again, delayed its own building campaign, and formally petitioned the state in February 1869 for the northwest corner of Penn Square.[25]

Such were the stakes when the Governor signed the bill into law on August 5, 1870, establishing the Public Building Commission. Once again McArthur's plans were set aside and a third building committee once more set about the tedious business of finding a suitable design for the public buildings.

The Building Commission consisted of the Mayor, the presidents of Select and Common Council, and ten other members. These included some of Philadelphia's best-known citizens, including three prominent lawyers: Henry M. Phillips (1811–84),[26] Theodore Cuyler (1819–76), and Samuel C. Perkins (1828–1903), a Yale-educated attorney.[27] As chairman, the committee chose its only member with practical building experience, John Rice (1812–80), the influential contractor who had worked with Walter on the extension of the U.S. Capitol.

The membership of the commission was inclusive, with both Democrats as well as Republicans, an unusual gesture in the highly partisan postwar era. But two factions were conspicuously absent: the city's social elite as well as its cultural and intellectual leadership. The commission was not filled with the Episcopalian and Quaker gentry (such as Nicholas Biddle) who had set the agenda up until now but by the newer mercantile and legal elite, who made their mark in the city's industrial economy; instead they tended also to be Presbyterian and Freemasons.

The commission met for the first time on September 12, 1870; its first order of business was the selection of plans for the new building. A subcommittee was established to choose an architect, and it considered the possibility of holding yet another competition, to which six architectural firms would be invited. They would be asked to submit plans for both the Washington Square and the Penn Square site. But, it was quickly pointed out, no architect could possibly provide detailed plans in the thirty days before the site referendum. Instead the subcommittee turned once more to John McArthur, the one architect with a detailed set of plans that might be adapted to either site. He was engaged to make plans, without the ritual of a competition whose result was a foregone conclusion. There was evidently no protest by the city's architects.

As the referendum drew near, the city's most important newspapers tilted toward the Washington Square site, following the lead of an outspoken editorial in *The Day*. By the time of the referendum, the *Public Ledger*, the *Philadelphia Press*, and the *Evening Bulletin* were all champions of the Washington Square site, and the institutional acropolis at Penn Square that this would make possible.

Believing that the choice of Washington Square was inevitable, McArthur spent the weeks before the referendum adapting his 1869 design to this site. All that was necessary was to convert his U-shaped building into a square, reprising one of his symmetrical wings in the place of Independence Hall. Working briskly, he had a completed design ready for the committee on October 7, 1870. As it happened, he chose wrong. Four days later the city decided overwhelmingly in favor of the Penn Square site, by a vote of 51,623 to 32,825.

"The intersection plan has been abandoned"

The matter now seemed settled. McArthur promptly dropped his plans for Washington Square and began adapting them to Penn Square (which hardly required any major changes). T. U. Walter was called in once more as referee to help the committee assess the newly revised drawings, which he did on October 24. He spoke warmly of McArthur's abilities and the merits of the design.[28] This, and the quality of the design itself, carried the day. McArthur was appointed the architect of the public buildings at an annual salary of $6,000, effective as of January 1, 1871.

Privately, however, Walter had his doubts. With the addition of a massive fourth wing, McArthur's building had grown into a hulking foursquare leviathan. The same evening that Walter praised McArthur's design to the building commission, he was more honest when speaking to his fellow architects in the rooms of the newly formed A.I.A. chapter. There the topic of discussion was the new City Hall site, and whether there ought to be a single building upon the square. Walter joined his professional colleagues in arguing for a group of smaller buildings, arranged in a picturesque ensemble. Here he was heartily seconded by the young Gothic enthusiasts of the A.I.A.: Frank Furness, George Hewitt, Henry Sims. The only man to champion a single monolithic structure was McArthur himself.[29] It was a playful argument among friends, but it showed how high feelings ran.

The same misgivings were voiced in the city at large. The Penn Square project was dubbed "the intersection building," because it would stand athwart the city's principal intersection. The *Evening Bulletin* led the anti-intersection campaign, which raged with increasing fury throughout late 1870 and into 1871. By March 1871, the more moderate *Philadelphia Inquirer* was lamenting that "the Public Buildings question has degenerated at last into mere personal abuse."[30]

McArthur worked on his plans throughout the winter and spring. By March 3, 1871 they were advanced enough to be shown at a private evening organized by John Rice at the Continental Hotel.[31] McArthur used the new device of lantern slides to project his plans and elevations, to lobby in favor of the intersection building. His project had been considerably modified in the months since October. The tower had now grown to 292 feet and for the first time was to be capped by a monumental figure of William Penn. And it was no longer simply a major building in Philadelphia; it was now to be the central and dominant building of the city, locked into the crucial intersection of Penn's plan, and the largest and tallest building in the city. This was an order of magnitude greater than the more modest building that the city had set out to make in 1868.

In one respect the presentation of the vastly enlarged monument backfired. It spurred Henry Charles Lea to make one last heroic effort to stop the building. At first, he focused on declaring the Penn Square site invalid, but early in 1871 he shifted his aim higher: to the outright abolition of the Public Buildings Commission itself. Lea paid for much of the movement's expenses (which amounted to $20,000), including advertising, printing, and the renting of the Academy of Music.[32] There his campaign reached its crescendo on March 24, 1871, with a "Mass Meeting to Abolish the Public Buildings Commission."[33]

The campaign clearly alarmed the building commission, which was itself not entirely certain about the wisdom of building so monumental a pile in modest and unpretentious Philadelphia. Anxious to calm public outrage, it set about making the "intersection building" more palatable. John Rice proposed a pair of buildings, which would have monumental fronts on Broad Street but "plain" walls on Thirteenth Street.[34] Here he was joined by Theodore Cuyler, the prominent counsel for the Pennsylvania Railroad. Since Cuyler had been a member of the original building committee of 1860, his words carried special force. A narrow majority preferred the ensemble of four buildings, and McArthur was authorized to make yet another set of plans—his fifth since 1860. By mid-August 1871, the *Philadelphia Inquirer* could proclaim "the intersection plan has been abandoned."[35]

McArthur now submitted designs for four separate buildings, two larger ones to the north, measuring 208 by 290 feet, and two smaller ones to the south measuring 214 by 197. All were to be "Renaissance in style." The northeast building would have the Mayor's Office, District Courts, Court of Common Pleas, and office of the Police Chief, while the northwest would have the Supreme Court, and the registrar of wills and registrar of deeds. The southern buildings would contain the two chambers of City Council along with the municipal office.

The defeat of the "intersection building" ought to have been a triumph for Lea's civic-minded reformers, who dreaded an ostentatious and costly marble behemoth. And yet it was immediately recognized that four separate building campaigns might be costlier than one single concentrated operation. The chance for hiding graft and waste in four separate projects was all the greater. And so support for the four-building ensemble began to wane during the fall of 1871. Quietly the commission instructed McArthur to reconsider his plans for the intersection building. On April 17, 1872, he submitted his revised design for a single massive towered building, placed directly atop the intersection, although four large portals would permit traffic to continue through the building, if desired (fig. 6.7).

McArthur's presentation was effective, and he stressed the role of his building as an urban monument: "In Paris, a city which has lavished money, without stint, upon its architectural decorations, no single modern building, with which I am acquainted,

FIGURE 6.7 When the site of City Hall was moved to the intersection of Broad and Market streets, the U-shaped building became a square although it retained its basic form, including the cupola that had been inspired by the steeple of Independence Hall.

has been erected in a position that does not admit of a perfect view whether by the apparent termination of intersecting streets, or by the occupation of a park or square." In gridiron Philadelphia, McArthur's options were limited, although fifty years later the city would oblige him with the Benjamin Franklin Parkway to the northwest, finally granting the Parisian building a Parisian boulevard from which to approach it. This was far in the future, of course, but the commission was nonetheless persuaded by McArthur's drawings, and his estimate that the building would cost $6,250,000.[36]

Confident that public opposition had now subsided, the commission voted 9 to 2 in favor of the intersection building.[37]

The meeting ended on a fateful note. Having settled on the building's definitive design, commission president John Rice promptly retired—evidently to bid for its lucrative contracts. His place was taken by bland, self-effacing Samuel C. Perkins, who would maintain his grip on the reins for nearly thirty years, not relinquishing them until the dissolution of the commission in 1901. Step by step, McArthur's utilitarian courthouse and municipal building of 1860, estimated to cost not quite two and a half million dollars, metamorphosed into a civic monument costing ten times as much.

McArthur now repaid T. U. Walter the favor of choosing his design by hiring Walter as his chief assistant. Walter began work on June 1, 1874, his salary set at $2,500. It was just the sort of job for which he had lived his professional life, a vast civic monument to be built with almost European deliberation and slowness. Walter was one of the few American architects capable of such a project, having worked on most of the American buildings that were exceptions to the general rule of haste and carelessness: the Second Bank of the United States in the 1820s, Girard College in the 1830s and 1840s, and the United States Capitol in the 1850s and 1860s. McArthur had found the perfect assistant.

Perhaps too perfect, for the word gradually circulated in Philadelphia that Walter was the author of the design. The *Evening Bulletin* published an editorial "Concerning Architects" that

suggested that McArthur was simply a figurehead of sorts, over-
seeing the building of City Hall. Walter, it insisted, "is the real
architectural genius of the Public Buildings." Walter was horrified, and swiftly dashed off a reply to the paper, insisting that
McArthur "alone [was] the beginning and end of the design and
construction of . . . this his greatest work."

But the gossip was not entirely unfounded. As we have seen,
Walter had acted as design critic since 1869, and the results are
obvious. City Hall stands far above any of McArthur's other
works in quality, refinement of detail, massing and grouping
of parts, and the relationship of ornament to architecture (fig.
6.8). This does not mean that Walter was the secret author of the
building. Rather, he was the critic, guiding McArthur, challeng-

FIGURE 6.8 The facade of City Hall is no flat wall; instead, layered planes of
columns, entablatures, and sculpture project from it, giving it the play of
deep shadow that we associate with sculpture.

ing him, and forcing him to make his good ideas better. You do not need the ghostwriter when you have the right editor.

McArthur's own personality made this collaboration possible. He was unusual in nothing so much as his remarkable ordinariness. When contemporaries tried to sketch his character they became remarkably tepid: "He enters keenly into all boyish amusements, never attends the theatre, but takes delight in circuses and menageries."[38] Here there was nothing of the worldly Stanford White or sophisticated Wilson Eyre. Circuses and menageries indeed!—rather than an artistic cosmopolite, McArthur was an American Presbyterian, supported by the strong lattice of values of protestant America: respectability, sobriety, orderliness. If poetry was absent from this list it was perhaps not missed. After all, McArthur was not designing an art museum or a cathedral, but an American municipal building. And here his own values could not have been more in harmony with the character of his building.

The struggle over the site and architect is but one chapter in the long epic of Philadelphia City Hall. Still to be told is the story of its construction—each year's building campaign, accompanied by frenzied clashes over taxation and mounting expenses; the extraordinary engineering of the masonry and metal tower; the artistic decoration of the palatial chambers for the mayor and City Council. There is also the story of the sculpture, how Alexander Milne Calder transformed a modest program of conventional foliage and a stock figure of *Liberty* into the most ambitiously encyclopedic allegory ever to grace an American building, with a cast of colossal marble figures large enough to fill several opera companies (fig. 6.9). And then there is the mystery at the heart of the building, how all this architectural and sculptural idealism was carried out by a ring of municipal lawyers and politicos, against a backdrop of unconcealed patronage.

By the time McArthur died in 1890, his Second Empire confection was distinctly dowdy; by the time it was finished—and 1901 will serve as a useful benchmark—it was laughably unfashionable. But fashionableness is only one architectural virtue,

FIGURE 6.9 Alexander Milne Calder, the Scottish-born sculptor, worked on City Hall continuously from 1872 to 1894. Here his studio, housed in City Hall's Courtroom no. 2, is visited by architect John McArthur, Jr. (in the jaunty straw hat).

and by no means the greatest. Walt Whitman stumbled upon it coming home late one night and was enchanted with the vast presence looming in the moonlight; it was "a majestic and lovely show, . . . silent, weird, beautiful."[39] Rudyard Kipling visited it in 1890 and was captivated by the sculpture at the base of the tower (fig. 6.10): "The figures representing the races of man on top of the large granite columns excited his merriment at what he called their agony at having such a great weight upon them."[40]

What critics like Whitman and Kipling could sense was that City Hall was more than another bloated pastiche of Second Empire stage scenery. It is pleasant to discover that for many de-

FIGURE 6.10 Rudyard Kipling visited City Hall during his first visit to America, spending "nearly a half hour" admiring the sculpture at its base. Here the theme of Four Continents culminates in heroic figures that represent the races of Africa, America, Asia, and Europe all working together to carry the mighty load of the tower, assisted by infant putti in the corners.

cades City Hall followed an odd ritual that began in 1899. Every night at 8:57, the yellow lights in the four clock faces of the tower would suddenly be turned off. For three minutes they would remain dark, then, promptly at nine, the lights would be turned on. Even those far out of sight of the clock hands would be able to set their watch. For this one moment each evening, City Hall united the sprawling grid of Philadelphia—Southwark, Kensington, even far West Philadelphia—much as cathedral bells once united medieval towns.

Crisscrossed by the city's two major streets, its four facades equal, City Hall is itself an image of gridded Philadelphia, extending evenly in all directions. And unlike its Parisian counterparts, McArthur's building was not an imperial building, with a show facade, a mighty flight of stairs, and a long gilded hall converging at some central climax. Instead the building remained profoundly, even chronically Philadelphian, anchored at street level and not hoisted above it, egalitarian and not governed by an axial hierarchy of corridors and grand rotundas, and holding at its center not a royal chamber but a place of public circulation—itself a directionless space, but from where four portals offered views of limitless extent (fig. 6.11). It is the definitive Philadelphia building—un-Quaker in its extravagance but resolutely Quaker in its open and non-hierarchical geometry, as open and non-hierarchical as the Quaker meeting houses that made it possible.

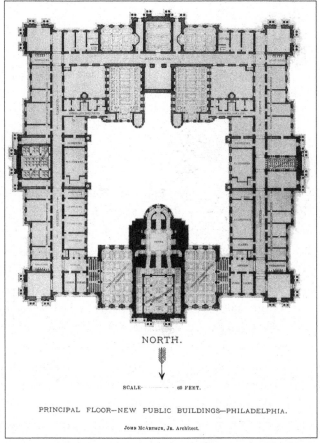

NORTH.

SCALE ———— 60 FEET.

PRINCIPAL FLOOR—NEW PUBLIC BUILDINGS—PHILADELPHIA.

John McArthur, Jr. Architect.

FIGURE 6.11 The most remarkable—and most quintessentially Philadelphian—feature of City Hall is that there is no single monumental entrance leading to a great chamber. Instead, four monumental portals lead to an open space of the people.

CHAPTER 7

The Carpenter

Owen Biddle

■ IN 1805, the Philadelphia architect Owen Biddle, Jr., published *The Young Carpenter's Assistant; or, A System of Architecture,
Adapted to the Style of Building in the United States.*

It is the second work of architectural instruction written and
published in this country, preceded only by Asher Benjamin's
The Country Builder's Assistant (1797).[1] Each was directed at the
aspiring carpenter who, by learning to draw and to manipulate
the classical orders, might become an architect. The authors, who
were born within a year of one another, had themselves made
that transition. And yet Benjamin wrote from central Massachusetts and Biddle from Philadelphia, and their books emerge from
architectural cultures of radically different character.

Of Biddle's life we have only the barest sketch. He was born
in 1774, the son of a Quaker clockmaker, and trained as a house
carpenter. In 1800 he became a member of the Carpenters'
Company. From 1799 to 1801 he practiced with fellow carpenter
Joseph Cowgill but for most of his life he worked independently.

His early works were houses—like the "convenient well-finished three Story Brick House" he built at 23 Powell Street in 1799—while his mature work included several large public buildings.[2] Late work was not to be: Biddle died in 1806 at the age of 32.

Biddle was never a professional architect in our modern sense. He was capable of making a perfectly serviceable design for a house or a Quaker meeting but only in order to build it. Sometimes we find him acting only as builder, as at the first Pennsylvania Academy of the Fine Arts, and sometimes as both builder and designer, as at the Arch Street Meeting House, but we never find him acting only as designer. Had he lived longer, perhaps he would have given himself over entirely to design, perhaps not; we cannot know.

Biddle's sphere of action widened beyond mere house-building with the Arch Street Meeting, for which he served as both designer and builder, and which still stands on Third and Arch streets. In 1803 a committee was formed to build a "Home for the Year Meeting of Women Friends" with a capacity of 1,000. Benjamin Henry Latrobe was consulted and recommended "a circular, domed meeting house," while grumbling that his suggestions had "never . . . been of any use to your Society."[3] But this time his advice might have been taken, for while Biddle designed an absolutely plain and sober brick meeting house, there is a superb sense of balance and proportion in the three cubic masses of its facade, suggesting the abstract geometric discipline we know from Latrobe (fig. 7.1). The central block and eastern wing were built in 1803–5, the western wing in 1810–11, after Biddle's death.

Biddle's design survives in two drawings, a signed plan and perspective at the Athenaeum of Philadelphia and a plan and elevation at Haverford College (unsigned, but certainly by Biddle). The perspective is skillfully rendered in ink wash with well-constructed cast shadows, a handsome staffage of foliage and trees, and that clever Baroque ploy of making the corner of the drawing curl inward like a scroll (fig. 7.2). But his plan is quite lucid, and it perfectly illustrates the advice he would give later in

FIGURE 7.1 Quaker worship is largely silent, and Owen Biddle's Arch Street Meeting House gives us its equivalent in architectural silence. He built the east wing in 1804 and the identical west wing, used for the Women's Monthly Meeting, was added in 1811 after his death.

his book: "it will considerably enliven the drawing to give the appearance of a shadow on one side of the wall, by drawing one line thicker than the other."[4] The shadow was to be cast, as architectural convention required, from a light source at the upper left hand corner, projected at a 45 degree angle. The drawings are quite accomplished but while we may admire the artistry, Biddle would never have thought of them as *designs*, that is, as formal artistic compositions, but rather as *drafts*, practical plans for a building of conventional construction and detail in which personal expression had no place.

While the Arch Street Meeting was under construction, Biddle was pulled into another project, the Schuylkill Permanent Bridge (later the Market Street Bridge). In 1798 a stock company was incorporated to build the bridge, under the direction of Richard Peters (1744–1828), a prominent judge and one of Philadelphia's most enterprising civic leaders. He was also a gentleman-amateur architect who had designed Belmont, his Palladian

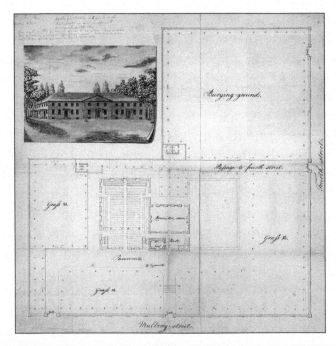

FIGURE 7.2 The Quaker meeting house rejected not only ornament and extravagance but all spatial hierarchy. Instead of a grand portico that opened onto a dramatic axis to reveal a magnificent altar or pulpit, there were two absolutely equal spaces for the men's and women's meeting, reached through a profusion of identical entrances.

mansion in Fairmount Park, and he was knowledgeable about building matters. After several false starts, in which he considered several designs for a stone bridge, including "a very elegant one by Mr. Latrobe," he settled on Timothy Palmer, a bridge-builder from Massachusetts.[5] Palmer devised a highly original arched wood truss, 550 feet in length and resting on two stone piers.

Judge Peters significantly modified Palmer's design for the masonry piers and frame but his greatest contribution was in convincing the dubious stockholders that the bridge needed to have a superstructure to cover it. Moreover, its particular situation "compelled ornament, and elegance of design, lest it should disgrace the environs of a great City"; no perfunctory shed would do.[6] Peters himself "furnished several sketches for covers (as no person better qualified would do it)," which he had drawn to scale by Adam Traquair (1782–1851), a stonemason and assistant to Latrobe.[7] After securing a preliminary estimate of $8,000, he had Traquair revise the design, working in consultation with amateur architect John Dorsey (1759–1821).[8] Their proposal was further modified by Biddle, the fourth to work on the design but the first trained carpenter.[9] This final design was approved and Biddle was engaged to build it. He used white pine, and as it was painted, "an adroit hand dashed on the sand and stone dust" to imitate stone; convex strips were then nailed regularly across the boards and painted white to represents the joints of stone masonry.[10] The entire structure, bridge and cover, was built in 1804 and opened on January 1, 1805 (fig. 7.3).

The Schuylkill Permanent Bridge was extraordinarily influential and it heralded a long succession of American covered bridges. It also brought Biddle into contact with the highest levels of patronage, which helped make possible the publication of *The Young Carpenter's Assistant.* Judge Peters was an advance subscriber, and his name carried weight. Dorsey subscribed as well and he also engaged Biddle to serve as the builder of his new Pennsylvania Academy of the Fine Arts, America's first building expressly built as an art museum (fig. 7.4).[11] Dorsey designed it as a neoclassical temple of the arts, a domed cube fronted with a

The *Evangelical Intelligencer*

The *SCHUYLKILL Permanent BRIDGE High Street* Philad.^a

FIGURE 7.3 Biddle designed the walls and roof that protected the wooden structure of the Schuylkill Permanent Bridge, making it the first of America's many covered bridges.

FIGURE 7.4 The Pennsylvania Academy of the Fine Arts was America's first building expressly devoted to the arts, and its solemn temple character would inspire countless successors. It was by the amateur John Dorsey, one of fifteen plans he produced in 1806 ("because he charges nothing for them," Latrobe grumbled).

pair of Ionic columns in antis and guarded by carved sphinxes, and it could hardly have looked more different from the plain style Arch Street Meeting. But this did not trouble Biddle, who, even after it was completed in 1806, still identified himself as a "House Carpenter and Teacher of Architectural Drawing" on the title page of his book that appeared that same year.

We do not know where Biddle received his advanced architectural education. Private architectural schools came and went in Philadelphia throughout the 1790s. Regular courses of instruction were launched by Falize and Lacour (1794), Joseph Bowes (1794), Stephen Hallett (1796), and Christopher Minifee (1797), and suspended just as quickly. These are only those who purchased advertisements in the newspapers; perhaps there were more. At any rate, by 1800 or so, Biddle was sufficiently accomplished to begin teaching "the rudiments of architecture" to his fellow carpenters. In 1804 he tried to formalize his school and to affiliate it with the Carpenters' Company. In January of that year he proposed that

> a Committee of five Members be appointed to take into consideration the expediency of forming an establishment under the patronage of this Company, for the purpose of Teaching the different branches of Architecture &cc. and if in the opinion of this Committee such an establishment should be proper, they are directed to draw out a plan for carrying the same into efect [sic], and lay it before the Company at the next stated meeting.[12]

Biddle's proposal was studied, and defeated in a vote the following November. It seems the Company was more concerned with regulating competition than with the grooming of competitors.

Who would be happy to be put off for ten months and then abruptly turned down? Biddle was not; he instantly turned his energies in a different direction. Two months later he was advertising for subscribers to underwrite the making of an architectural textbook. It was to be lavish: "one neat quarto volume, strongly bound, printed in a handsome style, on a superfine paper, illustrated with upwards of forty engravings."[13] Although subscriptions cost four dollars, a hefty sum, Biddle was able to secure 198 buyers, who between them bought 221 copies. Besides Peters and Dorsey, he found buyers among his fellow carpenters, including John C. Evans, John Ogden, and his former partner Joseph Cowgill. (Conspicuously absent was Latrobe himself, who might well have had nothing but scorn for the book, were it not that it also marked his first appearance in an American architectural book.)

Although the majority of Biddle's subscribers were concentrated in and around Philadelphia, there were far-flung patrons in Lancaster, Pittsburgh, and even Bristol, Rhode Island, where a certain David Leonard bought one. Seven carpenter-builders in Baltimore subscribed. The single biggest subscriber was an enterprising patron named Lewis Sanders in Lexington, Kentucky, who ordered ten copies to sell to the builders of the backwoods region.

Between working on the Schuylkill bridge and canvassing for subscriptions, Biddle managed to finish the book, perhaps by candlelight, by July 5, 1805. On that date the manuscript was copyrighted by the printer Benjamin Johnson, whose shop was on 31 Market Street. In his preface Biddle explained the book's *raison d'être*:

> Having been for some time past in the practice of teaching the rudiments of Architecture, I have experienced much inconvenience for want of suitable books on the subject. All that have yet appeared have been written by foreign authors, who have adapted their examples and observations almost entirely to the style of building in their respective countries, which in many instances differs very materially from ours.[14]

The Young Carpenter's Assistant was aimed at the young carpenter rather than the young architect; Biddle was teaching men like himself, who had already swung tools and formed calluses, who knew how to build, but not how to render or design. And to judge from the text of his book, his curriculum was crafted to produce men like himself, that is, to produce Biddles rather than Latrobes—carpenters who could devise serviceable designs, and could communicate them effectively in graphic means.

This accounts for some of the oddities in Biddle's book, which does not pretend to present a complete education in architectural design. Instead it is intended as a supplement to classroom study, a reference book devoted chiefly to drawing and the classical orders. Following the ancient model of architectural treatises since the Renaissance, it begins with a design for a drawing board and T-square, progressing to the laying out of ellipses and arches; plates four through six depict standard moldings and cornices; at plate seven the orders commence, beginning with the Tuscan order and proceeding apace through the Doric, Ionic and Corinthian orders. Following the orders comes a succession of porticos, pedimented frontispieces, dormer windows, Venetian windows, mantles, roof trusses (fig. 7.5) and stairs. In all these

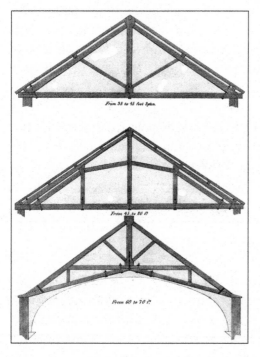

FIGURE 7.5 Biddle's *Young Carpenters' Assistant* (1805) was America's second original manual of architecture and Philadelphia's first. It mixed old and new: the raised tie beam truss at bottom copied a design by Robert Smith from the 1786 *Carpenters' Company Rule Book*. But the middle truss, used for the sixty-foot span of his Arch Street Meeting, innovatively used screwbolts that could compensate for shrinkage in the wooden bottom chord.

examples, Biddle's proportions are the same as Palladio's, or *pretty nearly* so, as he tells us:

> Paladio has been allowed to have been the best judge among the Moderns, who have given the proportions of the remains of Antiquity; the proportions in this book are pretty nearly the same as his . . .[15]

Biddle was no slavish copyist, and through his book runs the pragmatism of the experienced carpenter. Where circumstances forced him to alter his proportions, as with a townhouse of constricted frontage, he was willing to do so, although he still upheld the notion of ideal proportions:

> [If] the door is for a town house with a narrow front, . . . the true proportions of the Orders may be dispensed with, and regard had to the general proportion of the building; but in country houses where the front may be well proportioned, the nearer we adhere to the Orders, the better will be the appearance in general.

But Biddle also conceded that the rules of proportion were somewhat subject to the vagaries of changing taste; here too he recommended a posture of discriminating flexibility. When showing, for example, his cornice design on plate 28, he recommends that it be gauged at one nineteenth the height of the building. But, "every thing is in some degree regulated by fashion," he observed, "and the present fashion would be something smaller than the above proportion" of 1/19th.[16] Whether by the present fashion he means the bold neoclassicism of Latrobe, or the general shift in taste to the attenuated forms of Federal architecture is not entirely clear. Nor did Biddle necessarily distinguish between these categories.

From time to time glimmers of Biddle's own taste peeked through. In a discussion of mantle-pieces, he recommended that the design should "always have a due proportion of plain surfaces, as a contrast to the ornamented parts."[17] By all means he should "not cover his work with unmeaning holes and cuttings of a gouge." In this is something of the voice of a conservative Philadelphia craftsman, for whom a mantle must always remain an architectonic composition, in good Palladian fashion—as in Thomas Nevell's Mount Pleasant—and not an overwrought piece of Federal woodwork (of the sort that still survives in a number of houses in New Castle, Delaware).

Biddle himself made no claim for originality, freely acknowledging his debt to English sources. He acknowledged that he took the proportions of his orders from William Pain (ca. 1730– ca. 1790), whose *Builder's Companion* (London, 1762) was among the most accessible of eighteenth-century architectural manuals. The geometric exercises at the start of Biddle's book he credited to the Scottish architect Peter Nicholson (1765–1844), "whose works are held in deserved estimation." Likely Biddle meant *The Principles of Architecture*, Nicholson's chief work. However he did not accept these works, products of a different building culture, uncritically: his plate 25 depicts a wooden dome, copied, as he tells us, from Nicholson, but which, he complained, "to me appears abundantly too strong."

Biddle had to have owned these books. According to his estate inventory, he owned fifteen "books of Archititure [*sic*]" which would have included the works by Pain and Nicholson, and surely an edition or two of Palladio. Perhaps also the works of James Gibbs, Colen Campbell, William Chambers, and William Halfpenny. For a competent carpenter-builder that would have amounted to a well-stocked reference library. It was dispersed, alas, one month after his death, and sold along with his carpenter's tools at public auction in June 1806.[18]

Biddle also drew from local sources. Many of his designs, including his classical frontispieces and roof trusses, closely follow the illustrations made by Thomas Nevell for the *Articles of the Carpenters Company of Philadelphia: and Their Rules for Measuring and Valuing House-Carpenters Work* (1786).[19] Until the end of the eighteenth century, these designs had been precious commodities, but their appearance in Biddle's book shows how the company's role and influence was changing. The company had dominated the building trades in Philadelphia since 1724, acting much like a medieval guild, enforcing standards of workmanship, consistent fee scales, and corporate solidarity among its members. Not only was the company guild-like in its organization, but also in its secrecy; it treasured its trade secrets, guarding them as the arcane knowledge of a privileged conventicle. In fact, it could be argued that the *Articles of the Carpenters Company of Philadelphia* is America's first architectural book, although it is a publication without a public; copies were numbered and signed, and on the death of a member his widow would find herself visited by a somber delegation from the Company who would reclaim his volume.[20]

Biddle was hardly risking expulsion by publishing variants of the plates from the Carpenters' Company rulebook. Those plates were themselves stolen goods, for the most part, cribbed from English originals.[21] Furthermore, a pirated edition of the rulebook was already published in 1801.[22] And so Biddle's book, with the exception of a few plates at the end, was essentially derivative. He was original only in the selection and arrangement of his borrowed pieces. But even this is a category of originality, and he took great pains, he emphasized, in eliminating the unessential information that clogs European books.

Up to plate 36, Biddle presented little that would have been out of place in a book half a century older. Only in the final section of the book is there any awareness that he was writing in a time of extraordinary architectural change. Here he depicts the recent architecture of Philadelphia, including Samuel Blodgett's Bank of the United States, Benjamin Latrobe's Bank of Pennsylvania, and his own bridge over the Schuylkill River.

Plate 56, the final illustration in his book, is an anomaly, depicting the steeple of Christ Church, designed and built by Robert Smith in 1753. This tribute to Smith, a fellow Carpenters' Company member, and designer of its building, showed that he was still held in high esteem, although he died in 1777. In fact, his description of the steeple scarcely noticed its venerability:

. . . for the justness of its proportions, simplicity and symmetry of its parts [it] is allowed by good judges to be equal if not superior in beauty to any Steeple of the spire kind, either in Europe or America. . . . The superstructure of this steeple is composed of three distinct well-proportioned parts of Architecture, the first story, with its small Pediments and Attics, forming one; the octagonal part, with its ogee formed dome, being the second; and the spire and its pedestal, the third. These three parts are very dissimilar, no one having any thing in it that is common to the others; and yet they agree very well with each other, forming one complete and consistent whole.[23]

For him the steeple was no superannuated curiosity; it was to be judged as a piece of design, on its own merits. An exhibition of architectural drawings in 1795 at the Columbianum (or American Academy of Painting, Sculpture and Architecture) had shown several of Smith's drawings; perhaps they were lying around in the collections of the Company.

Perhaps there was also some sentimental attachment to the most venerable symbol on the Philadelphia skyline. To be sure, William Strickland himself made a drawing of the same mid-Georgian relic a few years later. But in an architecturally conservative city, the study of the Georgian past was not useless knowledge. It was this very immersion in local tradition which made Strickland's own neo-Georgian steeples so satisfying— those he later added to Independence Hall and St. Peter's Episcopal Church.

Clearly it was no contradiction to Biddle to bring together America's most modern building, Latrobe's bank, with a steeple a half a century old. The two buildings were shown in elevation, and apparently based on the original drawings of their respective architects rather than measured drawings. As new and prominent public buildings these designs would have been of intense interest to Biddle's pupils. The more recent architecture, the two banks by Latrobe and Blodgett, were judged on the same neutral scale. Latrobe's building was a "beautiful building" and "a neat specimen of the Ionic order, taken from an ancient Greek Temple," while Blodgett's was a "superb building" and "an elegant specimen of the Corinthian Order; the proportions taken from a Roman Temple called the *Maison Quarree*, at Nismes, in the south of France."[24] To our eyes these buildings leap apart as if electrically charged, but Biddle did not think in categories of the sort we do, in those rigid stylistic divisions of Neoclassical, Federal, and Georgian architecture. His understanding of architecture permitted him to judge all of these things, even Smith's steeple, as part of the same flexible, elastic system, so that even Latrobe's building was a neat Ionic "specimen" rather than a revolutionary essay in correct classicism and America's first great masonry-vaulted dome.

The Anglo-American Palladianism that ruled Philadelphia architecture permitted an extraordinary latitude in the design of details, but within certain conventional channels. Such a system could absorb the stylistic innovations of George Dance or the Adam Brothers, and yet remain in the end fundamentally unchanged. In this mixture of permissive eclecticism and underlying conservatism, we find the peculiar character of Philadelphia's architectural culture. It was the very conservatism of Philadelphia which allowed it to absorb fads and innovations with abandon, but without ever losing its strongly local character. But this was possible in a city for whom style was simply a dressing of carpentry that was applied to a brick shell; while the style of the portico or cornice might change according to the vagaries of taste, the underlying brick building did not.

This is apparent with Biddle's own designs for a freestanding urban townhouse (fig. 7.6). Here a bewildering variety of lunettes, bull's eyes, and fanlights cluttered a facade which was otherwise a taut planar form, in substance not that different from his laconic meeting house.[25] Here is the taste, above all, of a carpenter. Although he understood the orders, he understood them as two dimensional affairs, not plastically, as sculpture. But this is no surprise. After all, the sculptural handling of the orders cannot be separated from masonry construction.

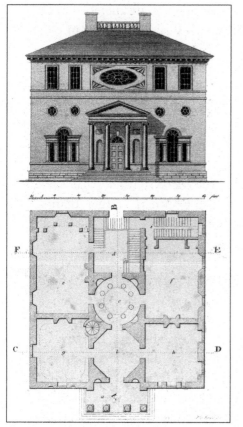
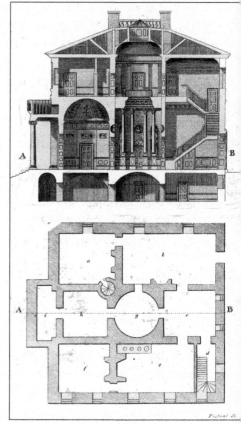

FIGURES 7.6 (left) AND 7.7 A carpenter can quickly learn to carve neoclassical ornament and motifs, but it is a different matter to deploy them gracefully. Biddle's project for a townhouse shows him awkwardly mingling window sizes and shapes, as he tries earnestly to master the new language of neoclassicism.

To be sure, Philadelphia's brick Palladianism had always tended towards planarity, its ornamental motifs always resting lightly on the surface of the building. But even in his interior planning Biddle languished behind the vanguard of taste. The geometric sequence of spaces throughout the house is varied (fig. 7.7), but more in the interlocking Palladian sense than the dynamic sense of Woodlands, a local building that was already sixteen years old when Biddle wrote his book. With these competent but rather ungainly and additive designs, which recall much of the anonymous architecture of turn of the century Philadelphia, Biddle's book closes.

BIDDLE PRACTICED in a swiftly changing world, in which competent professionals such as Latrobe would increasingly shape architectural culture. But his response to these changes was not so much to embrace the new, but rather to solidify the old. He strove to elevate carpenter builders to the level of their professional competitors, regularizing the informal system of education, even as the substance of that education remained that of the eighteenth century.

Nonetheless, in conservative Philadelphia, where the vast bulk of building activity remained the domain of bricklayers and carpenters, such a response was entirely appropriate. In fact, Biddle's book remained a useful compendium for at least another generation.[26] As late as 1833, at the apogee of the Greek Revival, John Haviland produced a second edition of it (adding a few plates of his own at the end "particularly adapted for country use").

Haviland's relationship to Biddle indicates how complex the relationship was between those supposedly distinct categories, architects and builders. An English émigré who arrived in Philadelphia in 1816, Haviland had benefited from an apprenticeship to the English architect James Elmes. But though he was a professional like Latrobe, Haviland also learned from the example of Biddle. He too conducted a drawing school where architecture was taught, running it together with Hugh Bridport from 1818 to 1822. And, like Biddle, he published a book aimed at the ambitious, upwardly mobile carpenter. This was *The Builder's Assistant, containing the five orders of architecture . . . for the use of builders, carpenters, masons, plasterers, cabinet makers, and carvers,* which appeared in three volumes between 1818 and 1821.[27]

The Builder's Assistant was a more substantial book than Biddle's, with a more sophisticated text, but its basic conception was still that of a book of the orders, augmented with the customary leaven of original designs. And Haviland seems indeed to have followed Biddle in becoming Philadelphia's principal architectural educator, for upon closing his own school of drawing he became chief instructor at the Franklin Institute's school of architecture.[28] Throughout this time Biddle's book evidently remained in constant use; why else would Haviland work so diligently to republish it in 1833?

In that same year, the Carpenters' Company at last established the architectural drawing school that Biddle had proposed in 1805. Thus the eighteenth-century system of architectural education—aimed at builders and based on the drawing of simplified versions of the classical orders—passed into the mainstream of Philadelphia architecture in the nineteenth century. The story of American architecture is told primarily as a triumph of professionalism, but it is equally remarkable how enduring and adaptable the country's builder-architects remained. Many of Philadelphia's key figures of mid-century design, including Samuel Sloan, John McArthur, Jr., and even T. U. Walter, enjoyed much the sort of education that Biddle and Haviland provided.

Against this backdrop, Biddle's book plays a more prominent role than its humble wood engravings might suggest. Even up to the end of the eighteenth century, American architecture was a regional affair, based on local building practices and materials. Training was controlled by the building trades, making building a local affair in much the same way that medieval architecture was local. This is not to say that ideas did not move from place to place, but they moved on foot, and through individuals. If there was an overall national character to American architecture—a collective set of typical ideas and forms—it was only that borrowed from England. The means with which Americans learned about English architecture were modern—that is, through publications and mass-produced, accurate prints; the means with which Americans learned about their own architecture were medieval, that is, through personal travel, through second-hand accounts, through drawings and sketchbooks. American carpenters were more reliably informed about the buildings of London than about those of their peers in Boston, Baltimore, or Charleston.

But not all aspects of American culture were still regional in character. America had already achieved a national political culture by the 1790s. The various local models of self-government had been interacting for a generation, throughout the Revolution and Constitutional Convention, during which period there came into being a national political literature of vigor and vitality. These means were not yet available to American architects; American builder-architects worked within a limited radius, and even a city such as Philadelphia was still profoundly provincial, so far as its building went, into the eighteenth century.

Until Biddle, that is. Before 1805 was out, *The Young Carpenter's Assistant* could be bought in Philadelphia; two months later it was being advertised for sale in Hartford, Connecticut, and the shipment of ten copies was on its way to Lexington, Kentucky.[29] Its audience was national. From the standpoint of the history of ideas, Biddle's book itself is not remarkable. It is a provincial variant of a long-established European publishing genre, and is thoroughly conventional in form and content. But with its publication, and that of Benjamin's book, the character of American architecture changed decisively and permanently, for these books are nothing less than the beginning of a national architectural culture.

CHAPTER 8

The Namesake

Peter Angelo Nicholson

■ WHEN SIXTEEN-YEAR-OLD P. A. Nicholson arrived in Philadelphia in 1845 he had nothing to show but his name. But what a name! Every architect, carpenter, or builder in the city knew it. He was the grandson of the legendary Peter Nicholson (1765–1844), the Scottish architect and author of one of the most successful builder's manuals in history, *The Carpenter's New Guide.* From the moment it appeared in 1795, it was constantly in print. American publishers pirated it shamelessly; Lippincott, the Philadelphia publisher, printed at least sixteen editions, the latest in 1871.[1] This alone guaranteed Nicholson's grandson a respectful interview whenever he chanced to knock on an architect's door.

And once in the door, young Nicholson would have needed only a few minutes to demonstrate his training and talents, which included lithography. In no time at all he won a position as draftsman; at twenty-three he would establish his own practice. Few architects begin their careers on such a convenient launching pad. And yet Nicholson's rocket fizzled out. He made all the right moves but while the first years of his practice show a sharp upward curve, the next four decades trace a long slow descent. The few buildings that survive are undistinguished and they cast a grim light on the dynamics of an architect's career.

Nicholson bore the burden of living up to the reputation of his grandfather. Peter Nicholson was one of those Scottish polymaths of boundless energy and curiosity, whose *Carpenter's New Guide* was just one of some two dozen books he had written and illustrated with his own engravings. He also designed buildings, taught engineering, and invented a curious device for making perspective drawings when the vanishing point falls off the page (he called his invention the *centrolinead*). Dreaming of an architectural dynasty, he burdened his son with the name Michael Angelo Nicholson (ca. 1796–1841).

Michael Angelo Nicholson inherited his father's versatility but not evidently the prodigious energy. He had a modest career as architect and engraver, and ran a school of architectural drawing on Euston Square in London. He died young, and his large family fell upon hard times. Two of his daughters eventually found architect husbands, the brilliantly imaginative Alexander "Greek" Thomson and his partner John Baird, whom they married in a double ceremony. But this happened in 1847, too late to benefit their brother Peter Angelo, who was already seeking his fortune elsewhere.

P. A. Nicholson (1829–1902), as he signed himself, chose his destination purposefully. Philadelphia was the home of one of his father's pupils, John Notman, a Scot who emigrated to Philadelphia in 1831.[2] Notman had recently won the competition to design Philadelphia's Athenaeum and needed draftsmen "capable of lining and tinting neatly."[3] Somehow word came to Nicholson, and whether or not arrangements were made before he sailed, he soon found himself in Notman's office. This was at 1410 Spruce Street, in Notman's brick house, and there Nicholson drew the handsome lithograph that introduced the Athenaeum building to the public (fig. 8.1).

The Athenaeum was founded in 1814 as a subscription library by a few young men who wanted a place to pass "their leisure

FIGURE 8.1 John Notman's brownstone Athenaeum introduced the Italianate style and gave Philadelphia something much like a fashionable London Club.

hours . . . without danger to their morals or taste."[4] Setting aside its morality, Notman's dignified building was certainly a temple of taste, although it takes an act of imagination to see how something so stodgily respectable as the Athenaeum could ever have been revolutionary. But the Italian Renaissance palazzo type was unprecedented in Philadelphia and even in London, where the style originated, it was still a recent innovation. Notman distilled the two best examples, the Travellers Club and the Reform Club, into a superbly scaled and detailed gentlemen's library. Just as novel was the material. Had it been built a few years earlier, it would have been of white marble or limestone, like the Reform Club. But instead the facade on Washington Square was of Connecticut River brownstone, a ruddy and warm material. This was the task of Nicholson's lithograph, to make gorgeously palpable the warm and picturesquely textured surface of the stone.

It is noteworthy that the men who built this prodigy of the Italian Renaissance were all Scottish immigrants. Besides Nicholson, there was Notman (Edinburgh), his superintendent of construction, John McArthur, Jr. (Bladenock), and even the publisher of his lithograph, Thomas Sinclair (Orkney Islands). McArthur would soon open his own architectural office, as would John Fraser, yet another Scottish immigrant, shortly thereafter. Philadelphia's architectural scene in the 1850s was shaped by these Scottish overachievers and their German peers, formidable competition if Nicholson was to claw his way to the top. Whatever knowledge he brought to Notman's office in 1845, it can hardly have been much more than lithography, given that he was only sixteen. The next seven years are obscure, apart from a return visit to Scotland in 1851; perhaps he spent the entire time toiling for Notman.[5] Whatever it was he did, by 1852 he felt he knew enough to go into private practice as an architect.

Meanwhile, another émigré found himself in much the same situation. Theodore Wadskier (1827–98) was born on the Danish island of St. Croix and later studied architecture in Copenhagen. In 1850 he emigrated to the United States, where his uncle was the Danish ambassador. And like Nicholson, Wadskier had a situation with an established local figure. This was Samuel Sloan, that ambitious builder-turned-architect who also ran an "architectural drawing academy" and needed an instructor.[6] The arrangement lasted for only a year, just long enough for Wadskier to learn Sloan's hustling style.[7] Central to this was tireless self-promotion, chiefly through publication. Sloan aggressively promoted himself with a ceaseless stream of pattern books, of indifferent originality but marvelous comprehensiveness. (One of these was Nicholson's *The Carpenter's New Guide*, which Sloan reissued in pirated versions in 1854, 1856, and 1860.) As soon as he was on his own, Wadskier did the same.

Every month between December 1851 and June 1852, Wadskier published a design for a suburban villa in *Sartain's Union Magazine of Literature and Art*, along with floor plans.[8] The houses were variously Italianate and Gothic, and of utterly conventional

COTTAGE AND VILLA ARCHITECTURE.

BY T. WADSKIER.

DESCRIPTION OF A DESIGN FOR A VILLA IN THE ITALIAN STYLE.

FIGURE 8.2 For Theodore Wadskier, the Italian villa style was neither urban nor rural, but mingled the traits of each in a way that suited suburban houses. Because it was "capable of the most varied and irregular, as well as very simple, outlines, it is also very significant of the multiform tastes, habits, and wants of modern civilization."

character (fig. 8.2). Just as conventional was the accompanying text, which was filled with platitudes familiar to readers of A. J. Downing's *Architecture of Country Houses* (1850). For example, "the object of all real art is to elicit truth," or it is the duty of art to "give a moral significance to objects," or it is "reprehensible" for one material to pretend to be another material, or a cottage is "a dwelling of limited accommodation" and must be distinguished from a villa. None of this was controversial, and should be taken as the polite background noise of respectability, reassuring the reader that these restless new styles were unimpeachable, morally and aesthetically.

How Nicholson and Wadskier met remains uncertain. Did Nicholson visit Sloan's office, demanding some sort of royalty arrangement on behalf of his grandfather's estate? Whatever the occasion, the ambitions of the two young immigrants ran higher than serving as draftsmen and renderers to more prosperous men. In 1852 they made their gambit and launched the firm of Nicholson & Wadskier, renting rooms at 103 Walnut Street. At the same time Nicholson joined the St. Andrew's Society, where fashionable Philadelphians of Scottish descent met in state, a social investment of the sort that architects still make and perhaps made in the days of Im-Ho-Tep.

Since both Nicholson and Wadskier knew how to make prints, it is natural that their first career move was to bring out their own pattern book. In 1852 they began to issue *The Practical Sculptor, Comprising a Series of Original Designs for Monuments, Mantles, Balustrades, Adapted to the Present Taste and Style of Architecture,* which was meant to be completed in twelve monthly fascicles. Only three were issued before the project sputtered out.[9] Soon they were advertising for "Day Pupils" to help meet their expenses.[10] It was not enough, and in late 1853 they moved to a cheaper office at Seventh and Sansom.[11] None of this helped— not the book, not the school, not the low-budget office—and not a single building, not even an "original mantelpiece," has come to light in Philadelphia. In 1855 they closed up shop and Nicholson moved to Chicago.

Nicholson practiced briefly with the Chicago architect William B. Olmsted (1807–ca. 1881), serving as junior partner in "Olmsted & Nicholson, architects," an ominous demotion and the first sign that his career might not have the glorious arc that his name suggested. Together they built the William Reddick House in Ottawa, Illinois, which still survives, a proud, deep-corniced Italianate cube in the Sloan style. They also built the Ross & Foster Dry Goods store on Chicago's Lake Street, a colossal five-story marble palazzo.[12] The partnership was short-lived and by 1856 Wadskier came west to reestablish Nicholson & Wadskier. He arrived just in time to sign the Architects' Code of Chicago, a pioneering statement of professional solidarity in the United States.[13] They immediately went to work, designing the J. R. Jones House in Galena, a paraphrase of one of the Italianate designs for *Sartain's Magazine*. But the happy times did not last, and once again Nicholson & Wadskier dissolved, this time in the wake of the financial panic of 1857.[14]

Nicholson now made a brave attempt to practice on his own, relocating to Cairo, Illinois. There he worked throughout the Civil War (in which he declined to serve), while the city flourished as a military entrepôt. By the end of the war he had amassed a list of ten clients and designed a fire house.[15] And yet this was not enough; around 1867, he returned to Philadelphia and found work in the office of James H. Windrim, this time not even as junior partner but as draftsman.

Perhaps Windrim (1840–1916), who had also trained with John Notman, was happy to assist a fellow Notman protégé. He certainly needed the help, having won the competition for Philadelphia's Masonic Temple that year. But from this time onward, the remainder of Nicholson's career shows a downward trajectory. He exhibited a fire escape of his own design in 1881 but otherwise shows up only in accounts of chess competitions.[16] During his final years he drifted to the office of Otto Wolf (1856–1916), the brewery specialist with a prodigious national practice but certainly a less prominent figure socially than Windrim. There can have been little glory in this professional end game. Nicholson retired and died in the suburb of Germantown in 1902.

What are we to make of this career, which by the measure of its ambitious debut must be deemed a failure? Nicholson had both a famous name and skill in print-making, which he exploited to start a private practice. But we find him moving to progressively more provincial locations, from Philadelphia to Chicago to Cairo, perhaps to shun the competition of better-trained and more capable competitors. Before the age of forty, all personal ambition seems to cease, and he is content to live the low-pressure life of a draftsman and idle away his hours playing chess.

In architecture, as in other fields, the ingredients for success include training, connections, and talent, but these alone are not sufficient. One might make every professional decision correctly and still fail abjectly. There is the intangible leaven of temperament—the ability to communicate solidity and sobriety to clients, a capacity for sustained work, and a certain discipline with the checkbook. Evidently Nicholson lacked one or all of these qualities. His frequent changes of address, beginning with his impulsive emigration to America, bespeak a certain restlessness of spirit. Did he lack ambition? Or did he suffer from one of those personal demons, such as depression or alcoholism, that are invisible to the historian? It is a burden to feel compelled to live up to a great name; ask Randolph Churchill or Frank Sinatra, Jr. In the absence of any personal papers, or archival discoveries still pending, all we know is what the newspaper record shows. And here the record is clear: the last architectural design by Nicholson to be mentioned in the press comes in 1865. After that, nothing—nothing, that is, except for a great many well-played chess games. What is it we are missing?

CHAPTER 9

The Impresario

Edwin Forrest Durang

Impresario (noun): a person who runs a business
arranging different types of public entertainment,
such as theatre, musical, and dance events.
—*Cambridge Dictionary*

■ IF YOU GREW UP Catholic in Pennsylvania you have spent
time, whether you know it or not, in a building by E. F. Durang
(fig. 9.1). If you are a Philadelphian, you were likely baptized in
one of his churches, attended one of his parochial schools, were
sick in one of his hospitals, and will be buried from another of
his churches. For half a century Durang controlled the architecture of Catholic Philadelphia, a denominational monopoly that
no other American architect has known, or ever will. This is
not to say that he was a great architect, or even a good one. But
he made the most of his limitations, and what we now see as his
faults were to his loyal patrons his greatest assets.[1]

Edwin Forrest Durang was born in New York to a family of
actors and singers on April 1, 1829.[2] He maintained the family
tradition, designing music halls throughout Pennsylvania.[3] And

FIGURE 9.1 Technical skill must be based on knowledge, and so Edwin F. Durang's portrait of 1874 shows the tools of the architect's trade—a pair of dividers, a flexible tape, and a sheet of drafting paper—resting on a book. The painter was Lorenzo Scattaglia, who frescoed many of Durang's church interiors.

he seems to have passed on the theater tradition to his descendants: his great-grandson Christopher Durang is one of America's most prominent playwrights. The last thing one would predict for Durang is that he would emerge as a prolific designer of Catholic churches.

As it happened, Durang came to architecture belatedly, and indirectly, through show business. He first appears as a Philadelphia artist and lithographer in 1848, making satirical political cartoons.[4] We know nothing about his early training as an illustrator but can assume that it came naturally, as it were, in a family constantly involved with stage scenery and costume design. After the election of 1848, the market for political cartoons collapsed and Durang moved to Cincinnati. There he worked on a series of moving panoramas, that nineteenth-century form of popular entertainment that united popular illustration and theater. A massive painted backdrop was slowly unspooled before the audience, accompanied by music, lecture, and dramatic lighting. A staggering amount of painting was required—the *Mammoth Panorama of the Mississippi River* (1849), said to be the largest painting in the world, consisted of 45,000 square feet of canvas (fig. 9.2).[5] Durang would have drawn a great many riverside trees and houses.

Having grown up amidst the commercial side of the entertainment business, Durang felt confident enough to try his hand at the making and marketing of his own panorama. Together

FIGURE 9.2 Durang painted a substantial part of Henry Lewis's *Mammoth Panorama of the Mississippi River,* claimed to be the "largest painting in the world." The original painting is lost but it was recycled to provide the color lithographs for Lewis's *Das illustrirte Mississippithal* (Düsseldorf, 1854–57).

with a fellow assistant on the Mississippi panorama, he created the *Panorama of the Old and New Testaments* (1849), which toured Cincinnati, Louisville, and Philadelphia.[6] It is a venerable show business tradition that every commercial success is immediately followed by a sequel. Durang provided this with *The Mirror of Our Country* (1850), depicting "all the events from the landing of Columbus to the occupation of California" in *three* moving panoramas. It is also a venerable tradition that sequels generally flop. Perhaps the patriotic theme was ill-chosen for a time of growing strife over slavery, and perhaps the accompanying "descriptive lecture and appropriate music" left the audience underwhelmed; in any event, by the summer of 1851, Durang was reduced to offering shares in the enterprise as "a splendid speculation."[7] If any investors were foolhardy enough to advance money to Durang, there were too few to save the project. Deciding abruptly to change careers, he entered the office of John Carver, a Philadelphia architect with a lively practice.[8]

Durang was a curious apprentice, for his previous experience was entirely graphic: lithography, popular illustration, scene painting. His one deficiency was in practical building, which, as it turns out, was Carver's strength. He is a type we see throughout Philadelphia history, the highly driven carpenter-builder who transforms himself into an architect by dint of effort and private study. Born in 1809, John Ellicott Carver trained as a wheelwright in Doylestown before practicing as a carpenter and stair-builder in Philadelphia. He learned architectural drafting, perhaps at the drawing school of the Franklin Institute, for it later judged him "competent to teach architectural drawing in all its branches" and engaged him as instructor.[9]

That was in 1838, and three years later Carver promoted himself in city directories from house carpenter to architect. His newspaper advertisements give the picture of an architectural polymath able to do anything—or give it a try:

J. E. Carver, Architect and Engineer . . . Gives Drawings and Specifications or contracts to erect Dwellings, &c., and lay out the grounds for Country Seats or Cemeteries; together with the arrangement of Trees to give the proper effect.—Also, Churches, Hospitals, Prisons, Water Works, Gas Works, &c., on the latest and most approved plans, including heating, ventilating, &c.[10]

Carver also knew how to ingratiate himself with big-spending clients, such as P. T. Barnum, who engaged him to alter an existing building to house his Philadelphia museum, "as strong and substantial as any similar structure." (Strong and substantial, but not fireproof; it burned to the ground within two years, but this was not judged Carver's fault.)[11]

It was in this versatile office that Durang learned the practical business of architecture. After three years, he felt capable enough to strike out on his own. When a competition was announced in 1854 for the Academy of Music, he decided he would not sit idly by while Carver prepared his project but make an independent design. It is the earliest project we have by Durang, and it failed to impress (see fig. 5.4). He followed it up with something much more consequential, the National Guards Armory of 1857 (fig. 9.3).

Officially an armory whose large hall was intended for military exercises and drills, it was designed in such a way that it could be rented out "for all kinds of exhibitions, balls or concerts, conventions and other large public meetings."[12] If used as a ballroom, its great drill room could seat 1,800, and to carry its floor it required "10 trussed girders . . . the most powerful that have ever been put in a building of this kind, being 60 foot span and 7 feet deep." In consolation for the armory's 1959 demolition, we have a photograph of those powerful trussed girders (fig. 9.4). Here in embryonic form was the solution for all of Durang's subsequent churches, theaters, and halls: a clear open span under a mighty trussed roof, carrying a plaster ceiling of segmental form, "divided into compartments" and tastefully frescoed. He would repeat the formula, at varying scale and for varying budgets, over the next half century.

FIGURE 9.3 The urban armory was a new building type in the 1850s, and its image had not yet been established. Durang's National Guards Armory could easily have been a music hall or storefront, which in fact it became.

FIGURE 9.4 The National Guards Armory, which stood at 518–520 Race Street, was demolished in 1959 to make way for Independence Mall and, eventually, the National Constitution Center.

Upon completing his armory Durang returned to Carver, now as partner.[13] But Carver died unexpectedly on April 1, 1859—Durang's thirtieth birthday, as it happened—and he took over the business. He ran it as a sort of Dickensian one-man office, occasionally hiring out Samuel Rumer as a kind of part-time Bob Cratchit for additional drafting by the day (or half-day) when the tracings were needed in a hurry. All was done along old-fashioned lines. While the practice of charging on a percentage of construction was now well established among Philadelphia architects, Durang charged his clients a daily rate: five dollars for a full day of drafting, three dollars for a half day. This had definite advantages. For example, it let him wrest the commission for St. John the Evangelist (1867) from Henry A. Sims, a much more talented architect, because—as he grumbled in his diary—Durang's "charges were so much lighter than mine."[14]

His office ledger for that first hectic year survives, and shows him designing the same madly eclectic variety of objects that Carver proposed—a row of houses on Chestnut Street and a set of "heavy marble railings" for Woodland Cemetery, an insane asylum in Baltimore (unrealized), a design for Fairmount Park (also unrealized), and even a set of "oyster boxes"—some fifty projects in all.[15] Significantly, not one was for a Catholic church.

Durang's church-building practice developed from out of the shadows of bitter and longstanding anti-Catholic sentiment. Quaker Philadelphia's celebrated tolerance did not extend to Catholics and not until 1733 was Catholic worship officially permitted. Churches were built, gradually at first (four by 1808), and then more quickly as Irish immigration surged. When nativist hysteria flared up in 1844, these churches drew the fury of the mob. Two were burned to the ground, others vandalized, and more than a dozen Philadelphians died in the street fighting.

Catholic Philadelphia straightaway reasserted itself by building a great cathedral, Saints Peter and Paul (1846–64). It stood apart from America's other mid-century cathedrals, most of which followed the Gothic example of St. Patrick's in New York. Instead the Philadelphia cathedral took its inspiration from the churches of Renaissance Rome. Except for its facade, which is by John Notman, the cathedral was designed by Napoleon LeBrun, a staunch classicist who had trained under T. U. Walter. If Nativists suspected that Catholics were secretly loyal to Rome, LeBrun taunted them with a cathedral that was defiantly Roman. While it grew, new parish churches followed throughout the city, at first designed by LeBrun but then, after 1850, by John T. Mahoney, an immigrant from Cork, Ireland.[16]

This left Durang out of the picture until 1864. Mahoney died suddenly and was buried at the start of the year; a few months later, the cathedral was consecrated and LeBrun also departed the scene, moving to New York. By default and certainly to his surprise, Durang now found himself the principal Catholic architect practicing in Philadelphia.[17] When Catholic parishes sought to build, he was the obvious choice. (It is possible that Carver and Durang had already established some connections with LeBrun and his Catholic clients before the Civil War, for Carver for a time served as superintending architect for the cathedral.)[18]

Because of the centralized nature of the Catholic archdiocese, he was handed what was in effect a monopoly. Durang's practice was instantly transformed. In short order he was "up to his eyes in work."[19] This was the age of massive immigration from eastern and southern Europe, as Catholic workers and families poured into the factory neighborhoods of Philadelphia and founded parishes. Each meant a cluster of buildings, a church, rectory, and school, and frequently a convent—and Durang designed almost all of them. By 1875 he was wealthy enough to own a gold pocket watch worth $125 (enough to entice an enterprising pickpocket).[20] An early portrait captures him in the flush of prosperity, looking thoughtful as he holds a pair of dividers (fig. 9.1). The artist was Lorenzo Scattaglia, who painted many of his church interiors.[21]

Durang made his debut as a Catholic architect with a pair of oversize parish churches, St. Anne (1866–69) and St. Charles Borromeo (1868–71). Each was a stone leviathan, with a sculptural prodigy of a facade. At St. Anne's, Port Richmond, this was a Baroque portal, with Corinthian columns projecting boldly before the triple portals of the entrance, their movement repeated with vigorous breaks in the entablature above to ascend into triumphal urns.[22] It was not terribly original: it was a paraphrase of the Philadelphia cathedral, even in such details as the round returns in the corners of the entablature, but it was a paraphrase with verve and dash. It was to have been even grander, with "one of largest towers in the city," but even in its truncated form it was sumptuous. Its facade was scraped clean in the twentieth century but that of St. Charles Borromeo, at Twentieth and Christian, survives intact (fig. 9.5). Here the Baroque theme was carried out with High Victorian restiveness: a pair of asymmetrical towers bracketed the round-arched entrance, the loftier one rising on impossibly spindly columns.

St. Anne and St. Charles Borromeo established the model that Durang would follow without significant modification for the next 45 years: a spirited frontispiece, plain but solid walls to the sides, and a roomy auditorium of a space within, "divided into compartments by ribs resting on corbels," decorated more or less richly as the parishioners could afford. They were built to hold enormous crowds, but even so there was frequently standing room only (so I knew them in the 1960s). A typical specimen was Our Lady of Visitation (1876), a twin-towered Gothic Goliath that held 1,300.[23] Even larger was St. Francis Xavier (1894), which seated 1,370 and another 80 in the gallery.[24] (Its Richardsonian Romanesque bulk is visible from the front steps of the Philadelphia Museum of Art.) In spatial terms, there was little difference between a Durang auditorium and church (fig. 9.6): each was a capacious gathering space, with clear lines of sight and vision, its seats (or pews) facing a raised stage (or chancel). When he added galleries, as he did at St. Charles Borromeo, the resemblance to an auditorium was even stronger.

Gothic churches posed a special problem for Durang, especially when arranged in three aisles, divided by rows of columns. This violated his impulse to make his churches as auditorium-like as possible. Where columns were necessary, as in St. James (1880) at 38th and Chestnut, he made them as slender as possible,

FIGURE 9.5 Durang believed churches should be ecstatic in silhouette. The facade of St. Charles Borromeo at Twentieth and Christian streets cheerfully ignores the sober box of a building behind it as it leaps up to announce the presence of its parish in the sky.

almost like pipes. And in a sense they were pipes, since he used cast iron columns, grouped in spindly shafts, grained to simulate granite. The next step was to dispense with the columns altogether. In Our Mother of Good Counsel, Bryn Mawr (1896), he suspended the clerestory on internal steel beams so that no columns were necessary. Only the florid capitals remain beneath the clerestory arches, dangling in midair as if resting on hypothetical columns.[25] As with his National Guards Armory forty years

FIGURE 9.6 If one scraped all the Baroque pageantry off the walls and ceilings of a Durang church, only a simple box of space would remain. His Nativity of the Blessed Virgin Mary (1890), at 2535 East Allegheny Avenue, shows how theatrical devices could accentuate the splendor of the Mass.

earlier, Durang was keen to use efficient modern construction to make a roomy, spacious hall—and utterly indifferent to the artistic expression of that construction.

Durang was concerned with expression of another sort: how to give a community a tangible symbol that conveyed its presence in proud, distinctive visual terms. If possible that symbol should be at least as tall as the smokestack of the neighborhood factory (or the spire of the local Presbyterian Church). He routinely gave his churches lofty towers; 170 feet was normal. The loftiest is over St. Peter the Apostle (the shrine of St. John Neumann), rising more than 230 feet.[26] Had it been completed, the one above St. Anne's would have risen even higher.[27]

Durang's towers showed where a parish was, his facades showed *what* it was. And in an age of immigration, that meant ethnic iden-

tity. For a church like St. Mary Magdalen de Pazzi (1883–91)—
"the first in the United States used exclusively by Italians"—the
Roman Renaissance was appropriate (fig. 9.7).[28] For German
Catholics it was the Gothic, that traditional symbol of German
nationhood. German Catholics, who felt themselves besieged in a
Germany increasingly dominated by protestant Prussia, found in
Cologne Cathedral, the largest of all Gothic cathedrals, a symbol
of Catholic identity. Durang's German churches were typically
Gothic: St. Joachim (1874), Visitation of the Blessed Virgin Mary
(1876), and St. Bonaventure (1894), all built in the historic German neighborhoods to the northeast of Penn's original city (fig.
9.8). There is a notable exception: St. Peter the Apostle on Girard
Avenue is a romanesque colossus, but here Durang was con-
strained by the proportions of the older classical church building
that he was refacing.[29]

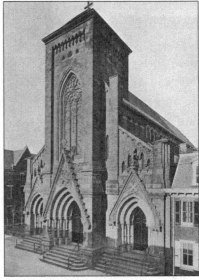

FIGURES 9.7 AND 9.8 In Philadelphia's immigrant neighborhoods, Durang's Catholic churches were typically the chief marker of ethnic identity. St. Mary
Magdalene de Pazzi (*left*) spoke of Rome to an Italian community in South
Philadelphia while St. Joachim's Gothic facade was a reassuring reminder
of Germany. (Its parishioners would have been indignant to learn that
the Gothic was a French invention, something still not widely known.)

If German Catholics felt themselves persecuted in Europe, the same was even truer of Poles and Irish. Here the question of style was even more fraught. There was no independent Poland, which was then partitioned between Germany, Russia, and the Austro-Hungarian Empire, and no obvious choice of style. Durang's Polish parishes opted for the Gothic: St. Laurentius (1885) and St. Adalbert (1903). But for the Irish the Gothic held distressing associations. It was introduced by the English following their conquest of Ireland in the Middle Ages and could be seen as a foreign imposition. The Gothic Revival further complicated matters, since both the Anglican Church in England and the Episcopal Church in America were energetically championing the Gothic. Durang occasionally built a Gothic church for an Irish parish (after all, St. Patrick's Cathedral in New York offered the most respectable of models) but in general he chose historical styles that came earlier or later. The Romanesque suited as the indigenous Irish architecture before the English conquest, hence Immaculate Conception (1871) and St. Francis Xavier (1894). Likewise the Renaissance or Baroque styles were acceptable as nods to Rome, hence St. Anne's, St. Charles Borromeo, and St. Michael's, Kensington (1865), whose parish still remembered how its first building had been burned to the ground by a protestant mob in 1844.

ALL THAT I have written here implies that Durang was a static artist, and in some sense that is true. The rites and rituals for which he designed did not change during his lifetime, nor did the social circumstances confronting his patrons, especially those in his immigrant parishes. Intense but unchanging pressures result in highly specialized buildings, and there is a pleasing consistency in Durang's work—right up to his last day of practice. He spent the morning of June 12, 1911 measuring the site for a new convent, then headed to the church where his daughter was to be married. After walking one block he collapsed and died "from heart disease, aggravated by heat exhaustion"; Durang was eighty-three years old.[30] The wedding proceeded without him.

Durang's churches may vary wildly in style but in one crucial aspect they are the same: their facades have nothing whatsoever to do with the space behind. Like a piece of stage scenery, the extravagance ended at the front wall and did not go around the sides, which presented nothing more than an austere march of round-headed windows. It is so unusual for the facade of a Durang church to express its interior that when it does one wonders if outside influence is at play. The Church of the Gesú (1879) certainly stands out (fig. 9.9). The centerpiece of a vast

FIGURE 9.9 Durang's Jesuit clients wanted their Church of the Gesú to be "of pure Roman architecture similar in design to the Church of the Gesú in Rome." But it was also American in expression: to each side of the nave were four alcoves, each with an altar to be dedicated to an American saint.

Jesuit complex that includes Saint Joseph's Preparatory School, it is modeled on Il Gesù in Rome, the mother church of the Jesuit order. Its mighty barrel vault, with a 76-foot clear span, carried on the robust wall piers that Germans call *Wandpfeiler*, easily makes it Durang's finest and most sumptuous church interior. Even more remarkably, the volumes of the interior are carried right through to the facade: the central section marks the barrel vault while the towers mark the side chapels and galleries above. The scholarly quality of the whole, and its unity, suggests the guiding hand of Rev. Burchard Villiger, the Swiss-born rector of the Gesú. (Perhaps it was he who suggested that Durang look at the church of St. Sulpice in Paris as a model for his facade.)

But the Gesú is an exception to the rule, and the rule was that Durang's churches generally look like stage scenery. In a sense they *were* stage scenery; their spritely animated movement had nothing to do with the facts of their construction. They have their origin in the fanciful tableaux that Durang painted on his panoramas, those riverside towns he sketched on the endless panorama of the Mississippi or his fairy tale reconstruction of Solomon's Temple or Belshazzar's Palace. Carver had taught him to build solidly, and the panoramas had taught him to doodle imaginatively, but Durang never successfully integrated the two lobes of his mind. But this was true from the beginning of his mature career. One returns again to St. Charles Borromeo to see the practical builder working side by side with the scenographic artist. Its sanctuary is substantial architecture, as solid as it comes, but its wonderfully fidgety silhouette is graphic invention, like one of those dream visions gliding past on the painted canvas of the rolling panorama.[31]

CHAPTER 10

Incognito at Haverford

George Senneff

■ WE WERE PREPARING for our graduation procession when someone asked the college marshal when we should slide the tassel of our caps to the other side. His answer came instantly: "We don't do that at Haverford; that's High Church folderol."

High Church folderol—is there a better summary for the Quaker view of pageantry and pomp? The phrase helps us understand the building where that graduation took place, Founders Hall of Haverford College. Proud in its humility, extravagant in its plainness, it is by far the most important educational building in Quakerdom. It takes a great deal of intelligence and forethought to make a building so anonymous, so completely vernacular in character, perhaps as much as it takes to make a self-consciously original building.

Venerable colleges make much of the authorship of their first building; William and Mary has Christopher Wren, Princeton has Robert Smith, and the University of Virginia can boast of Thomas Jefferson. Yet Haverford itself has never shown the slightest interest in its designer; none of the college histories of the college even records his name. There is something fitting about this; after all, the authorship of a building that is plain to the point of anonymity scarcely matters. But it is a historical injustice that needs be righted, and we now can belatedly celebrate—folderol though it may be—the architect of Founders Hall, the unjustifiably forgotten George Senneff (1795–1872).[1]

Senneff, like virtually every architect of pre-Civil War Philadelphia, began as a carpenter.[2] Between 1821 and 1823 he took classes at the "Evening Draughting School" run by James Clark, where he would have learned rendering and perspective.[3] After completing his apprenticeship he began building houses; one from the 1820s survives intact, tiny 318 South Fawn Street, a "trinity" measuring 12½ by 13½ feet.[4] He soon began taking in his own apprentices.[5] Senneff's obituary gives us a brief but charming account of his early life:

> Mr. Senneff was noted for his mathematical attainments, in which he was excelled by few, and surpassed by none. He was also a fine German scholar, the rudiments of which language he mastered by studying in the evening, while working in the daytime as a journeyman carpenter. He was a member of the ancient and honorable Carpenters' Society of Philadelphia, and was the fifth living member on the list, he having joined the association in the year 1823. This fact alone speaks volumes of the worth and reputation of the man, as the man who is admitted to that company must show a very clear record . . . At one time Mr. Senneff taught architecture, conducting an architectural school in one of the rooms belonging to the Carpenters' Society.[6]

Lucrative as house carpentry may have been, Senneff yearned for more. In his early thirties he made a determined effort to establish himself as a professional architect and he entered competitions for the Philadelphia Almshouse (1829) and for Wills Eye Hospital (1831).[7] The almshouse was an especially prodigious undertaking, in effect a small city of the poor. The Blockley Asylum, as it became known, occupied a campus of 187 acres on the banks of the Schuylkill River, today the site of the hospital of the University of Pennsylvania. It comprised five colossal buildings, including an almshouse for "1,250 paupers," a workhouse for 500 inmates to be housed in separate rooms, and a hospital for 600 patients, "including lunatics." Senneff's design was bested by that of William Strickland, but he was not entirely unsuccessful. He was given the asylum hospital to build, while the remaining four buildings were assigned to other carpenters. As Strickland was too overworked "to give my exclusive attention as architect to the building," Senneff was entrusted with "all of the general jobbing work required previous to the commencement of the new buildings."[8] It was a mighty undertaking and, apart from Strickland's grand Doric portico, it wallowed in Dickensian severity, but not much more so than Senneff's building at Haverford College, for which it served as a kind of dress rehearsal (fig. 10.1).

FIGURE 10.1 Quaker philanthropy and Dickensian sternness came together in the program for the Blockley Almshouse: an almshouse building for "1,250 paupers," a hospital for 600 patients, "including lunatics," an asylum building for 400 children, and a workhouse for 500 inmates, within "a wall sufficiently high to prevent escape."

In 1831 the newly formed Board of Managers of Haverford College, having acquired a farm tract of some 200 acres to the west of Philadelphia, appointed a "Committee on the plan of Buildings." By the time of their meeting of December 17 they had given the program for the building to "a competent person for the purpose of obtaining an estimate of the cost."[9] Next came a tentative plan ("an outline of a plan arranged with a view to the erection of single dormitories"), which was approved at the meeting of January 21, 1832, with the understanding that the committee's unnamed designer would now draw up detailed plans and elevations. On February 3 these "drafts of the proposed buildings" were approved and a building committee appointed to carry them out.[10] The plans were put out for estimate and must have exceeded the $18,000 that managers had budgeted for the building; on February 18, a revised plan was approved that left the third story unfinished for the moment.[11] Satisfied at last, the Board of Managers decided on March 8 to have a lithograph made of "the elevation plan of the buildings" in order to give it to donors (fig. 10.2).[12]

FIGURE 10.2 Oscar Lawson was paid $37.97 for his copperplate engraving of Haverford College's Founders Hall, more than George Senneff was paid for designing the building.

Nowhere in these records do we find the name George Senneff. Not a single history of Haverford College has ever credited
him with the design of Founders Hall. We know of his work
because of a single document, his receipt dated March 22, 1832,
for "thirty-five dollars in full for making drafts & estimates of
building for Central School."[13] Obviously he was a logical choice
as both draftsman and practical builder, and he was then working
on the almshouse, where he would have up to date information
on prices and materials. But the reason he was chosen is closer at
hand: the decisive figure was Thomas Pym Cope (1768–1854),
who served both the Blockley Almshouse and Haverford College in an identical capacity, as a member of the committee to
secure plans and enter into contracts.[14] When he needed "a competent person" to estimate the cost of Founders Hall and draw up
a practical plan, the first name to occur to him would have been
Senneff's.

The college site was on a slight elevation, sloping to the south,
and in order to capitalize on the southern exposure, Senneff
designed an extended horizontal block, 110 feet long, flanked by
two short end blocks; between, a continuous porch ran across
the front of the building. The site itself provided the materials:
a quarry on the original farm supplied rubble and the "north
woodlot" the lumber. Senneff was strictly charged to avoid "useless ornament and extravagant expenditure" in favor of "that
Plainness and simplicity which are alone consistent with the religious profession of friends." In other words, there was to be no
showy Greek temple front or any use whatsoever of the classical orders.

Senneff divided the principal rooms into squares and double
squares: to the left were two classrooms, measuring 24 by 24, and
to the right was the "collection room" (meeting room), 24 by 48
(fig. 10.3). Above this, the students were lodged in 32 unheated
tiny cells measuring nine by five and a half feet, each getting only
half of a window.[15] (That half the student body was condemned
to cold north-facing rooms troubled no one.) Their dining room
and kitchen were in the above-ground basement. At each end

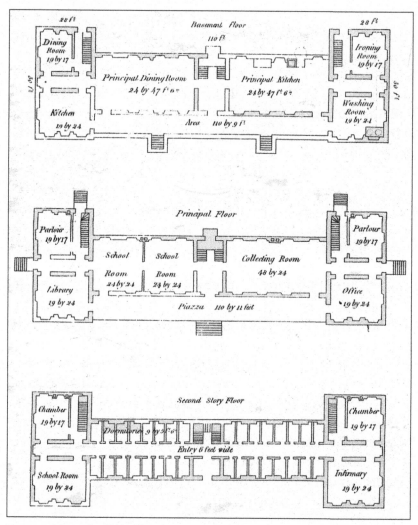

FIGURE 10.3 Haverford's student accommodations were little better than monks' cells; each of the 64 chambers in the top two stories of Founders Hall measured 9 by 5½ feet.

of the main block or "school building" Senneff placed a smaller wing measuring 50 by 28; the east wing contained the offices of the manager and the infirmary, while the west wing housed the library and another classroom. Above this were two modest apartments; one for the superintendent, who was expected to live on the premises (after all, he had to send the students to bed every night at nine, after having closed the day with "suitable serious reading").[16]

Senneff ran a continuous axis lengthwise through the main floor, passing through seven doors, but this was no ceremonial enfilade of a Baroque palace, merely the plainest possible sort of planning: boxes of space in round whole numbers, arrayed in orderly fashion. Apart from the cupola, suitable for astronomical observation, nothing served to emphasize the center: no portico, no central pavilion, no projecting block. Even the Friends Asylum in Frankford, built by philanthropic Quakers in northeast Philadelphia in 1817, had a grander entrance. At Haverford absolute plainness governed all, even the treatment of the rubble walls. Should they be "rough-dashed" with a coat of lime mortar, so that some of the projecting stone showed through, as on a Pennsylvania barn? Or was it better to "rough cast the outside of the building in imitation of granite," as the building committee proposed in early 1833? Senneff would have had his views but he was no longer in the picture, the execution of his design having been assigned to carpenters and masons who lived closer to the site.

Perhaps it was just as well that he did not build Founders Hall, for Senneff soon found work closer to home. In 1833 he applied, along with ten other builders, to superintend the construction of Girard College; he was unsuccessful.[17] In 1834 he had better luck. At that time the Schuylkill Navigation Company had begun to ship anthracite coal along the Schuylkill River to its terminus in Philadelphia. John Price Wetherill (1794–1853), a manufacturer and real estate developer, expected the riverfront to develop quickly, and he conceived the idea of building a 40-room hotel at the corner of Twenty-fourth & Chestnut streets along with "a row of houses . . . for the use of the clerks and officers of the company who might desire to live in the vicinity."[18] Senneff built the entire complex, for which he was honored by having the spine of the complex named Senneff's Court (today Ionic Street). A portion of the project survives in the houses at Samson and South Bonsall streets.

The location was as perfect as the timing was dreadful. The Philadelphia & Reading Railroad had just been founded in 1833 and was already laying tracks toward Reading. Within a few years, coal was moving by rail and the Schuylkill Navigation Company began its decline. In 1841 the hotel failed, dragging Senneff down with it. Soon he was offering to rent the "large commodious hotel . . . for manufacturing purposes"—a sad indication that he had made the mistake of investing his own capital in the project.[19] This misfortune at the age of 46 effectively ended his career: "After this time Mr. Senneff virtually retired from active business, for, besides being crippled in resources, he was a victim of an illness which confined him for the greater part of the time to the house."[20]

Although confined, Senneff hardly sat still for he was preoccupied with matters religious. These were the years when the Society of Friends was riven by the Hicksite/Orthodox split. The followers of Elias Hicks tended to be more urban and liberal, while "the orthodox portion" tended to be rural. (It is the same division, *mutatis mutandis*, between Unitarians and Congregationalists or between Reform and Orthodox Judaism, for that matter.) Haverford was stalwartly orthodox, and so was Senneff. In 1836 he published a pamphlet whose title certainly followed the Quaker practice of speaking plainly: *The Bible Advocate; or, an Answer to Elias Hick's Blasphemies and others*; he signed it humbly as "G. Senneff, a Mechanic." It evidently did well; a second edition appeared in 1837. Was Senneff chosen by Haverford because of the ardor of his religious convictions? These sectarian passions cooled later, and by the time Swarthmore College was founded as a Hicksite institution in 1864, it took for its architect Addison Hutton, an Orthodox Quaker who would work for Haverford and Bryn Mawr.

Senneff's Founders Hall has left a long legacy at Haverford (fig. 10.4). The college's stringent plainness relaxed briefly when Founders came to be flanked by a pair of sober Gothic Revival buildings in gray stone.[21] But then followed the Colonial Revival, which gave Haverford a half dozen superb buildings in

FIGURE 10.4 Founders Hall inverts the usual model of a college's main building by emphasizing the end wings and making the center as modest and reticent as possible.

local fieldstone with wood trim, invariably by Quaker firms.[22] These neocolonial buildings happened to be quite fashionable, which would have delighted Haverford, which could pretend that this was an accidental side-effect of their plainness. The last of these was "Dutch Colonial" Leeds Hall (1954), by which time the style had long since outlived itself. The awkward dormitories of the 1960s were modernist-colonial hybrids, and even their ostentatious plainness was of a hybrid sort: modernist cinderblock within and colonial fieldstone without.[23]

But for the fiasco of the Wetherill Hotel, Senneff might have ascended into the ranks of other Philadelphia carpenters who made themselves architects, as John McArthur and Samuel Sloan would do. Yet personal vanity does not seem to have been part of his makeup, and he could hardly have been troubled that the central achievement of his career, the design of Founders Hall at Haverford College, was performed incognito. It is fitting that the author of this defiantly anonymous building has remained anonymous for so long. If we could ask, I am certain he would be utterly baffled at the existence of this article.

CHAPTER 11

The Bibliophile

Henry A. Sims

■ Two CHARGES are routinely made against Victorian architects and they can't both be true. Either they were shameless
copyists or capricious fantasts; either they copied their designs
out of books or from year to year never opened a book. Of course
the truth is somewhere in between, for the High Victorian era is
distinguished by a peculiar mixture of bookishness and furious
originality. Its architects certainly owned books but how exactly
did they use them?

Which books did they consult for reference, which did they
fold flat to trace a detail, which did they browse for inspiration?
Or did they use them at all? The study lined with bound journals and folios was itself an object of prestige, telling of sophistication and refinement. Burnham & Root dazzled their clients
with their library, which doubled as a reception room, and which
filled a corner of the Rookery Building. The architects had
themselves photographed there, beneath a cast of the Venus de
Milo, books and portfolios strewn on the floor about them in

studied casualness—and yet it is hard to imagine a pair of less bookish architects.

Henry A. Sims was uncommonly bookish (fig. 11.1). We know this not only from the inventory of his library but also from his diary that tells us how he used it.[1] His is not the only library from the era whose contents we know—we have inventories of the architectural libraries of T. P. Chandler, James H. Windrim, and Joseph Koecker—but it is the only one cut short by sudden death. It shows none of the pruning and updating that working libraries constantly undergo; it gives us a scene as instantaneously suspended as at Pompeii.[2] Sims died on July 10, 1875, one year before the Centennial Exhibition changed the architectural landscape, sweeping in an enthusiasm for Queen Anne and Old English architecture, the rediscovery of the colonial, the first Japanese currents. His quirky and intelligent library gives us the High Victorian at its zenith.

The auction of Sims's library was a subject of public interest and was covered widely in the press:

> Mr. Sims was an artist not only of unusual ability but of unusual culture, and his refined professional taste found expression in the books which he gathered, embracing the choicest works upon architecture and decoration, especially of the revived Gothic school. At this time, when so much interest is felt in the study of architecture, these beautiful books, and especially the photographs of furniture and household decoration, will command unusual attention.[3]

That furniture, another news item specified, was that of "the private rooms of the well-known London architect, Mr. Burgess [i.e., William Burges]."[4]

The catalogue of Sims's library and his diary of 1866–68 give us the picture of the architect as dedicated bibliophile. They leave us with an enigma, how an architect could have spent so much of his time with his nose in books and yet make buildings that were dramatically charged with life.

FIGURE 11.1 Three of Philadelphia's leading architects were photographed on November 29, 1871, in their capacity as officers of the Philadelphia Chapter of the American Institute of Architects. At center was Thomas Ustick Walter, president, flanked by John McArthur, Jr. (left), and Henry A. Sims, both vice presidents.

FORGOTTEN TODAY, Sims was a prominent Gothic Revivalist who practiced in Canada and Philadelphia.[5] Born in 1832 in Philadelphia, he moved to Canada in 1851 and served four years on the staff of the Bytown and Prescott Railroad; another year was spent in Brunswick, Georgia, as an engineer for the Brunswick and Florida Railroad. In 1858, after some false starts, he traded engineering for architecture, practicing first in Prescott and then in Ottawa. After the Civil War he returned to Philadelphia, counting on his prominent family for work.[6]

Sims was "a warm admirer of the Gothic styles."[7] So he declared in a public lecture of 1860, peppered with extracts from the writings of John Ruskin and John Henry Parker. His churches were archaeologically fastidious affairs, and when he arrived in Philadelphia he confided to his diary that "I am the only architect here making any pretensions to a knowledge of Gothic."[8] The language is revealing. It was not that there were no Gothic Revival architects in Philadelphia but that they had no *knowledge*. And by knowledge he evidently meant books. His defensiveness was understandable, though, for his "pretensions" to Gothic proficiency were just that. He had not seen Europe and never would, his conception of medieval architecture remaining second-hand and bookish. The bookishness shows up in all he did. In 1869 he was a founding member of the Philadelphia chapter of the American Institute of Architects (and the first foreign correspondent of the national organization), and tried "to establish a Reading Room of Architectural and general Art periodicals—a Library of Reference of works of a similar character."[9] But while scholarly, Sims was also gregarious: he helped form an Aesthetic Club in 1872 and served as its first president (the club faltered in the Depression of 1873).[10]

Sims's architectural taste ran to the High Victorian Gothic at its most Anglophiliac. His clients were typically Episcopalians of the High Church sort, who delighted in the revival of medieval ritual and symbolism—what their Low Church critics derided as "bells and smells" (the smell being incense). And so it is ironic that his most important High Victorian church, and the one with his richest iconographic program, was for a Presbyterian congregation. This was Philadelphia's First Presbyterian Church at Twenty-first and Walnut streets (planned 1867–68; built 1869–72).[11] A vibrant essay in architectural color, it took the form of a basilica with transepts and a polygonal apse, rising to an emphatic corner tower, as high as the church was long. The daring spire was never realized and it would have been deeply unfashionable thirty years later when Frank Furness brought it to a bold termination with a defiant belfry (fig. 11.2).

Sims's program of iconographic sculpture, if not literally medieval, was medieval in spirit. Just as Gothic stone masons carved the flowers and foliage they knew, and the demons they imagined, so Sims's clients created a sculptural program from their

FIGURE 11.2 During the High Victorian Gothic era, the highest praise for a building was to say that it had *go*—a slang term for vitality, muscle, sheer pizzazz. Sims's stony, musclebound First Presbyterian Church was certainly not short of *go*.

contemporary world. In it mixed the ethnic and the patriotic, a conflation of Presbyterianism, Americanism, and a kind of fictitious pan-British identity. On the main portal to the north (the "west" in traditional ecclesiology) was an interlace of the Scottish thistle, English rose, Welsh bramble, and Irish shamrock. Along the side aisle the principal crops of America were depicted: corn, wheat, grapes, sugar, cotton, and tobacco (against which the pastors had no qualms). The carving was executed by two Scotsmen: Alexander Kemp and Alexander Milne Calder, who would soon create an even more sweeping allegorical program for Philadelphia's City Hall.[12]

The First Presbyterian Church is an example of what was known in the Gothic Revival as *muscularity*. This was the Early French Gothic craze of the late 1850s, which drew its inspiration from the example of Viollet-le-Duc in France and William Burges in England. Unlike the nearly skeletal construction of the fully developed Gothic, the Early French exulted in the wall in all its sheer silent massiveness. It had a quality of archaic power that one English architect described as "nervous manliness." Leaving aside the question of whether Sims's transept, with its sweeping mass of blank masonry, is manly or even nervous, it is certainly as fine an example of American muscularity as we have.

Without broad spaces of blank wall, Sims's 1871 project for the Pennsylvania Academy of the Fine Arts merely looked nervous. He had obviously studied the building program, which urged the competitors to "break the straight line of a front on so great a length," for his proposal was so restless as to be twitchy (he told the building committee, unnecessarily, that its "outline was as much broken as possible").[13] This was conventional Gothic Revival doctrine, that the external composition should express the free and functional arrangement of interior spaces; less conventional was the glass roof carried on an iron truss, and the use of terra cotta. Sims's considerable experience in railroad engineering meant that he conceived his designs not as pretty pictures to be handed to the contractor to figure out how to build, but instead thought in terms of structure and materials from the begin-

ELEVATION

FIGURE 11.3 It is curious that a fanatical Goth like Sims would shift to the Romanesque when making a design for the Centennial Exhibition. Did he think the Gothic too specifically Christian, and the Romanesque a more appropriate style for what was a secular national celebration?

ning. In one instance, his would-be clients were more impressed with his engineering than his architecture. In 1873 he made a design for the main hall of the Centennial Exhibition and won a $1,000 premium (fig. 11.3).[14] Whatever the judges thought of his design—a veritable mountain range of Romanesque—they recognized its clever engineering, and although they decided to build the project of Calvert Vaux and George K. Radford, they proposed to modify it by introducing "the much more simple construction" of the Sims project.[15]

FIGURE 11.4 The Girard Avenue Bridge (1873–74) measured 1,000 feet long and at 100 feet was the widest in the world. "A very attractive feature of the work is that each kind of material used is allowed to show what it is, iron not being treated to resemble stone, and color being applied only to distinguish parts."

The Vaux-Radford design was never built, but the incident shows how much Sims's engineering acumen was appreciated by his contemporaries, so much so that he was chosen to collaborate on the Girard Avenue Bridge (1874), which crossed the Schuylkill River to link Fairmount Park with the new Philadelphia Zoological Garden (fig. 11.4). Samuel L. Smedley was the structural engineer but the architectural features were designed by Sims and his brother, and for once we have the architects' own statement of the principles that informed their design: "there should be no sham ornamentation"; ornament should accentuate "the prominent lines of construction"; each material should "suggest for itself its appropriate treatment"; and that color should "do what nature uses it for—to distinguish parts from one another."[16] All this was taken almost word for word from A. W. N. Pugin's *True Principles of Pointed or Christian Architecture* (1841), the book that served as the conscience of the Gothic Revival and gave the clearest statement of the doctrine of truth in materials. The doctrine consumed Sims; his pocket notebook of 1871 shows his struggle to distill it into a personal motto; *Design with Beauty/*

Build in Truth was one version; another was *Beauty in the Design/Truth in Execution.*[17] (Strangely, given the central importance of Pugin to Sims, his library catalogue did not list a single book by Pugin, although it did include Benjamin Ferrey's *Recollections of A. N. Welby Pugin.*)

The principle of truth in materials held that the language of arches and buttresses is different from that of beams and rivets; a Gothic church built in iron would look nothing like one built in stone. Sims's final work, his Holy Trinity Chapel, Twenty-second and Spruce streets (1874–75), shows this in the most radical way.[18] Above its brawny brownstone torso rises an astonishing display of flying buttresses, executed not in stone but in slender iron girders (fig. 11.5). Here Sims the Railroad Engineer merged with Sims the Gothic Revivalist. Perhaps he was inspired

FIGURE 11.5 The *Philadelphia Times* raved over Holy Trinity Chapel: "the roof is of novel construction, having a clerestory, but no columns, the thrust of the upper part being carried by iron flying buttresses . . . this is the only roof of this construction in the world."

by Furness & Hewitt's Pennsylvania Academy of the Fine Arts, which brandished its iron truss on the exterior, flaunting its bolts and rivets with the same cheekiness with which a contemporary barista flaunts her tongue stud. But Sims was even more daring. It is as if he was trying to imagine what an architect of the twelfth century would do if he had the iron beams of the nineteenth. One wonders how much further he might have gone in expressing all-metal construction, had he not died just before its completion in 1875.

FOUR MONTHS ELAPSED between the death of Sims in July and the auction of his library in November.[19] A printed inventory survives, listing a large collection of fiction and history as well as seventy-odd architectural items. It seems strange that the architectural books did not go to James P. Sims, his brother and erstwhile partner. Was there bad blood?[20] Or did Henry's widow, who had two children, need the money? If her brother-in-law wanted the books, he had to bid against other architects, and pay full market value.

The printed catalogue is scrupulous, and includes frequent notes on condition and rarity. Unfortunately, it is irregular in giving dates and full titles. It is impossible, for example, to know if the item listed as Humphrey Repton's *Landscape Gardening* refers to his *Sketches and Hints of Landscape Gardening* (1798), *Observations on the Theory and Practice of Landscape Gardening* (1805), or his *Fragment on the Theory and Practice of Repton's Landscape Gardening* (1816). But even in its abbreviated form, reproduced below, the catalogue is revealing (see pp. 350–53).

Sims's books fall into four broad categories: those of antiquarian interest; English books, almost exclusively medieval in scope; American pattern books; and a smattering of miscellany, mostly German. The antiquarian books seem to have sat on Sims's shelves for prestige value. He scarcely had the minimal reference library necessary to design in Greek or Renaissance classicism, even had he wanted to. For example, he had neither Stuart and Revett's *Antiquities of Athens* nor Paul Letarouilly's

Edifices de Rome moderne. His few works by Palladio, Alberti, and Vitruvius were in editions that were venerable rather than valuable. These were apparently haphazard acquisitions, so that he owned Palladio's study of ancient Roman baths but not *I quattro libri dell'architettura*. His one classical compendium, Domenico de Rossi's *Studio d'Architettura Civile*, looks like a stray.

The largest category of books, comprising about forty of the seventy, are English and form an exemplary compendium of Gothic Revival theory and practice. Besides the principal theoretical works of Ruskin, he owned key works by George Gilbert Scott, John Henry Parker, and F. A. Paley, as well as the *Instrumenta Ecclesiastica*, the comprehensive manual of church furnishing published by the Ecclesiological Society. He also had the groundbreaking work of Richard Norman Shaw and W. Eden Nesfield, who urged the Gothic Revival in the direction of a gentler pictorial picturesque, and who helped bring about the Queen Anne fad of the 1870s. Some of Sims's English books came from a penurious English architect in the same Ottawa boarding house where Sims stayed: "Bought a lot of books and drawings which an English architect named Edmunson left . . . for his board" (April 21, 1866).[21]

Sims assiduously collected books about the practical design of suburban or country houses. He owned Robert Kerr's *The Gentleman's House*, C. J. Richardson's *The Englishman's House*, and Thomas Morris's *A House for the Suburbs*, popular works that went through several editions. Books such as Kerr's provided practical suggestions for designing houses on the largest scale, requiring platoons of servants and capacious service wings to operate. It is not clear how Sims made use of these texts; although his obituaries credit him with several large country houses, none have been identified.[22]

The pride of Sims's library was his trove of illustrated English periodicals. He had nearly complete runs of all three English architectural journals, *The Builder* (1850–75), *Building News* (1864–75), and *The Architect: A Weekly Illustrated Journal of Art, Civil Engineering, and Building* (1869–75). With their regular woodcuts of English architecture, he would have been as well informed about the new buildings of London as those of New York or Boston, and perhaps more so. He even had a complete run of J. C. Loudon's *Architectural Magazine* (1834–38), although it was long since defunct. So enthusiastic was Sims about the usefulness of journals to the professional health of architecture that he tried to persuade the American Institute of Architects to launch one, although it came to grief on the sensitive issue of illustrating the work of non-members.[23]

The second pillar of Sims's library was his collection of American books. Of course, American architectural literature was on a much less sophisticated plane than that of Europe and consisted almost entirely of illustrated pattern books, but here he purchased diligently. He owned A. J. Downing's five most important books, as well as volumes by Richard Upjohn, Gervase Wheeler, and A. J. Bicknell. He owned Martin Field's *City Architecture* (New York, 1853), a comparatively rare work. He even owned Orson Squire Fowler's absurd *A Home for all, or the . . . Octagon Mode of Building*, but while he bought avidly, he did not buy indiscriminately. Strangely, for a man who loved books, he owned none by Philadelphia's most assiduous producer of architectural literature, Samuel Sloan. Sloan's national reputation was based on the aggressive hustling of his pattern books but Sims had no use for him. Or so his behavior suggests: Sims once asked facetiously in a lecture before the local A.I.A. if "the architect of Horticultural Hall" (i.e., Sloan) should, for reasons of its architectural sins, be hanged.[24]

Sims's smattering of German books is intriguing. Since the failed revolution of 1848, which brought a considerable number of German architects to the United States as refugees, German sources had enjoyed a certain vogue. Because of the language barrier, however, publications that consisted chiefly of images rather than text were most popular. The *Architektonisches Skizzenbuch*, a periodical with generous color plates of picturesque palaces and country villas, was particularly coveted during the 1850s and 1860s, and it shows up in the libraries of an extraordinary variety of American architects.[25] But not that of Sims. His curiosity extended rather to those German Goths who were exploring the relationship between the materials of construction and architectural form, above all Georg Gottlob Ungewitter (1820–64).[26] Sims owned Ungewitter's pioneering *Vorlegeblätter für Ziegel und Steinarbeiten* (Leipzig: Romberg, 1849)—Model Designs for Brick and Stonework—which showed how forms of extraordinary vigor and plasticity might be extracted from the facts of construction. He also owned *The Workshop*, a Hanover-based journal published by Ungewitter's disciples that applied Gothic Revival dogma to furniture and the decorative arts.

Rich as the list is, it must once have been larger. Several books that Sims most certainly owned (according to purchases recorded in his diary) are missing.[27] And a whole array of books that we know were essential to the Gothic Revivalist are strangely absent. Where is *The Ecclesiologist*, the articulate and acerbic journal that was the mouthpiece of High Church medievalism? And what of George Edmund Street's *Brick and Marble in the Middle Ages* (1855), Owen Jones's *Grammar of Ornament* (1856), Christopher Dresser's *Principles of Decorative Design* (1873), or any of the books by Edmund Sharpe?

Also entirely missing is any French literature, a surprising gap since Sims was an astute observer of recent French architecture. The inventory lists neither Viollet-le-Duc's *Dictionnaire raisonné de l'architecture française* (1854–68) nor his *Entretiens sur l'architecture* (1863–72)—books obviously known to Sims, who wrote perceptively about French architecture. Is it possible he bequeathed these Gothic Revival essentials to his brother?

Sims's most important acquisitions were not his books but his photographs. Architectural photographs, unless pasted into albums or otherwise preserved, tend not to survive. And not surviving, they tend to be neglected in the scholarship. But Sims's inventory shows that photographs circulated briskly among architects, and that they were at least as important as periodicals in showing new buildings. Besides his photographs of the rooms and furniture of William Burges, he had photographs of com-

FIGURE 11.6 Long before Trinity Church in Boston made architect H. H. Richardson a national sensation, Henry Sims decided he was a young man to watch. He acquired this photograph of one of Richardson's first buildings, Grace Church, Medford, Massachusetts (1868), with its animated play of rough rubble and finely cut stone.

mercial buildings in Boston by Cummings & Sears and Memorial Hall by Ware & Van Brunt. These do not survive but we do have his photograph of Grace Church in Medford, Massachusetts (1867–69), one of H. H. Richardson's earliest works (fig. 11.6). But one can see why Sims was interested, for Richardson's hefty masonry, clinched by alternating smooth courses in the tower, suggested his own experiments with masonry texture in his First Presbyterian Church. Richardson was only just beginning to achieve recognition when Sims died in 1875, and the appearance of the photograph in his library shows prescience on Sims's part.

But even more prescient was his acquisition of a photograph of the tomb of the Duc de Morny, at the cemetery of Père Lachaise, Paris (fig. 11.7). Built in 1866, it is perhaps the most startling object ever designed by Viollet-le-Duc. It is a remarkable synthesis of the two most fertile sources of architectural inspiration of the day, the *néo grec* and the Gothic, and Sims, like all thoughtful architects, wondered how their lessons could be combined.[28] The tomb is an almost violent collision of the two, and it comes closer to the work of Furness than perhaps any other single work of European architecture. It is telling that Sims owned the photograph, and that Furness did not see fit to buy it at auction.[29]

FIGURE 11.7 Eugène Emmanuel Viollet-le-Duc gave the Duc de Morny, half-brother of Napoleon III, one of the oddest tombs in Père Lachaise Cemetery. Sims owned this photograph but his friend Frank Furness seems to have spent the most time studying it.

ONE MUST BE CAREFUL when speculating from an inventory. To own a book is not necessarily to admire it, or even to read it. Sims owned *Builder's Jewel* (either the edition of 1751 or that of 1768) by Batty Langley even though he savagely mocked its author in print; evidently the book was there for laughs.[30] Likewise, G. G. Scott's *Remarks on Secular and Domestic Architecture, Present and Future* (1858) was the most cogent argument for the applicability of the Gothic to the problems of the modern world, yet it is listed in the auction catalogue as "an uncut copy"!

But to turn from the inventory to the diary is to see that Sims was constantly immersed in his library, especially after he "had my book case and books brought up to the house where they will be of more service to me than at the office."[31] His nighttime reading, except for the occasional Charles Dickens novel, is chiefly architectural: on June 10, 1867 we find him reading J. B. Denison's *Lectures on Church Building*; on November 11, 1867, he "looked over a volume of the *Builder*"; on March 31, 1868, he amused himself with *Memoirs of Sir Charles Barry*. If he thought a British book essential, as he did Bruce Talbert's *Gothic Forms*

Applied to Furniture, he had it imported (this was on August 31, 1868 and it cost a hefty $25).

Sometimes he needed a book more swiftly, in which case he borrowed it from a friend. On February 1, 1868 we find him needing a good reference source for wooden roof trusses and so he "borrowed Brandon's *Open Timber Roofs of the Middle Ages* from Hewitt. Read it tonight."[32] This was George W. Hewitt, and his loan of the book shows professional generosity of a high order, for the architects were at that very moment competing to design the Church of the Holy Apostles. (Sims later bought the book, for it shows up on his inventory.)

But Sims's great ambition was to publish a Gothic Revival treatise of the sort that formed the heart of his collection, and to place it on the shelves with them.

On April 27, 1867 he drew a section of a church roof: "The first of a series of drawings for illustrating a book on small churches which I think of publishing. I have been thinking it over for some months past. This evening made out the heads for the letter press." Throughout the rest of the year and into 1868 he toiled over the book whenever business was slack: "engaged all day on one of the plates for my book—that showing different styles of walling" (June 21); "worked all day on drawings for seats which I now make for Cape Island but will use the drawing for my book" (June 26); "This evening worked on my book drawings—made gd. [ground] plan for a log church" (October 18); "Each evening have been engaged writing on book" (January 31, 1868); "This evening completed writing the chapter on sites. I have much enlarged it" (July 9).

As the year went on, Sims's business increased and we find him working less and less on the book. At some point he set it aside, never to return to it; the manuscript and drawings are missing and should be presumed lost. But it is revealing just how much thought and effort he lavished on it, which bespeaks an inordinate reverence for the printed word and image. Given his peculiar education, it could hardly have been different. As a seasoned railroad engineer, charged with superintending the construction

FIGURE 11.8 Sims took heraldry as seriously as architecture, and while composing the arms that he placed on his bookplate he followed its rules scrupulously. Among other things, it tells us that he was a married man, the eldest son, and that his father was still living.

of minor service buildings as well as making viaducts, embankments, and trestles, Sims had a thorough education in construction before he lifted his thoughts to architecture. When he did this, at some point in the mid-1850s, it was through the bracing and urgent literature of the Gothic Revival. These books gave a sense of vital purpose and meaning to the forms he designed, and it is poignant that he wished to add to them.

Sims did one more thing that marks the authentic bibliophile: he designed his own bookplate (fig. 11.8). It bears the full coat of arms modified in strict accordance with the rules of British heraldry (it shows, for example, that Sims was a commoner, a married man, the eldest son, and that his father was still living).[33] At the base was the Sims family motto, *Ferio, Tego* (I strike, I defend). Both the arms and the motto were taken—and what could be more appropriate for a bibliophile?—from a book: James Fairbairn's *Crests of the Families of Great Britain and Ireland* of 1860.

CHAPTER 12

"He was not a connoisseur"

Willis Hale and the Widener Mansion

■ FOR A TYCOON of the Gilded Age, the building of a great mansion on New York's Fifth Avenue was sport, duty, and investment. Seldom was pleasure so serious. Here the shabby secrets of the boardroom, the desperate gambles and hidden partnerships, were put aside, and the American plutocrat stood forth as a public citizen, as if presenting himself for public inspection. For the Vanderbilts and the Astors, the Goulds and the Fricks, to build a rich town house was also to build a civic image. It marked the moment the capitalist emerged as statesman, no longer the frenetic speculator, but now a man with the pledge of permanence and solidity about him.

Of all the mighty gilded townhouses, Peter A. B. Widener's turreted brownstone in Philadelphia stood apart.[1] With its north German scroll gables, bizarre woven stone pattern, and roofline bristling with peculiar ventilators and chimneys, it was absolutely unlike anything on Fifth Avenue, or anywhere else (fig. 12.1). Most of the great townhouses were assertive and fashionable in

FIGURE 12.1 Peter A. B. Widener's Germanic mansion at North Broad Street and Girard Avenue reminds us that we swagger most arrogantly when we are most insecure.

their time, some looked vulgar, and all soon dated, but the Widener mansion was perhaps the only one to look odd the day it was built. Widener himself realized this, and within a decade moved out, having built himself a second house as unlike the first as could be. In America's lengthy rolls of architectural follies and men made bankrupt by their dream houses, Widener's brownstone earns a place of honor, the most lavish of mansions to have been discarded for no other reason than an unhappy but monumental miscalculation of fashionability.

"Republican, Capitalist, Episcopalian"

To his native Philadelphia Peter A. B. Widener (1834–1915) remains the greatest and gaudiest of the robber barons: the German butcher-turned-tycoon, the art collector, the traction magnate who ruled the streetcar lines, and the builder of a vulgar mansion on the wrong side of the tracks in North Philadelphia. He was of that class who so totally exhausted the descriptive possibilities of English adjectives that its behavior could only be encompassed in French words: *parvenu, nouveau-riche, arriviste.* And yet Widener was no more parvenu than any of the other plutocrats thrust forward by the great Civil War boom, his wealth no newer than that of a Vanderbilt or Carnegie, and his ancestry no more German than the imperious Astors. And far from coming from the wrong side of the tracks, Widener owned the tracks themselves.

Born to a family of Philadelphia butchers, Widener was made by the Civil War. His main chance came with a franchise to supply mutton to all Union soldiers within a ten-mile radius of Philadelphia, a major staging point for the Union army.[2] Fifty thousand dollars richer by war's end, he began buying interests in streetcar lines. And as city treasurer after 1873, he made sure that the city's fiscal interests and his own did not diverge too widely. By the end of the decade he and his partner William Elkins had established a virtual monopoly over the city's trolley lines, changing the horsecar lines first to cable and then electricity. He next invested his vast dividends in the United Gas Improvement Company (now UGI) and a fleet of other companies, helping to organize the U.S. Steel Corporation and the American Tobacco Company. Each of these diverse activities recapitulated the same formula for success: begin by buying shares and then establish a monopoly on a necessary service or utility, first the traction syndicate, then the gas syndicate, next the electric syndicate, and so forth. It was as if Widener again and again reprised his Civil War experience, perpetually seeking to recreate his first fortune, his humble mutton monopoly, ever expanding his ten-mile radius.

In the 1880s Widener enjoyed national prominence, ruling large interests in the traction lines of Chicago and New York. Swaggering in his newfound status, he captioned himself boldly in social directories, "Republican, Capitalist, Episcopalian," as if they were the same thing. Crucial, of course, to a role as a great capitalist was the ability to provide formal entertainment on the most profligate and uninhibited scale. Therefore, to crown his newly won stature, Widener decided in early 1886 to exchange his old-fashioned townhouse for a mansion in the grand manner.

As architectural patron, Widener was no novice. He had been building speculative rowhouses throughout North Philadelphia, positioning them cunningly to support his network of trolley lines. His architect was Willis Gaylord Hale (1848–1907), an architect of shameless and gleeful idiosyncrasy. Hale was born in Seneca Falls, worked in a variety of architects' offices, including those of Samuel Sloan and John McArthur, Jr., whom he assisted on the early plans for Philadelphia City Hall.[3] From 1873 to 1876 he practiced in Wilkes-Barre, Pennsylvania, where he once impulsively declared that he was renouncing architecture to "join the Italian opera," a first inkling of the eccentricity that would mark his buildings.[4]

Eccentricity, if properly deployed, generates public interest and Hale proved to be a genius at getting attention. He certainly knew how to thrust himself forward, and he practiced the high art of insinuating flattering items about himself in the newspapers: Hale entertaining the Athletic Club of the Schuylkill Navy by accompanying himself at the piano and singing "The Last Watch," or launching into an impromptu fencing match, or inventing something called "Hale's Twin Star Pneumatic Seat," a bicycle seat that "completely removes all pressure from vital parts"; so shameless was the self-praise that one almost suspects the editor was having a laugh at Hale's expense: "The Apollo-like figure of Willis G. Hale . . . disported himself in a stunning suit, mounted upon his spangled and glistening wheel."[5]

HALE CAME TO THE attention of the city's real estate speculators through the *Philadelphia Record* (see fig. 12.2). William Singerly (1832–98) inherited the stumbling paper from his father and daringly lowered its price to a penny; by 1882 circulation jumped from 5,000 to 90,000. To project an image of verve and energy, he enlisted Hale to design new newspaper offices. The result was astonishing, a granite cage below which bursts into an odd campanile at the roofline, a campanile that seems to have wandered in

FIGURE 12.2 The *Philadelphia Record* was an aggressively modern newspaper that relished investigative journalism, qualities that Hale celebrated with his high-keyed nervous building: a cage of granite piers, its corner sporting curved windows instead of solid wall, and a spikey armored head poking up at the skyline.

by accident from another building entirely—perhaps a "Hindoo" one, as one baffled critic proposed. For the first time we encounter the bizarre Hale touches: the absolute physical dematerialization of the corners, at which he set curved expanses of windows, unerringly placing a gesture of weightless crystalline elegance at just the spot where the viewer expected a show of strength.

With this figurehead looming over Chestnut Street, the newspaper surged. And as fast as the money poured in, Singerly poured it back into house-building. No sooner was the *Record* building completed than he announced a development of eight hundred houses (!) at Twenty-second and Diamond Streets; another hundred went up simultaneously on the 2300 and 2400 blocks of Berks and Norris. This brought Hale to the attention of other real estate developers, including Widener and William Weightman, the quinine tycoon.

Widener was even more audacious than Singerly, and he unleashed Hale to turn blocks of mass-produced speculative rows into fashionable, upscale neighborhoods. These were sprawling operations, with hundreds of houses rising by concerted industrial processes, whole city blocks turned into brick yards and sawmills. Hale's genius was to take these essentially identical rowhouses, with their mass-produced industrial parts and lathe-turned woodwork, and make them distinctive. It is not altogether unfair to call Hale a facade architect, more interested in clever walls than intelligent plans. And when compared to Frank Furness, his better-known peer, Hale falls short. Furness's best works are based on a single motif, inflated to heroic scale, but Hale's are riddled with passages of ornament, invention, and incidental detail: like a musician who is more interested in his trills and tremolos than the line of the melody. Nonetheless, for his new house Widener seems to have wanted only a facade architect, for much of his interior was to be the work of another man entirely.

George Herzog (1851–1920) was a German decorative painter who had trained in Munich before emigrating to Philadelphia in 1871, ostensibly to paint some landscapes.[6] He quickly became its principal decorative painter, presiding over a large staff of assistants. In such works as the interiors of the Masonic Temple and City Hall, Herzog brought the extravagant Munich decorative tradition to Philadelphia. This was a system of great discipline, brought to a high pitch of perfection by the royal building projects of Bavaria's ambitious kings, and reinforced by rigorous academic training. Painters learned to divide their walls and ceilings into an architectonic lattice, within whose geometric panels wafted languid figures and foliage, all executed with the delicacy and sentiment of Germany's Nazarene painters, the counterpart to England's Pre-Raphaelite movement. Sentiment, strong colors, and a preference for literalness over subtlety: here were qualities that the blunt Widener could appreciate.

Throughout the spring of 1886 Widener saw Hale and Herzog, foisting on them his own sketches. The idea of the house soon expanded to take in a similar house for his son next door, forming a kind of family compound. This second house was a monument to the multi-generational Widener and Elkins partnership: in one half would live George Widener, who was married to

Elkins' daughter, while her brother would live in the other half. Widener's location for these new houses seemed odd but made sense. The city's finest new mansions were built near fashionable Rittenhouse Square, but there the downtown streets were carved into 25 by 100 foot lots; even a couple of these lots put together would yield but a cramped house, shouldered between the fussy brick fronts of neighbors. It would have felt small, not only physically but perhaps even psychologically. Only on Broad Street, where the city was expanding beyond William Penn's original grid, was there a generosity of scale that could compare with Fifth Avenue. (After all, New York's grid dates from 1811 and Philadelphia's from 1682—New York shows a nineteenth-century bigness that a seventeenth-century grid could not match.)

But Widener had even better reasons for moving north: here ran his streetcar and here too were his new rowhouse operations. To move to this neighborhood (with his partner Elkins across the street and both their sons next door) would be a colossal act of real estate promotion, a personal guarantee to buyers that the new northern districts would be prosperous, stable, and, above all, fashionable. On July 31, 1886, he finally showed reporters the design of his new houses. A tried hand at manipulating the press to promote his real estate and traction ventures, he evidently felt no qualms about exhibiting his private life to public scrutiny. Nor was he troubled by any taint of discretion when it came to his finances. Instead he shamelessly trumpeted his costs, bragging that he was paying an additional $50,000 for stone carving on his facades when it was not necessary. Only one reservation draped this epic of financial exhibitionism. The enormous outlays for his house, so he assured reporters, would be spent locally: "every stone and every stick of wood and all the labor" would come from Philadelphia. As far as he went, Widener was telling the truth, and perhaps every brick did indeed come from Philadelphia, but virtually every idea in his house came from New York.

From the first Widener had been brooding over photographs of Fifth Avenue houses, particularly the new mansion of William H. Vanderbilt (1880–81), a Renaissance palazzo with an exceptional amount of surface sculpture, and probably the most famous house in America in its time.[7] Widener boasted to reporters that he had carefully studied the mansion, having had it photographed inside and out. More likely he had simply bought a four-volume set of *Mr. Vanderbilt's House and Collection* which showed every room of the house.[8] Vanderbilt's house was the work of the Herter Brothers, decorators rather than architects. Many of their best ideas resurfaced and, where possible, were made bigger, in Widener's house.

For his builder Widener chose William T. B. Roberts, who had been building his speculative housing projects in North Philadelphia.[9] Roberts broke ground in August 1886, and by late fall spectators had their first clear picture of the house—or at least thought they did. For several months Widener appeared to be building a Romanesque house, with rusticated brownstone walls, brawny projecting bays, and muscular round arches. Then, above the level of the second story cornice the form abruptly changed. Gone were the Romanesque arches and moldings, and in their place a frothy display of gables soared up three full stories in mighty curving lines, freighted with sculpted hermes and fantastic grotesques. It was as if the original architect and drawings had been banished overnight, replaced by a second man with another vision, who immediately and without transition commenced his design on the abandoned work. The perplexed *Philadelphia Inquirer* decided that the first story was Romanesque while the upper stories were "Elizabethan." In fact, the upper stories with their north German gables were drawn from the Weser Renaissance of Hamelin and other cities along north Germany's Weser River, a source of forms seldom used in America and never on such a scale.

Turrets under conical caps marked the four corners, the whole roofed in vivid red tile, while a wing to the rear terminated in a glazed conservatory. These turrets bowed outward from the building, undulating, as if raised up by a passing wave from within the brownstone. The brownstone was as remarkable as the gables and turrets, for it was not laid in conventional horizontal courses, but in alternating vertical and horizontal joints, as if woven rather than bonded together. These brownstone walls were modeled as richly as sculpture, juxtaposing shadowy voids against boldly projecting volumes, the bays and turrets offset by the cavernous entrance and the shadowy loggia above it. Here was no sense of timeless forms in restful equipoise, but all stood in dynamic tension—accomplishing with shadow and mass the nervous expressiveness that a preceding generation would have achieved through colors and materials. Of course, the historic charade ran only so deep. Within, behind the basement smoking den and billiard room, was a dynamo supplying power to run the electric lights and lift Widener's elevator. For all the medieval drapery and the whiff of aristocratic splendor, the house was as mechanized and up-to-date as one of Widener's streetcars.

"That enchanted world of form and color"

Despite the German flourishes overloading its walls, the Widener house was profoundly American in plan, organization, and conception. Within was the center hall plan of eighteenth-century tradition, with a formal stair hall flanked by principal rooms at either side and a service wing to the rear (fig. 12.3). Widener's imagination went no further than the houses of his Philadelphia childhood; he could multiply the rooms and magnify their dimensions, but could not envision other types of living. Nevertheless, out of the traditional center hall arose the house's most astonishing feature. This was precisely the effect that the cramped urban interior usually ruled out—the sense of endless, luxurious vista. Hale commenced his great hall at the tiled vestibule, marched it through a screen of onyx columns into the stair hall, and carried it into the great banquet hall, teasingly interrupted it with a fountain throwing up spray, then passed it through the rear wing where it terminated in the greenhouse. The entire length of the view, from vestibule through column screen, portals, and fountain to the distant light of the greenhouse, was 194 feet. There was nothing like this view in any townhouse in America (fig. 12.4).

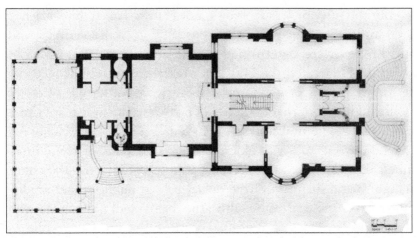

FIGURE 12.3 As outrageous as the facade of the Widener House was, its plan could not have been more conventional: a broad center hall passed between the principal rooms to culminate in the dream world of the banquet hall. Subtlety was not the point.

FIGURE 12.4 Hale put Widener's grand stair in the middle of the hall, coyly blocking the view of the banquet hall beyond.

But the interior was Herzog's, not Hale's. The architect delivered unfinished spaces and raw construction; walls, ceilings, and furnishings were determined by Herzog's ceaseless torrent of sketches. He treated the house not in architectural but pictorial terms, as a series of vivid and constantly changing vignettes, "a household interior that is a series of pictures as artistic as anything on canvas." The movements of parvenu social life were choreographed by Herzog with clocklike precision and Germanic literalness. Each room was impeccably adjusted in material and color, hangings and furniture, to its social role as public spaces graduated to ever more private realms: the formal hall ("stateliness and sociability") yielded to dignified reception rooms ("cheerfulness and sociability") and parlors ("elegance"), which in turn gave way to the dining room ("hospitableness"), the library ("tranquility"), and, at last, the family sitting room ("domesticity"), and the sleeping chambers ("repose").[10] But despite all his orchestration of public and private, the demands of formal entertainment counted for everything. Even the central passage outside Widener's second-story bedroom was furnished as "the promenade or rendezvous of guests after a banquet or a dance." For Widener, *repose* must wait for *sociability* to run its course.

And sociability certainly ruled the first story. Guests would glide from main hall to reception room while Herzog's "incomparable" murals hovered above the wainscoting. These were softly luminous paintings, with the nearly smoky colors of the Munich mural school, showing "glimpses of far off, shadowy but gilded and rose-tinted celestial cities, appearing like a mirage of dream castles in the air." To the left was the Empire style drawing room and to the right the well-wainscoted library. But Herzog's consummation lay beyond. Astride the main axis was the banquet hall, the centerpiece of the entire house, measuring thirty-two feet square and rising twenty feet to a cove ceiling (fig. 12.5). Above the entrance was a so-called minstrel gallery, an internal balcony with a florid balustrade from which one might spy into the conservatory. (For once Widener did not crib from Wil-

FIGURE 12.5 Hale's last surprise: as guests passed into the banquet hall, they would realize they were being serenaded from the minstrel gallery above.

liam H. Vanderbilt but from his nephew, William K. Vanderbilt, whose dining room had a similar musician's gallery.)

Above the deeply paneled walls ran a continuous mural. Once again the idea came from Vanderbilt's mansion, and once again Widener trumped Vanderbilt. While the New York drawing rooms showed a procession of mere knights and troubadours, here were portraits of Widener's own family, gamboling in seventeenth-century costumes: Widener's wife Josephine, in a jeweled bodice, and, beneath a plumed hat, son George, one day to drown on the *Titanic*. This was the triumph of the mansion and the one most cited by visitors. While Herzog typically left his assistants to execute his deft sketches, the painting of the banquet hall murals he reserved for himself. The sycophantic critic of the *Times* swooned over Herzog's murals, perceiving in them "the beautiful and fertile realm of the Renaissance . . . that enchanted world of form and color, full of mysterious existences and fanciful beings, incongruous, grotesque, attractive, that express as in a painted language the many phases of human thought and feeling."[11] It was a breathless and fawning tribute, and not until a century later would critics again be so appreciative, but too late to save the house.

"The week has not been noteworthy for its gaiety"

Widener had announced that his house would be completed by June 1, 1887, well in advance of the social season when genteel Philadelphians would return from their summer homes in Newport, Bar Harbor, and Cape May. But September passed and work languished. The Belgian sculptor Edward Maene had not yet finished the colossal hermes carrying the gables, and as late as November Widener's artists were still assembling bits of friezes in their studio.[12] Not until early 1888 were the Wideners ready to position themselves beneath Herzog's painted trellises and arbors and receive guests. On Wednesday, January 25, Mrs. Widener held her long-anticipated evening reception. Thinking perhaps of New York—as her husband seemed incessantly to do—she addressed precisely four hundred invitations, doing so at the very moment that the concept of the First Four Hundred was being coined. (The idea that there are "only 400 people in fashionable New York Society" is usually attributed to Ward McAllister in 1888 but the Wideners seem to have anticipated him by a year.)

Widener made his great gesture to Philadelphia and in return was met with Philadelphia's great snub. The fashionable society columns ignored his grand unveiling and even the *Philadelphia Inquirer*, generally obsequious to the wealthy, rubbed in the insult. Looking over the social calendar, they sniffed that "the week has not been noteworthy for its gaiety."[13]

Widener's bad press was perhaps inevitable, and it distinguishes him from men such as Vanderbilt and Carnegie. His counterparts in New York, America's great financiers, were vigorous rivals and often inspired great passion, but they were seldom in direct conflict with civic property interests. Americans were affected by the price wars and stock swindles but these typically occurred at a distance or involved abstract quantities. Yet Widener's operations immediately affected urban property holders, his trolley lines directly influencing land values. Philadelphians were quite vocal in defending their property rights, their acerbic newspapers at the vanguard, and Widener and Elkins were choice targets. No chance was missed to pummel them. When the *Philadelphia Inquirer* celebrated the centennial of the American constitution in 1887, it cast a prophetic look ahead at the Philadelphia of 1987. The key event of the century was to be the breaking of the monopoly of a fictitious "William Peter Elkener."[14]

The most earth was scorched, however, by Widener's friends. The ever-eager *Times* wrote an overwrought review of the house so ludicrous as to approach parody: "The sky is not pierced with pinnacles nor do towers and turrets confront the attention. No mansard roof overweights the top and there is no useless cupola as a resting place for the birds of the air. It is by no means a congregation of queer forms and devices presenting a medley of the mythologic and marvelous architectural monstrosities of many ages."[15] Finally, it assured readers that the house was not "conspicuous." Was this deadpan irony? Or the nervous guest who blurts out inadvertently just what he is trying not to say? In either case, the critic unerringly listed the house's weakest points, perhaps by malicious design.

Widener's house was not yet complete. By temperament he was not so much maker of things as acquirer. Now he turned from architecture to art, which he had begun buying seriously in 1885. Dispatching buyers and agents to Europe, and stealing away when he could himself, he began to amass the enormous collection which eventually became the mainstay of the National Gallery. During these early years he seemed to want one of everything, and like the prudent financier who wants to diversify his portfolio, Widener purchased across the board: seventeenth-century Dutch, eighteenth-century English, nineteenth-century

French. After half a dozen Gainsboroughs and Constables came as many Vermeers and Van Dycks, and then a dozen Corots and Courbets. There were some American works—the odd George Inness and Mary Cassatt—but otherwise his collection was as European as the motifs on his house.[16]

In 1892 Widener's collection was too big to be adequately hung on the overdecorated walls of his house. He now demolished the glass conservatory to the rear and set about building a picture gallery. Once more Herzog was called to furnish the interior, delivering the most astonishing drawing with which he ever flattered a client. Rather than simply detailing the strapwork ornament of the cove ceiling and the gilded frieze below, he created little cameos of nineteen paintings—some of them representing works in Widener's collection and others apparently in the style of well-known artists (fig. 12.6). It was a labor of love—absolutely unnecessary for the design of the space or the approval of the furnishings—but a virtuoso performance of stupendous versatility. At the heart of the drawing appear Widener and his

FIGURE 12.6 George Herzog's design for the interior of Widener's picture gallery was a spirited piece of showmanship, assuring his client of his place in this world of ease and elegance—where he could forget for a moment his origin as an enterprising butcher.

wife, admiring their own taste. Just as they walked into the wall murals of their banquet room, they now strode onto the actual design drawings. Small wonder that Widener enthusiastically commended Herzog to all his friends (although, still the penny-conscious butcher at heart, he told them that the artist could be coaxed into doing extra work for nothing, as long as it might improve the design).

"He was not a connoisseur"

Widener's house, augmented by the 1892 picture gallery, was a veritable Louvre at the corner of Broad and Girard. Still, a Louvre in the backyard does not a Paris make. The first hint of unfashionability came wafting in. In 1893 the Columbian Exhibition inaugurated a vast and spacious classical revival. Picturesque brownstone arches yielded to white marble columns, and the distinctly north German character of the Widener house aged poorly. The great prestige that things German had enjoyed in the 1870s and 1880s began to wane. Immigration made America less charitable to central Europe and the rising temperance movement took on a nativist cast in which Germans were viewed warily. The Wideners crafted their family history to show that the ship in which their great-great-grandfather had arrived in the US sailed from Holland. Widener's German antecedents were left unmentioned (although much was made of a stop in England during the passage!).[17]

Widener's personal taste began to change after the completion of his gallery, and he started to jettison his nineteenth-century paintings for Old Masters. It was as if he feared the ridicule leveled at Vanderbilt, an indiscriminating collector who had a shrewd eye for a phony business deal but none for a phony Rembrandt. Widener's trading in paintings appalled fellow collectors such as the scrupulous John G. Johnson. For them collecting was an act of great integrity and discipline, and a collection was slowly to mature, polished and rounded off decade by decade; it was not a stock portfolio, held speculatively to be traded off at the first whiff of opportunity or danger. The elegant dealer and collector James Henry Duveen, who tried to keep his mouth shut when Widener showed off his occasional fake, spoke the last word: "Widener had a great eye for beauty, but he was not a connoisseur; he had begun too late in life."[18] It was not meant unkindly.

As his art seemed out of fashion, so did his house. When the *Architectural Record* began profiling the works of his architect, Willis Hale, in its blistering "Architectural Aberrations" feature, Widener sensed it was time to move on, perhaps dreading the appearance of his own house in an article (fig. 12.7).[19] On October 24, 1897, less than a decade after the completion of the house, he told a hastily summoned group of city officials that he would give his mansion as a gift to the city for use as a public library. This bequest spared him the humiliation of placing the property

FIGURE 12.7 Polite opinion turned against Hale in the 1890s when his Keystone National Bank (later the Hale Building) was singled out by the *Architectural Record* as "irrational, incongruous and ridiculous," with a tower that might have suited a country house but which was "violently incongruous" in downtown Philadelphia.

on the market, and the inevitable comparison between his original outlay and his sacrifice price. Three years later the Josephine Widener branch of the Philadelphia Free Library opened.

Widener moved on to build a new house in Elkins Park. Hale did not move with him. The spoils went to up-and-coming Horace Trumbauer and Hale had to make do with the crumbs. To him fell the demeaning task of tidying up the now dowdy mansions. In 1901 he was hired by the real estate entrepreneur Solomon Greenberg to lop the picturesque top off George Widener's neighboring house, transforming it into the Royal Apartments. Meanwhile, Trumbauer built the palatial Elkins Park villa, whose tasteful Renaissance style would better suit the Old Master paintings that were arriving to decorate its walls. Hale died six years later, destitute, pawning his collection of musical instruments and architectural books, waiting in vain for the return of his fickle clients.

Widener's house stood apart from the great parvenu mansions, differing in a way that brought against it the harsh judgment of a later age. Unlike the great Fifth Avenue houses, where tycoon shouldered against tycoon, Widener built his family enclave in the midst of his real estate ventures. His North Broad Street address was almost a warranty, a personal pledge, that his new housing operations would fall under the mantle of polite society. But not long after the last field was developed and his last house sold, Widener abandoned his mansion. His flight could not be reassuring to those who remained. By the turn of the century the surrounding neighborhood, developed with such dash and élan by Widener, lost its fashionability and began the long plunge into poverty and collapse that still, more than a century later, has not hit bottom.

To House the New Wealth

America had seen nothing like the great fortunes of the 1870s and 1880s, and there were no ready answers to the question posed by the new wealth: how to live? Like an English peer, a

Medici merchant, perhaps a Bourbon king? The great houses of these years were to some extent noble experiments, an attempt to create in a decade or two an aristocratic way of life which in England or France was the natural outgrowth of centuries. But this architectural improvising was not random, and it rested upon a strong code of manners and decorum. This was paramount, for after the great upheaval of the Civil War, and after the rise of dozens of spectacular fortunes, those who had most recently entered the ranks of the elect were most anxious to shut the door behind them. Hence the deep concern about codifying rules of behavior, of etiquette and manners—and hence the idea of numbering the Four Hundred as if there could be no more, as if foreordained and predestined: all was to shut and bar the vast door of mobility that the Civil War had opened.

Of course, this required the fiction that the recent fortunes were much older than they appeared. And all of the houses, the art treasures, the hangings and Old Masters, and Louis XIV chairs, all of this was the great and serious business of manufacturing patinas. Seldom was so much wealth so new, and never was it wrapped in so much that was old. The Widener house, like the best of the Gilded Age mansions, was a dazzling guess at how the new wealth might be housed: the guess proved wrong but it was nonetheless dazzling.

There is a strange coda. In 1980, after a long downward spiral of neglect, the Widener House was destroyed, apparently through arson. I learned this in mid-air, while flying to Germany for my Fulbright year. In my suitcase were notes for an article I planned to write about the house, which I fondly hoped might help preserve it. Here, with tragicomic lateness, is that article.

CHAPTER 13

The Last Quaker

Robert Venturi

■ ROBERT VENTURI, the Philadelphia architect who died last month at the age of ninety-three, left a twofold legacy. On the one hand, he demolished almost entirely by himself the prestige of the modern movement in architecture, whose moral authority had gone unquestioned for a generation. He did to it precisely what Andy Warhol did to Abstract Expressionism: make its heroic claims seem laughable. On the other hand, Venturi also created—again, almost entirely by himself—a rich architectural language that would take the place of laconic International Style modernism. By making witty use of signs and symbols, plucked from across the whole range of history and modern life, he made buildings speak again, if sometimes garrulously. Here was the origin of architectural postmodernism, although in later years he would bitterly deny all paternity claims.

It is fitting that the most devastating critique of modernist orthodoxy should have been launched by a Quaker from Philadelphia. The city, which had been building red-brick rowhouses on straight streets for almost three centuries, was itself the physical manifestation of the Quaker doctrine of plain clothes and plain speech. Venturi was raised a Quaker, and he absorbed its dread of pomp and display. When his first buildings were mocked as "ugly and ordinary," he adopted the phrase as a badge of honor. Since Quakers have no formally trained ministers, and so did not, as did the Puritan colonies, immediately found universities to produce them, Philadelphia's intellectual culture tended to be pragmatic and empirical, rather than abstract and theoretical. And so when Venturi came to write theory, its hallmark was a complete absence of utopian ambition and an insistence on accepting the basic facts of modern life.

In 1944 Venturi began to study architecture at Princeton; three years later he enrolled in its graduate program. These were the years when International Style modernism reached its zenith of postwar influence. But the doctrine of functionalism, imported by German refugees from the Bauhaus and adopted by their American disciples, had not taken over Princeton, where he was marinated in the history of architecture. As he liked to tell the story, he took the survey course three times: as a student, slide projectionist, and teaching assistant. It has been pointed out that his celebrated *Complexity and Contradiction in Architecture* is itself like an art history lecture, with its tiny images scaled like 35-mm slides and artfully arranged to show startling parallels.

After graduation, Venturi worked in turn for two architects whose interest in expressing the specific nature of building types put them outside the high-modernist camp: Eero Saarinen's airports looked like airports, and Louis I. Kahn's biological laboratory looked like a biological laboratory. But Venturi's formative experience came in 1954, when he received a fellowship from the American Academy in Rome. He spent the next two years in and around Rome, where he became enamored of the Italian Renaissance, particularly in its mannerist phase, when the forms of classical architecture were imaginatively manipulated for expressive purposes. If Venturi had an architectural philosophy, it was that of Mannerism, which treated architecture as a language with its own vocabulary, syntax, and grammar, and whose rules could be violated for expressive effect. His architectural heroes were actual mannerists like Michelangelo and Giulio Romano, or their rule-breaking successors over the centuries, e.g., Nicholas Hawksmoor, Frank Furness, or Edwin Lutyens.

In 1966 Venturi published *Complexity and Contradiction in Architecture,* whose effect on the architectural world was like that of a stone hurled from a catapult. It was quickly translated into sixteen languages, and Vincent Scully hailed it as "probably the most important writing on the making of architecture since Le Corbusier's *Vers une Architecture.*" Half a century later, that verdict seems truer than ever. As radical treatises go, it is as mild as can be. Venturi himself called it "a gentle manifesto." Its argument was a simple one, put forward with inexhaustible ingenuity and examples: that architecture is at bottom an expressive medium but that its expressive range had been drastically impoverished by a functionalist doctrine of universals and absolutes that had no sympathy for the complex and contradictory nature of life itself. Strangely, while the book was crammed with examples of historical architecture, as in a survey course, it was not in the slightest historical. Venturi juxtaposed examples from wildly different periods and cultures, the further apart the better—a seventeenth-century wooden synagogue in Poland and an outdoor theater by Alvar Aalto, an Egyptian temple and a Spanish church in Peru—to show that complexity and contradiction have always been the rule, not the exception, in architecture. The book's cruelest cut to International Style modernism was not to take it seriously. If Mies van der Rohe proclaimed "less is more," Venturi yawned that "less is a bore"—his book's most famous sentence.

Critics were baffled and young architects captivated by the portfolio of Venturi's own buildings and projects at the end of *Complexity and Contradiction.* They were at once goofy and esoteric. The small house he built for his mother looked like a child's cartoon of a house, all chimney and gable, but it was filled with sophisticated architectural quips. He alternately expanded and contracted his staircase as it made its way around the fireplace, giving it the kind of tortuous journey that might have delighted Michelangelo. And he placed a symbolic, nonfunctioning arch directly over the functioning lintel, as casually as a refrigerator magnet, gleefully subverting the Modernist insistence on truth in materials. Just as startling was his Guild House, a Quaker-operated retirement home whose main facade was an abstraction of a heroic Roman portal and whose rear was as plain as the brick factories nearby.

The quirky Guild House embodied another of Venturi's innovative ideas. If the forms of the International Style were meant to be universal, the same steel-and-glass box serving equally well for a school in Alaska or an embassy in equatorial Africa, Venturi insisted on the value of context. Buildings should not stand aloof in time and space, but should respond to their location. In fact, every architectural design needed to begin with a sensitive study of local conditions, materials, scale, and neighborhood character. If this idea is something of a platitude today, it testifies to how widely Venturi's ideas have triumphed.

For one brief moment *Complexity and Contradiction*, with its rich parade of classical buildings, suggested that humanist values might be restored to architecture, and the great Western tradition reinvigorated. But it soon became clear that this was never Venturi's goal. The decisive event was a 1967 pilgrimage to Las Vegas with Denise Scott Brown, the architect and planner who would soon become his wife and business partner (fig. 13.1). They returned a year later to study the visual language of casinos and their signs, a studio of Yale architecture students in tow. Where Venturi once condemned the American highway strip as a "honky-tonk [of] chaos and blight," he now looked at it with sympathy. After all, the Las Vegas billboard, for all its vulgarity, was nothing more than the modern counterpart to the mannerist facade, its elements cleverly abstracted and enlarged to be legible from a speeding vehicle.

Such was the argument he put forward in his jaunty *Learning from Las Vegas* (1972), written with Scott Brown and Steven Izenour, which famously categorized all buildings as either Ducks

FIGURE 13.1 Robert Venturi (1925–2018), the Philadelphia Quaker who found meaning in the least Quakerly of all American cities: Las Vegas.

or Decorated Sheds. Ducks were buildings that spoke by means of their iconic sculptural shape, which would be anything from the Parthenon to a roadside hot dog stand shaped like a hot dog; a Decorated Shed was a cheap utilitarian box that could be made to speak by applying decoration, either applied directly to the facade (more refrigerator magnets!) or detached in the form of a billboard.

To look without judgment at Las Vegas, in the detached manner of an anthropologist, was novel. It was probably made easier by virtue of Scott Brown having been raised in South Africa, which gave her an outsider's curiosity and insight about how things work. (It continues to rankle that Venturi alone received the Pritzker Prize, architecture's highest honor, and not jointly with Scott Brown.) As a sociological and semiotic analysis of America's visual culture, *Learning from Las Vegas* was brilliant, but as a program for architectural renewal it had unintended consequences. It gave permission to Venturi's followers to proceed directly to Vegas, skipping over the bracing history lesson of

Rome. In their work it soon wilted into a boorish commercial architecture of brazen cutouts, garish colors, and overscaled pastiches of historical motifs. Venturi, ever gentlemanly and soft-spoken, was properly horrified. In later years he would insist that "I am not now and have never been a postmodernist."

In retrospect it became clear that the buildings in *Complexity and Contradiction* were there for their graphic or spatial qualities, and not their cultural content. About the values and beliefs they expressed, or the spiritual or social yearnings they embodied, Venturi had little to say. It was a peculiar vision of the past, a great rummage sale of reusable graphic motifs, severed from their original owners and purposes, and innocent of any sense of tragedy. But for tragedy, Venturi had a ready substitute: irony. The owners of Guild House were appalled to read in *Complexity and Contradiction* that the classical acroterion crowning their facade was in reality a symbolic television antenna, meant to signify how the elderly "spend so much time looking at TV." They promptly removed it.

Ironic detachment, as it happens, is stony ground in which to plant an artistic movement. And while Venturi helped topple International Style modernism in its triumphant phase, the idiosyncratic personal style he cultivated did not amount in the end to a satisfying replacement. Had *Complexity and Contradiction* not seemed to promise so much, the architectural legacy would be less disappointing. And yet there are bright spots. Venturi's Franklin Court is the most significant act of architectural restoration since the controversial rebuilding of Colonial Williamsburg. Faced with the rich archaeological excavation of Benjamin Franklin's house but not a single image of the building itself, Venturi built a skeletal ghost structure above the site, marking its dimensions without building a spurious replica, inviting the visitor to imagine actively (fig. 19.1). Of similar high quality is his Sainsbury Wing addition to the National Gallery in London, which takes the festive neoclassicism of the original building and gradually relaxes its architectonic order as it moves away from it—his one great performance in high Mannerism. This was Venturi at his best, if not as pregnant with possibilities as those first provocative projects of the early 1960s.

One may admire the Roman Venturi even as one laments the Vegas Venturi. The highest standards were there, along with a stalwart probity. If his carefree buildings were free of tragedy, the man himself was full of it, deeply conscious of the fractured and anxious nature of modern life, and furiously determined to make an architecture that faced its reality fearlessly and joyously, and with the absolute sincerity that one is somehow comforted to find in architecture's last Quaker.

October 18, 2019

CHAPTER 14

Frank Furness at Thirty

The Armory of the First City Troop

■ THE FANCIFUL ARMORY of Philadelphia's First City Troop—
half Victorian clubhouse and half Crusader castle—is one of
Frank Furness's first successes.[1] It was built in 1874, the centennial of the Troop's founding, which it marked in duly martial
fashion. But four years earlier, Furness had made a very different design for the building, one so different that it looks like the
work of another architect altogether (figs. 14.1 and 14.2). That
first version, long missing, was unearthed by Dennis Boylan, the
Troop's archivist, in 2007. To have such a document for any artist
would be fortunate; with Furness it is a revelation. It shows him
tackling the same problem twice at a four-year remove, at the
precise moment he was discovering his creative powers.

Furness's armory was exceptional but no more so than his client. The First City Troop claims the honor of being America's
oldest independent military unit, and that the battle standard
in its collection is likewise America's oldest surviving flag, both
points of great pride. Formed during the American Revolution

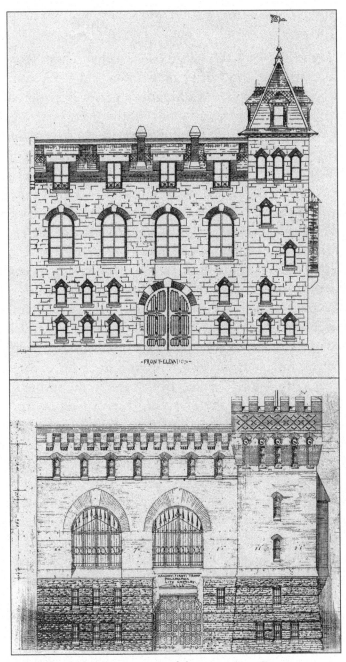

FIGURES 14.1 AND 14.2 The armory of the First City Troop, designed by Frank Furness in 1870, was never built. Four years later, without changing his floor plan, Furness devised a new facade, reducing the number of bays while swelling their scale to make a building of utterly different character.

as the Light Horse of the City of Philadelphia, the Troop distinguished itself at the battles of Trenton and Princeton; for a time it served as George Washington's personal escort. Its service in the Civil War was equally distinguished: it responded to Lincoln's call for three months of service in the summer of 1861, after which many of the members transferred into Rush's Lancers (later the Sixth Pennsylvania Cavalry). There they served as a cadre, the well-trained nucleus that would give experience and depth to the all-volunteer regiment; meanwhile, the Troop's older members remained in Philadelphia as part of the Pennsylvania Militia, and would see action at Gettysburg.

While the Civil War galvanized the Troopers, it also encouraged them to better their facilities. They had previously rented space for their drills but now they built their own parade shed, a simple brick block at the corner of Twenty-first and Barker streets in the city. It was set well back from the street, making for an attractive forecourt but also reserving space for expansion in better times (fig. 14.3). Construction began in the spring of 1863 and continued through the invasion scare of Gettysburg, when the Troopers abruptly decided a fireproof vault was needed for "preserving their books and valuable documents," presumably in the event of a Confederate raid into Philadelphia. The building opened on February 22, 1864.

Five years after the war, the Troop began to think of enlarging its quarters. After John W. Grigg died in 1869, bequeathing $10,000 to the Troop, a building committee was formed, headed by M. Edward Rogers, the Troop's captain.[2] The guiding spirit, however, would prove to be his cousin Fairman Rogers (1833–1900), his predecessor as captain and a man of surprising versatility. Fairman was Furness's first important patron, and as building committee chairman he steered the commission for the Pennsylvania Academy of the Fine Arts his way. (Furness also designed his city house and his summer house at Newport.)

Fairman Rogers was a professor of civil engineering at the University of Pennsylvania but his great love was the horse, to which he devoted the full force of his intellect.[3] He wrote *A*

FIGURE 14.3 The First City Troop built a parade shed on Twentieth Street during the Civil War, leaving room for a head house when times were better.

Manual of Coaching (1900), an encyclopedic guide to every aspect of the subject from the physics of turning a coach to the nature of road beds, to the performance of conical vs. flat wheels, to the best material for making riding breeches (it turns out to be moleskin). He even dilated upon the social etiquette of the salute:

> It is hardly necessary to say that a man when driving should always take off his hat to a lady; it is in bad taste merely to raise his whip in place of so doing. If he has not hands enough to spare one for his hat, he should continue to practise driving, until he can find one.[4]

This line is often quoted to show just how amusingly out of touch Rogers was with the modern world—and yet, his study of the horse was as modern and scientific as could be. As a photographer, Rogers was early to recognize the potential of rapid shutter speed to capture the physical action of the moving horse. Inspired by this, he commissioned Thomas Eakins to paint the celebrated *May Morning in the Park*, the first painting to show horses in motion with scientific accuracy. Later Rogers brought Eadweard Muybridge to Philadelphia to conduct his landmark motion-study photographic campaign.

Rogers was naturally concerned with the humane treatment of horses.[5] Behind his house he built a model stable, which was published as the frontispiece of the forward-looking *Gentleman's Stable Guide*.[6] In some respects it resembles the Troop's 1863 parade shed, particularly in the arrangement of paired windows, continuous brick archivolts, and marble sills carried on taut corbels. It is conceivable that Rogers himself designed both buildings; he was certainly capable.[7] But the design of a monumental public building was a problem of a higher order, and for this he and his cousin Edward turned to Frank Furness (1839–1912).

FURNESS WAS their only possible choice, for he was a relative, if only by marriage: their sister Kate Rogers had married Horace Howard Furness, Frank's brother. But even without that qualification, Furness would have been chosen. He was the only architect in Philadelphia (and perhaps in the country) who was a Civil War cavalry hero. When the war broke out, he was working in the office of Richard Morris Hunt, the eminent New York architect. He promptly enlisted in Rush's Lancers, where so many of the First City Troop also served. This was the most picturesque cavalry unit of the Civil War, the only regiment, North or South, to ride into combat bearing lances. There he learned what it felt like to have a horse shot out from beneath him while riding at top speed. He rose to the rank of captain and for his valor earned the Congressional Medal of Honor. To the end, he remained an inveterate rider, and in the poignant photographs of his final years he is invariably on horseback.

The First City Troop commission came to Furness at an opportune moment. He was a partner in Fraser, Furness & Hewitt, a precocious architectural firm whose members differed wildly in temperament and talent: John Fraser made hefty granite banks in the grave classical mode he had learned in Scotland, while George

Hewitt fashioned colorful churches in the English Gothic style. Furness, who had just turned thirty, had not yet hit his stride. Until now his work consisted mostly of unsuccessful competition entries and alterations to existing buildings.[8] The chance to flaunt his talents before the prosperous and fashionable membership of the Troop was a godsend.

The instructions given Furness were clear. He was to extend the Troop's old parade shed forward to Twenty-first Street, providing space for a formal meeting room, kitchen facilities, changing rooms, and a new fireproof vault. His only constraint was the need to retain the central passage, which he flanked with two low stories of service rooms. Above these he placed a grand hall for Troop meetings and receptions, which ran across four bays of the building and offered a dramatic view into the parade shed from an interior gallery. At the north end, behind the stair, was the fireproof vault, built into the thickness of the wall and projecting precariously out over Barker Street—a clever measure to ensure that the safe would not be crushed if the building ever collapsed in a fire. Finally, the topmost story was reserved for lockers and changing rooms.

Furness moved briskly: his rough sketches were submitted on April 11, approved by the Troop, and by June 7 he had completed the full set of plans and specifications. The specifications survive as does the front elevation, which was evidently engraved for fundraising purposes. It is this design that permits us to see Furness's mind in action (see fig. 14.1).

Furness's elevation shows a flat wall plane four stories high and some sixty-five feet wide. Three considerations seem to have governed his design: a desire to relate his addition to the original building, a desire to express its internal spaces on the exterior, and a desire to make something monumental and complete in its own right. Each he addressed in turn. To relate his building to its predecessor, he repeated its rhythm and organization, retaining the division into five bays. To express the interior, he adjusted the size and placement of the windows, indicating the grand ceremonial hall, the smaller service rooms above and below, and even the path of the rising stair. Finally, to assert the building's presence on the street, he pushed the corner bay slightly forward and treated it as a tower, capped by a low helmeted roof.

Each of these concerns was valid but what Furness did not see, and perhaps because of inexperience was unable to see, was that they conflicted to a great extent with one another. The bold tower that anchored the corner was at war with the steady, even rhythm of the original five-bay composition. And the array of windows was verbose without being articulate. He struggled to convey the character of a building that was at once a stable, an armory, and a social club—and so he expressed each of these roles with a piecemeal gesture, making his tower military, his over-sized windows civic, and his overly precious roofline domestic.

As if in compensation for these tentative gestures, Furness made his building as loud and colorful as possible. For his walls he specified the extravagantly green serpentine stone of Chester County, trimmed with bright yellow Ohio sandstone, and win-dow arches of red brick outlined with black mortar.[9] The chro-matic effect would have been stupendous. But muddles, however electrifying, do not inspire, and the design did not rouse the Troopers to generosity. A contract with the builders was drawn up in September 1870 but never signed.[10] Plaintive cost-cutting measures (e.g., the removal of the plaster cornice of the meet-ing room) shaved $2,000 from the estimate, but even the pared-down design cost too much, and as late as December the Troop was still dunning members for contributions. They did not come in, and soon thereafter Furness's drawings were quietly placed on a shelf and forgotten.

And there they might have languished except for the happy coincidence of the Troop's centennial. In the fall of 1873 a com-mittee was formed to determine how to mark the event, and once more the Rogers cousins played the decisive role. "After mature deliberation," the committee announced on December 1 that "the erection of a building as near as possible after the plans already presented and adopted by the company . . . is the most rational and proper mode of celebrating our approaching Centennial."

The Troop was willing to follow the original design "as near as possible" but Furness was not. His architectural judgment and taste had evolved so much in the previous few years that his first design now seemed amateurish. Using his drawings only as a rough guide, he spent the first weeks of 1874 completely redesigning it. By the time Edward Rogers reported to the Troop on March 2, he could announce he had secured "a new plan for the Front of the Armory . . . better suited for the purpose than the one originally intended." The Troop concurred, and except for some minor alterations—including the sacrifice of Furness's "bartisan," a slender watchtower that would have corbelled outward from one corner of the main tower—the armory was built according to the new design.

Although the facades of 1870 and 1874 appear radically different, very little had actually been changed. The plan was virtually identical: the central entrance, second-story formal hall, and corner tower were all carried over from the original design. But their meaning was utterly transformed by the change of scale and proportion. Instead of slavishly following the original division into five bays, each thirteen feet wide, Furness created three colossal bays, each of nearly twenty-two feet. Where the tower once took up a fifth of the building, it now took up a third, rising mightily from a strongly battered base to flare out again at its parapet. With the change in proportion, the nervous mincing rhythm of the first design turned into a massive elephantine stride.

Having amplified his scale, Furness next rethought his wall. What had been a sheer plane, rising without change in material or texture, now acquired an emphatic weightiness. At the bottom he placed a sturdy base of rock-faced bluestone that contrasted sharply with the razor-sharp brick walls above.[11] The original round-headed openings he converted to two bold Florentine arches (pointed above and round below) with deeply flaring voussoirs. Above the main entrance he inserted an odd lintel: a compact and spirited union of brackets, beam, and segmental arch. Finally, he shaved off the elaborate array of dormers,

FIGURE 14.4 Before 1874 it was not clear if an armory should look like a parade shed or a public hall. Furness & Hewitt's First City Troop singlehandedly created the architectural image of the modern city armory, a hefty, spirited, and yet purely symbolic fortress.

leaving a crenellated roofline that looked fully capable of defying a siege (fig. 14.4). (The crenellations, which were to have run the full length of the front, were restricted in execution to the tower.) These modifications brought about a radical change in the building's character. Surely the *Philadelphia Inquirer* was quoting Furness's own words when it observed that the "front view of the building will remind the spectator of an ancient fortress."[12]

The Troopers were clearly delighted with their ancient fortress and its air of stylish insolence.[13] In April they signed a contract with Williams and McNichol, who had been the successful bidders for the original project. Their bid was $26,700, a great deal higher than their 1870 bid, but in this centennial year contributions flowed more freely. (In fact, the armory would ultimately cost some $35,000.) The cornerstone was laid on July 4,

1874, and construction proceeded swiftly. Furness was now a more seasoned builder, and his handwritten specifications show an increasing industrialization of the construction process, specifying such materials as a readymade "Howe trussed girder" from the Keystone Bridge Company. (By contrast, his specifications of 1870 had such quaint provisions as a foundation of "two and three-man stones," presumably a vestige of the Scottish stone-building culture that Fraser brought to the firm.) One grace note was added at the last minute: the lintel over the entrance was given a sculpture of a cavalryman's helmet, with the distinctive crest that is the hallmark of the Troop.

By the time of the Troop's centennial, November 17, 1874, the Armory was sufficiently complete for the event to be commemorated in Furness's grand hall. The reviews were invariably complimentary, even outside Philadelphia. Furness's "little arsenal" was praised by the *American Architect and Building News*: "a parapeted building of red and black brick on a basement of gray rubble is designed with great spirit and signal success."[14]

But the armory did not stand very long: the roof of the parade shed—perhaps built with inferior materials during the Civil War—collapsed during a snowstorm in March 1899. The entire building was pulled down shortly thereafter and another armory erected on a nearby site, which houses the Troop to this day. Only the lintel over the entrance was salvaged to be reinstalled in the new building. Nonetheless, Furness's short-lived building looms large in his career, for it marks the beginning of his long and happy collaboration with Fairman Rogers. Over time that collaboration would also produce the Pennsylvania Academy of Fine Arts (whose building committee Rogers headed) as well as "Fairlawn," Rogers' exquisite villa in Newport, with its own sophisticated stable. Furness would have no other client so well connected with the intellectual and aesthetic currents of the day.

The armory would have one other consequence that neither man could have possibly envisioned. During the Centennial Exhibition of 1876 it would be seen by hundreds of thousands of visitors, who would carry back to their hometowns memories of Furness's plucky, colorful fortress. In short order there began a national craze for medieval armories, a fad that lasted well into the twentieth century and would place craggy battlemented regimental armories in most large towns in America.[15] In the history of architecture it is rare indeed that the image of a building type is so completely and indelibly transformed, and by a single monument.

What happened to Furness between his two designs for the First City Troop? How is it that he could triumph over an architectural problem in 1874 that had absolutely baffled him just four years earlier? The answer is that Furness in 1870 was still an unripe architect, a late bloomer who at thirty had not yet discovered the full and limber use of his powers. He had not yet designed a large and complex building, developed its details at large scale, and seen its construction through to the end. In the making of an architect, this is always the final lesson: the thoroughgoing and unsparing review of his own built work that helps solidify his personal sense of space, scale, and materials. For some architects, this lesson merely confirms habits and preferences that are already well established; for Furness, however, it would mean something rather more momentous.

For the first years of his practice, Furness's work was conventional, running to deferential paraphrases of the designs of his mentor Hunt. His firm's biggest work, the sumptuous Rodeph Shalom Synagogue (1868–70), was itself derivative, a studied pastiche of recent synagogues in Berlin, Budapest, and New York (fig. 14.5). When Furness made his first proposal for the Armory in the spring of 1870, he was still to a great extent a paper architect. And the weaknesses of that first version—its conceptual flatness, the additive quality, the absence of a palpable sense of weight and materiality—are those of a paper designer. His colleagues were aware of the diffidence; one friend observed that of all of Hunt's pupils, Furness's early work showed "the most timidity and the least promise."[16]

Furness did not shake off the timidity until the building of the Pennsylvania Academy of the Fine Arts. It was under con-

FIGURE 14.5 Furness was a capable designer before he was an original one. His Rodeph Shalom Synagogue (1868–70), a collaboration with George W. Hewitt, was a spirited Moorish performance—and yet showed that he was still fitting his buildings into specific stylistic categories.

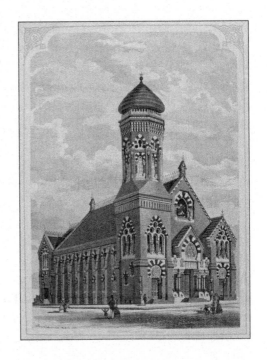

struction continually from 1872 to 1875, a raw hulk at first, with taut walls of brick and prodigious openings sliced through them. For Furness it was a process of discovery to watch his spaces take shape, week by week, revealing errors that only emerged when flat drawings were translated into unforgiving masonry. It was not long before the lessons of the Academy were spilling over into his new work. The buildings designed in early 1873—the Guarantee Safe Deposit and Trust Company, the Philadelphia Warehouse Company, and Henry Gibson's speculative office building at 310 Chestnut Street—all improvised exuberantly on the Academy, giving the distinct sensation of inhibitions being cast off and of sudden swaggering confidence.

In the end, it was perhaps not only architectural inhibitions that Furness needed to cast off. His family was somewhat of an intellectual pressure cooker, and his father was a plainspoken critic who did not spare even his own children. (Reverend Furness once told Emerson that his son William Henry Furness, Jr., a talented painter, demonstrated "no evidence of genius."[17]) Rev.

Furness and Emerson discussed Frank's plans for college—surely Harvard, where both men had studied, as had Frank's brother Horace—but the high expectations backfired. Frank shunned academics, taking refuge first in architecture and then in the military. But even as he won honors and recognition on his own terms, as a soldier, he could not easily free himself from the suspicion that he was a lesser light in the dazzling firmament of his family. Perhaps this accounts for the tentative, cautious quality in his first works—the "timidity"—as though he was afraid to make a mistake.

It is strange that all of this had been prophesied long before, when Furness was only fourteen. In 1853, his brother William wrote to their father, urging him to be patient: "Frank will be slow enough till he's going, but when he does, stand out of his way."[18] In another letter he rebuked Reverend Furness for making unfavorable comparisons between his son and, of all people, young Fairman Rogers: "You talk about Fairman Rogers and what a comfort he is to his father. I think that Frank has more natural capacity than Fairman, and if he were left to himself would be far greater."[19] In the event, both Furness and Rogers proved to be great, although—at least in the case of the First City Troop Armory—they needed one another to realize that greatness.

Furness had two distinct gifts that do not usually come together, a sculptor's sense for expressive mass, and an intellectual's appreciation for a building as a metaphysical idea. He could not unite these gifts in any meaningful way until relatively far along in his life, until he had won a measure of psychological independence from his overweening family. This is the importance of the two designs for the First City Troop Armory: in 1870 he did not know how to express the function of a building in metaphysical terms, as a freely imagined poetic caricature, and in 1874 he did. Between these two designs—made four years apart for the same site and the same floor plan—is the awakening of a slumbering spirit.

In Memory of Carolyn Pitts (1925–2008)

CHAPTER 15

Louis Kahn at Thirty

The Lenin Memorial in Leningrad

■ IN 1932 LOUIS I. KAHN designed a startling memorial to Vladimir Ilyich Lenin: two luminous red glass skyscrapers that would have loomed above the harbor of Leningrad, blazing at night as a harbinger of revolution. Yet the Soviet authorities were not impressed, and in years to come Kahn expunged the politically embarrassing project from his résumé, successfully concealing it from scholars until long after his death in 1974.[1] Recently a photograph of his lost competition entry, known heretofore from verbal descriptions, appeared at auction (fig. 15.1).[2] It is a startlingly imaginative performance, Kahn's first purposeful attempt to reconcile contemporary modernism with the Beaux-Arts system that had formed him. He would not make such an attempt again for thirty years, and when he did, he would return to the solution attempted here and in surprising ways.

The Lenin Memorial was but one of many ill-fated projects to come out of the three-year bout of unemployment that Kahn suffered at the trough of the Great Depression.[3] In January 1932

FIGURE 15.1 In 1932 it was acceptable for an American architect like Louis I. Kahn to propose a memorial to Vladimir Lenin but within a decade or two it was not. His project was conveniently forgotten and only after his death in 1974 was it rediscovered.

he was discharged from the firm of Zantzinger, Borie & Medary, where he had been making drawings for the Justice Department Building in Washington, D.C. (1931–34). Not until 1935, when the Ahavath Israel Synagogue project came his way, would he again have steady work. In the interim, he gathered around himself a dozen or so other jobless architects and draftsmen, rented a pair of rooms, and drew up a portentous "Outline of the Principles of the Society for the Advancement of Architecture."[4] This title, upon reflection, was evidently too bourgeois. Thinking perhaps of the ostentatiously objective acronyms that Soviet architectural collaboratives gave themselves during the 1920s, such as the ARU (Union of Architect-Planners) or Asnova (Association of New Architects), Kahn changed the name to the Architectural Research Group.[5] In press releases, it would be known as the ARG.

For the next two years, the ARG devised public housing projects, studied slum clearance in Philadelphia, and entered architectural competitions. All proved fruitless, and in May 1934 the group quietly disbanded. Its fifteen members went their own ways, in most cases into architectural obscurity.[6] The ARG's most enduring legacy was to have given Kahn methodical training in housing, a field that would sustain his practice for much of the next decade.

Kahn evidently heard about the Leningrad competition in May 1932, when it was announced in the English-language *Economic Review of the Soviet Union*.[7] (For some reason—political hostility?—it does not appear to have been announced in the principal American professional journals: *Architectural Record*, *Architectural Forum*, and *Pencil Points*.) The notice invited "the masses of workers" to submit their proposals for "a Lenin monument to be erected in the port of Leningrad," which was to cost six million rubles (then about $3 million). Designs could be submitted until September 15, after which the five best would receive prizes ranging from two to ten thousand rubles. The prospect was enticing, especially at a time when two young Philadelphia architects had won a major award in just such a contest: in March 1932 Alfred Kastner (1900–1975) and Oscar Stonorov (1905–70) placed second in an international competition for the Palace of the Soviets (fig. 15.2). Within a few years Kahn would be associated with both, and it may be that their victory spurred him to try his own luck in a Soviet competition.[8]

At least two other American competitors followed suit.[9] The modernist sculptor William Zorach proposed a statue of Lenin atop a spiral ziggurat, which he worked up into a three-foot plaster model and shipped to Leningrad in July 1932.[10] Like Kahn, Zorach was born in the Baltic (Lithuania) and emigrated to the United States as a child with his Jewish parents; perhaps he felt

FIGURE 15.2 Philadelphia architects, battered by the Depression, were happy to enter competitions in the Soviet Union. This proposal for the Palace of the Soviets (1932) was made by Albert Kastner and Oscar Stonorov; within a few years Kahn would be associated with both of them.

this gave him special insight into the project. Another project came from the Pittsburgh architect Michael J. DeAngelis, whose model showed a strenuously formal composition in which a slender reed of a skyscraper, cribbed from Eliel Saarinen's Chicago Tribune project, spurted joyously upward from between two squat blocks containing a museum and a library (fig. 15.3).[11]

FIGURE 15.3 Michael DeAngelis's well-mannered Beaux-Arts proposal for the Lenin Memorial could have fit comfortably in any American city and reveals how radical Kahn's submission was.

Kahn's submission was in keeping with the ARG doctrine of collaborative teamwork, and he insisted that everyone who worked on the project be cited. These included Hyman Cunin and Joseph Rovner, two fellow graduates of the University of Pennsylvania who had also worked with him in 1926 on the designs for the Sesquicentennial Exhibition.[12] He also added a consulting engineer, Henry Gravel, who helped determine the appropriate structural system for a complex that was to rise daringly over a river.[13] Gravel was not a formal member of the ARG, nor was Raphael Sabatini, the sculptor who sketched the relief sculpture.[14] Kahn claimed the role of principal designer for himself, and together with his team, he prepared the drawings, including the dizzying aerial perspective in which his proposal culminated.

The central motif of the Lenin memorial was a circular public plaza, built over the Neva River and approached via a raised causeway. Where the causeway met the plaza, Kahn placed a pair of 360–foot skyscrapers to form a monumental portal. His description of each of these elements survives in a typescript entitled "Design for a Monument to Lenin to Be Erected in the Port of Leningrad," which forecasts the powerful effect of the memorial on visitors and quotes carefully from the competition announcement:

> The primary concept of the monument is that of an open meeting-place for the masses of workers.
>
> The monument is simply and directly approached from the mainland by a lower level for vehicular traffic and an upper level for pedestrian traffic.
>
> Through the portals of two great towers of red glass one descends into the large circular plaza, enclosed by two sculptural arms of stone whereon is depicted the epochal emergence of the Proletariat and the Peasant—from Exploitation, though Struggle, to Victory and Achievement.
>
> The open approach from the sea and the encircling waters of the plaza assure the feasibility of marine spectacles and demonstrations on any desired scale.

The rostrum at the foot of the great towers, dominating the open plaza, assures adequate provision for addressing the masses gathered thereon.

Every point on the large open plaza is at a vantage to view and comprehend the sculptural realization of the epic of the Proletariat and the Peasant, culminating in two great towers of red glass, ever-present symbols of the triumph and achievement of Leninism.

The Monument, as conceived, expresses its functional efficiency in a circular form of continuing interest to the masses, focalized in the great towers of glass that mark the juncture of all avenues of circulation. Simplicity has been striven for throughout to assure a vividness and comprehension for the great masses of workers.

From the subsidiary promenades atop the circling arms, an unceasing variety of perspectives is afforded to the beholder. Seen from afar, on land and sea, the two great red towers, beacons of Leninism triumphant, dominate the horizon.[15]

Nearly every aspect of the proposal testifies to Kahn's close study of European high modernism. The memorial is conceived as an abstract city, in which a few isolated towers stand sentinel over broad plazas, paraphrasing Le Corbusier's *Ville contemporaine*. Likewise Corbusian is the multi-tiered array of viaducts, stacked to separate vehicles and pedestrians. Kahn was a lifelong admirer of Le Corbusier, whose office he had visited in 1929 during the course of his European study year.[16]

The towers are something else entirely. These were to be of red glass brick (the typed description called for 50,000 square feet of glass block), "held at frequent intervals by steel ledges projecting out beyond the face of the supporting frame." Behind this translucent curtain wall was "a solid reflecting surface" to make possible their illumination by night, making the design an early example of what Dietrich Neumann has called "the architecture of the night."[17] This idea of crystalline skyscrapers was hardly

Kahn's innovation, and it stems from the visionary projects made a decade earlier by Ludwig Mies van der Rohe and Bruno Taut. Kahn's contribution was to assign them a symbolic revolutionary function and to incorporate them into an urban ensemble in which they functioned chiefly as dazzling stage scenery (the project description failed to mention any function for the towers).

But the Lenin Memorial was more than a learned pastiche of French and German modernism, quoted reverently. Kahn took his borrowed motifs, flung them merrily into the air, and brought them to earth as explicit political allegory. In plan his memorial recapitulated the most celebrated work of art to come out of the Russian Revolution, El Lissitzky's *Beat the Whites with the Red Wedge* (1919), that agitprop abstraction of the Revolution in which a razor-sharp red blade pierces a white circle, causing it to splinter. Of course, the shard of red paving that punctures the central plaza can only be appreciated from above, which accounts for Kahn's uncharacteristic bird's-eye perspective, and the biplanes that fly dizzyingly below the viewer.

Yet this is not the only explicit symbolism of the memorial. Not only is there a literal hammer and sickle on the pavement, but the whole sweeping composition—a great crescent crossed at its center by an upraised shaft—is a freely rendered hammer and sickle. Here all the lessons of Kahn's study of modernism, his year of travel in Europe, and his deliberate manipulation of the symbolism of the Russian revolution, converged in a design of immense authority. It is remarkable that he was able to retain the legibility of representational art (necessary "to assure a vividness and comprehension for the great masses of workers") while achieving the formal poetry of abstraction. Of course, Kahn was not the only architect to try this; Soviet competitions of the time were rife with hackneyed Revolutionary symbolism. And yet few made the same intense effort to fuse simple geometric forms into a tightly drawn unity. These were Kahn's aesthetic fingerprints. The circle, wedge, and prism at the center of the composition, laminated and spindled onto the spike of the towers, is a harbinger of the spare geometry of the mature work, and a sign of terrific internal struggle. One can see why he invested such hope in the project.

And hope he did. As late as May 1934, almost two years later, Kahn was still awaiting happy news from Leningrad. In that month he insinuated a breathless profile of the ARG into the *Philadelphia Record*, which boasted that the Lenin memorial, "if accepted and constructed, will make the port of Leningrad the most striking in the world. Through the portals of two towers of red glass rising several hundred feet from the surface of the water the visitor would descend into an enormous circular plaza from which marine spectacles could be viewed."[18]

But this was not to be, as much because of bad timing as for any fault of Kahn's: 1933 was a tumultuous year in the world of Soviet architecture, as the avant-garde collaboratives Asnova and ARU were peremptorily disbanded and reorganized into a centralized bureaucracy. This was also the moment of Stalin's consolidation of power in Moscow and the crippling of the Leningrad establishment led by Sergey Kirov, whose assassination at the end of 1934 launched the Great Purges.[19] At this time of Stalin's disfavor, the Leningrad party was hardly in a position to make a self-aggrandizing statement in the form of 360-foot-tall columns of light. It is not surprising that the papers were soon reporting that "plans for a Lenin memorial in Leningrad have temporarily been shelved by the Russian government."[20] All of the entries disappeared into the Soviet archives, never to be seen again. Likely they were lost during the siege of Leningrad during World War II. But even before then, it might have been seen as a liability for an American to have pursued work in Leningrad. After the purge trials (1937–38) and the German-Soviet non-aggression pact (1939), the Soviet Union no longer seemed quite the progressive symbol that many had found so inspiring in 1932. Of course, prominent figures such as Henry Ford had dealt openly and frankly with the Soviets, without subsequent recriminations, so the changing perception of Russia cannot be the only reason that Kahn suppressed the project.

Perhaps his qualms were as much aesthetic as political. It is obvious that the Lenin Memorial, for all its sophisticated modernist phrasemaking, was still a piece of Beaux-Arts composition, in its axial symmetry, its tight interlocking unity, and its sequential spatial hierarchy (although Kahn sought to obscure this by describing the spatial hierarchy as "focalized," a pseudoscientific term). To project a monumental axis into the water and to mark its culmination with a portal was a gesture deeply classical in spirit. It had its origin in those monthly competition problems distributed by the Beaux-Arts Institute of Design, which formed the basis of the curriculum at Penn, where Kahn was trained. Like his classmates, he would have studied earlier problems for guidance, such as the 1913 one that proposed a Hall of Fame on the Washington Mall and would have extended its grand axis into the Potomac.[21]

This should not be in the least surprising. Kahn had been saturated with modernism since his 1928–29 study year in Europe, and he acquired its visual forms as a toddler picks up words: effortlessly and by osmosis. But how to put these forms together was a problem of a different order, a problem not of words but of grammar. And what was the Beaux-Arts, after all, if not a method of putting things together? By 1932, Kahn had spent nearly a dozen years under the shadow of the Beaux-Arts, four years as a student and another six or seven in offices that ran on Beaux-Arts lines. That his Lenin Memorial would not organize its modernist elements on axially symmetric lines was virtually unthinkable. And yet shortly thereafter Kahn eliminated axial composition from his formal repertoire, as if expunged by a tremendous act of will. None of his urban plans for the next three decades have anything remotely like a Beaux-Arts organization of space. Without exception they are exercises in flowing form, their relationships oblique or tangential, and skewed like the move of a knight in chess. When Kahn wrote an essay on monumentality in 1944, he no longer conceived of the subject in remotely classical terms, so thoroughly had he quashed his Beaux-Arts habits of mind.[22] Perhaps the Lenin Memorial was now purged from his résumé, not because its ends were radical but because its means were reactionary.

At last, in the 1960s, Kahn no longer felt the need to suppress the formal axis, and once the ban was lifted there came those buildings that we think of as most quintessentially Kahn, such as the Salk Institute. Now he felt free to evoke his Leningrad project more explicitly. His Memorial for the Six Million Jewish Martyrs (1966–72), which was to be built of piers of translucent block glass, recalls the Lenin Memorial. So does his Roosevelt Memorial (built posthumously 2010–2012) on New York's Roosevelt Island, which revisited its parti: a long processional axis leading to a plaza built out to the edge of the water.[23] Even his urban plans for Philadelphia, with their abstracted towers and colossal viaducts, again and again summon the haunting image of the hovering abstract plaza over the Neva.[24] The Lenin Memorial was Kahn's first experimental reconciliation of his modernism and his classicism. He seems to have deemed it a failure. But although he later worked to conceal that first attempt, he could not conceal the lessons it taught him, and throughout his career they rebounded, at first covertly and then with growing confidence in the classic-modern synthesis that is the central accomplishment of his life.

CHAPTER 16

Frank Furness, Perpetual Motion, and "The Captain's Trousers"

■ ONE OF ARCHITECTURE'S most tantalizing mysteries is the Bloomfield Moore house at 510 South Broad Street in Philadelphia, the remarkable building that propelled sixteen-year-old Louis Sullivan into the office of Frank Furness.[1] Half a century later (1924), when he wrote his *Autobiography of an Idea*, Sullivan remembered the encounter vividly—although he couched it in his strange third-person voice:

> Once settled down in the large quiet village [i.e., Philadelphia], he began to roam the streets, looking quizzically at buildings as he wandered. On the west side of South Broad street a residence, almost completed, caught his eye like a flower by the roadside. He approached, examined it with curious care, without and within. Here was something fresh and fair to him, a human note, as though someone were talking. He inquired as to the architect and was told: Furness & Hewitt. Now, he saw

plainly enough that this was not the work of two men but of one, for he had an instinctive sense of physiognomy, and all buildings thus made their direct appeal to him, pleasant or unpleasant. He made up his mind that next day he would enter the employ of said Furness & Hewitt, they to have no voice in the matter, for his mind was made up.[2]

That "flower by the roadside" was the Bloomfield Moore house, and it was Sullivan's tour of the house that won him a position in Furness's office.[3] In fact, had he not been able to discuss the house intelligently, it is very likely he would not have been hired because the interview got off to a very bad start:

So next day he presented himself to Frank Furness and informed him he had come to enter his employ. Frank Furness was a curious character. He affected the English in fashion. He wore loud plaids, and a scowl, and from his face depended fan-like a marvelous red beard, beautiful in tone with each separate hair delicately crinkled from beginning to end. Moreover, his face was snarled and homely as an English bulldog's. Louis's eyes were riveted, in infatuation, to this beard, as he listened to a string of oaths yards long. For it seems after he had delivered his initial fiat, Furness looked at him half blankly, half enraged, as at another kind of dog that had slipped in through the door. His first question had been as to Louis's experience, to which Louis replied, modestly enough, that he had just come from the Massachusetts Institute of Technology in Boston. This answer was the detonator that set off the mine which blew up in fragments all the schools in the land and scattered the professors headless and limbless quarters of earth and hell. Louis, he said, was a fool. He said Louis was an idiot to have wasted his time in a place where one was filled with sawdust, like a doll, and became a prig, a snob, and an ass.

As the smoke blew away he said: "Of course you don't know anything and are full of damnable conceit."

We have enough accounts of Furness's imaginative use of profanity to know that Sullivan had been given the full-bore treatment. But he did not wilt under the tirade and when Furness finally asked "what in hell had brought him there, anyway?" he saw his big chance:

> This was the opening for which Louis had sagaciously been waiting through the storm. He told Frank Furness all about his unaided discovery of the dwelling on Broad street, how he had followed, so to speak from the nugget to the solid vein; that here he was and here he would remain; he had made up his mind as to that, and he looked Frank Furness in the eye. Then he sang a song of praise like a youthful bard of old to his liege lord, steering clear of too gross adulation, placing all on a high plane of accomplishment. It was here, Louis said, one could really learn.

The rest is history: Sullivan talked his way into a one-week trial and was subsequently hired as junior draftsman. He remained with Furness & Hewitt throughout the summer and would have remained longer had not the Panic of 1873 forced them to cut the payroll. All this was set into motion by one sixteen-year-old's fateful stroll down Broad Street.

But what exactly was it about the Moore House that captivated Sullivan? No one knows. As thrilling as the house was in 1873, it was deeply unfashionable by 1895, when its new owner had it reconfigured as a French chateau (fig. 16.1).[4] Later it came into the possession of the brilliant art collector John G. Johnson, upon whose death in 1917 both house and collection were given to the city—on condition they remain together. Philadelphia wanted the collection but not the now dowdy house, and in 1933 the paintings were removed to the Philadelphia Museum of Art on the pretext that the house was unsafe. It was demolished a few years later.[5]

No scholar, despite decades of imaginative sleuthing, has ever found a photograph of the original exterior of the Bloomfield

FIGURE 16.1 Frank Furness's house for Bloomfield Moore was so brash and quirky that the next owners promptly recast it as a French chateau. Despite decades of sleuthing, no photograph of the original facade has turned up.

Moore house. Its interior, by contrast, is well documented, as the images reproduced here show. They first appeared in George William Sheldon's *Artistic Houses* (New York: D. Appleton and Company, 1883–84).[6] Apart from a few suggestive sketches for ornament in Furness's sketchbooks, they are all we have.

Until now. The chance discovery of a highly detailed, and highly opinionated, account of the house by its original client gives us for the first time a clue as to what it looked like. It also gives us something we never had before: a lively picture of how Furness interacted with his clients, his jaunty wit and charming impertinence. Perhaps it would have been discovered earlier if its author had not concealed it so discreetly in a book on the education of women, published under a pseudonym.

The house was built between 1871 and 1873 for Bloomfield Haines Moore (1819–78), who made his fortune in the paper-manufacturing firm of Jessup and Moore. Moore collected paintings and fine old books, as befitted a man in the paper business.[7] But the real intellect of the family was his wife Clara Jessup (1824–99), the daughter of his partner, whom he married in 1842. Clara was more interested in writing books than in collecting them, and soon after their marriage there poured forth a stream of novels, short stories, poems, and books of etiquette, all of which were coyly credited to either Clara Moreton or Mrs. H. O. Ward.[8]

After her husband's death, Mrs. Moore came under the baleful influence of John W. Keely, one of history's most successful charlatans, whose "experiments" in perpetual motion she would underwrite for the rest of her life. Keely was a former mechanic and a carnival barker, and both professions came in handy as he beguiled investors with double-talk about protoplasm, sympathetic vibrations, primitive atomic motion, and his lucrative "hydro-pneumatic pulsating vacuo machine."[9] Mrs. Moore fell hard for this patter and became his principal backer and public defender. Her *Keely and His Discoveries: Aerial Navigation* (London, 1893) is the most lucid statement of his ideas as well as a classic case study of childlike gullibility on the part of an otherwise first-rate intellect. All this was deeply distressing to her family, and her son publicly pronounced her insane.[10] Keely died in 1898, his promises unfulfilled, and few weeks later she died too. Wags could not resist the temptation of suggesting that she died of a broken heart.

If Clara Jessup Moore is remembered at all today, it is as Keely's dupe. But she turns out to have been an architectural patron of fierce intelligence and conviction. We now learn that she was deeply distressed by the house that Furness built for her and— more damningly—by his attitude. Of course, Victorian discretion ensured her respectful silence and for decades she smoldered quietly. This changed in 1892, when she decided to move permanently to London and to sell her Philadelphia house. She announced the sale the same week that she published her *Social Ethics and Society Duties: Thorough Education of Girls for Wives and Mothers and for Professions*. She wrote the book, reviewers noted, "under her usual nom de plume of H. O. Ward."[11] Here she addressed with startling frankness all the issues that a modern woman might face, from divorce to "home treatment of the insane." Whether or not she felt liberated by the frank subject matter or her farewell to Philadelphia, she now was able to tell the story of Furness and her house. She decently veiled it by anonymity, but anyone who knew her and her house (and all of Philadelphia society did) would know exactly whom she was talking about.

The extract should be quoted in its entirety:

Another opening for women is house architecture. No one knows so well as a woman the advantages and disadvantages of the arrangements of the interior of houses. The hundred little things thought trivial by a man, are by a woman known to be important. She knows the steps it saves to have the storeroom in the right place; the inconvenience of having her linen-closet without a window to light it, though it be but a small circular one, opening from a well-lighted bath or dressing room. A house, no matter how exquisite in ornamental details, may be made dark and dismal for want of proper forethought in its plan. It is easy to light dark closets from the rooms that adjoin them; but when the skylight has been wrongly constructed, it is not easy to light dark halls and staircases. For lack of forethought in an architect, one of the most beautiful homes that he built was wanting in the first requisites for cheerfulness, comfort, and convenience. A window had to be cut on the first flight of stairs, which was as dark as an underground passage in one part. A hot-air pipe passed through the wine-cellar. The enormous plate-glass windows would have required machinery to move them without breaking the chains; and consequently, until each plate was cut in two, they were always out of repair. The metal grooves of the sliding doors were placed below instead of above; and visitors invariably stumbled over them, even if the inmates of the house ever escaped. With four furnace fires in full blast, the house could not be kept comfortably warm, in the coldest weather, without closing the doors of the picture gallery and billiard-room.

The rooms which were to have been decorated to correspond to the furniture and hangings (Louis XVI., Louis XIII., and Greek the samples of stuff sent), were all in one architectural style, with no attempt to conform to the orders given. But the crowning error was in the position of the house. After the plan of building had been decided upon, which was a copy of a Boston residence, the wife of the owner of the site purchased an adjoining lot in order to have a southern exposure for the grounds, and to prevent the possibility of a wall being built up against the dining-room windows. Returning from abroad, she found that her forethought had been of no avail. The house was built with the lot on the north, and no way of entering it save from the street or from the stable ground. "How do you like your new house?" she was asked. The reply was, "I feel as a woman would feel who had ordered a comfortable home costume, and had received a ball dress."

When a man yields to his wife in the choice of an architect, giving up his preferences for one of more experience, the wife has a right to expect from the architect as faithful attention to her wishes in her absence as if she had been on the spot to see that they were carried out; and not leave to carpenters the selection of tiles for which shades of various colours had been sent,—nor decorations made *à fantaisie* when styles of certain periods had been ordered. Think of a library for which furniture and hangings had been commanded as purely Greek as they could be made, containing a fireplace in carved wood, reaching up to the ceiling, better suited for an English baronial hall! Of course, the Greek furniture was countermanded by cable despatch to Paris, where it had been ordered. The architect, in expressing his surprise at the evident disappointment of the wife, said, "I wonder that you do not like it. Every one who has seen it admires it very much." The only expression which the wife gave to the intense annoyance occasioned by this interference with her plans was manifested in the question she put in reply: "Did you, as the architect, construct your plans to please every one or to please me?"

"Oh, anything that you do not like I can change to please you," was the answer. "No, I will have nothing changed. I do not wish to have my husband troubled about any increase in the expense." "But I can make out the bills in a way that he will never know of the increased expense," was the answer. The wife looked her surprise, but said nothing; and the architect continued, "Did you never hear of the sea-captain who rendered an account one item of which was for a pair of trousers? 'No,' said the ship-owner, 'I can't pay for your trousers;' and he scratched the item out. The next time the ship came in, the captain's bill was looked over, and pronounced all right. 'No trousers here,' said the ship-owner. 'Yes, yes, they are there, but you can't find 'em,' chuckled the captain."[12]

What a trove of detail in 800 words! That Clara was speaking about her own house, there can be no doubt. It did indeed boast a painting gallery and billiard gallery to the rear, which could be shut off if necessary (fig. 16.2). And it was pushed to the south of

FIGURE 16.2 "With four furnace fires in full blast, the house could not be kept comfortably warm," Mrs. Moore lamented, "without closing the doors of the picture gallery."

FIGURE 16.3 Defended by heraldic lions with owls standing sentinel, all of it plunging down like a trash compacter on columns of tragic stubbiness, Furness's fireplace for Bloomfield Moore is a prediction of his mighty bank buildings.

its lot, leaving a vacant strip to the north, as one sees in the 1875 *Hopkins Atlas of Philadelphia.* It even had that "fireplace in carved wood, reaching up to the ceiling, better suited for an English baronial hall," intruding upon Mr. Moore's library (fig. 16.3).

We learn a great deal here about the Bloomfield Moore house, and we should take the items in ascending order of importance. First, Mrs. Moore confirms that the house was indeed by Furness himself, and was not a Furness & Hewitt collaboration, just as Sullivan concluded. Next we learn that it was Mrs. Moore who personally selected Furness, not her husband, who preferred an architect "of more experience." Mr. Moore was right to be concerned.[13] Furness had just left the firm of Fraser, Furness & Hewitt, where he had been subject to the counsel and criticism of his senior partner, architect John Fraser, "a well-regarded master of his profession through all its minutest details—practical & theoretical."[14] Fraser was not likely to bring a heated pipe through a cool wine cellar, or to put raised metal grooves in the floor, or to neglect the lighting of the stair hall, or to commit any of those other beginner's blunders that scandalized Mrs. Moore.

What we do not learn is how the Moores came to Furness. They were longstanding members of Philadelphia's First Unitarian Church, where Rev. William H. Furness, the father of the architect, preached. When Rev. Furness retired in 1875, Bloomfield Moore helped to organize the commemoration.[15] But this alone would have not have persuaded the Moores to entrust a young architect with a house costing $40,000 and involving a comprehensive scheme of interior decoration. Mrs. Moore had to have seen something that enticed her. Perhaps it was the nearby house of Lucy Hamilton Hooper, which had just been completed and which boasted walls "frescoed from the first floor to the roof" from Furness's own designs.[16] Hooper, her fellow woman writer, was an editor of *Lippincott's Magazine*, to which Mrs. Moore contributed. And Mrs. Moore likewise had Furness fresco her walls, as we see in the run of bright flowers skipping up alongside the stair (fig. 16.4).

If we do not learn the beginning of the story, we learn its astonishing conclusion. No sooner was the basic plan settled than Mrs. Moore went abroad, leaving Furness to carry out her instructions about decorating the interior.[17] She wished her rooms to be in certain period styles—"Louis XVI., Louis XIII., and Greek"—and the furniture and hangings were to be coordinated accordingly. But upon her return, and to her amazement, these various rooms were "all in one architectural style" and, what was worse, not in one that she recognized. Instead, Furness had inflicted upon her "decorations made *à fantaisie*." Of course, the principal reason that we admire Furness today is just that *fantaisie*, and presumably this is why Mrs. Moore sought him out in the first place.

In the end, it was Furness's jaunty highhandedness that most infuriated Mrs. Moore. When he offered to alter the house to

FIGURE 16.4 "Here was something fair," Louis Sullivan wrote of the Moore house, "a human note, as though someone were talking." The client felt differently: "dark and dismal . . . as dark as an underground passage."

please her, she haughtily refused, insisting that she did not wish her husband "troubled" by the additional expense. Here she played the martyr, burdening Furness with the knowledge that his poor client was suffering nobly at his incompetent hands. So she hoped. The very last thing she expected was that Furness would offer to conceal the cost of any alterations by juggling his accounts. The indecency of Furness's offer, and the sheer vulgarity of his anecdote (one imagines her stiffening at the word *trousers*) must have been deeply shocking. It is notable that this is the only time in her account that she provides dialogue, recalling words that she must have nursed resentfully across the decades.

Finally, we learn here something that is genuinely stunning, given our image of Furness as the most imaginative and original of Victorian architects: the Bloomfield Moore house was "a copy of a Boston residence." But even this should not surprise us.

FIGURE 16.5 Mrs. Moore claimed her house was "the copy of a Boston residence," presumably the Martin Brimmer house. It was by Furness's mentor Richard Morris Hunt, whose buildings he was still faithfully imitating in 1870.

Furness's architectural juvenilia is filled with pastiches of buildings by his mentor, Richard Morris Hunt. Perhaps the house in Boston was the richly carved one just completed by Hunt for Martin Brimmer, who like Moore was a great collector of art (fig. 16.5).[18] It is quite possible that Mrs. Moore saw the house and admired it; and it is certainly in keeping with her imperious character that she would have insisted on a copy of it. (This would explain the recurrence of details from the Brimmer house in Furness's work of the early 1870s.)[19]

If so, and it seems likely, then the Bloomfield Moore facade would have been an essay in what the critic Montgomery Schuyler referred to as Hunt's "staccato style," his highly animated version of the Neo-Grec style, characterized by deeply incised ornament, expressive linear detail, bold chamfering, and an abstracted use of Greek elements.[20] It is a theme that preoccupied Furness in the early 1870s, and we see it in his funeral monument

FIGURE 16.6 Furness's 1873 house for Rudulph Ellis, a fellow captain in Rush's Lancers, is in what one critic called his "staccato style."

to Edward Burd Grubb at St. Mary's, Burlington, New Jersey, and his Rudulph Ellis House at 2113 Spruce Street in Philadelphia (fig. 16.6). These are splinters of the same architectural ideas that he was exploring in more concentrated and lavish form in the Bloomfield Moore House.

It is a delight to have at last the record of a conversation between Furness and a client. One constant theme in all the reminiscences of Furness is his caustic, pungent use of language, frequently expressed in highly picturesque profanity. He was too well-mannered to curse in front of a lady, but as Mrs. Moore's remarks show about "the captain's trousers," he knew how to get a rise out of her, just at the edge of public decency. This adds to our picture of Furness's roguish charm, his raciness and also his instant ability to convey his point with an instructive parable. Clearly he absorbed the power of those parables from a childhood spent listening every Sunday to the sermons preached in his father's Unitarian church.

CHAPTER 17

Breakthrough at Bryn Mawr

Louis Kahn's Erdman Dormitory

◾ LOUIS KAHN'S Erdman Dormitory at Bryn Mawr College (1960–65) was one of his first masterpieces (fig. 17.1).[1] The three interlocking diamonds that define its plan are the culmination of a decade of experimentation with geometric forms and even longer musings about the character of private and public space. But because it is a dormitory at a private women's college, it is among the least accessible and least appreciated of all his works. One can more easily visit his capitol at Dhaka in Bangladesh. It is atypical in one other respect. Unlike any of Kahn's other buildings, with more or less linear design histories, Erdman's design history is the story of not one but two parallel schemes, pursued simultaneously but separately, which gradually converged to form the ultimate design.

At Bryn Mawr, Kahn faced one of his most capable clients, Katharine Elizabeth McBride, who had been president of the college since 1942. She built little during the early years of her

FIGURE 17.1 Erdman Hall at Bryn Mawr College (1960–65), Louis I. Kahn's study in three cubes, joined at their corners.

presidency but by 1959 a new library building and a new dormitory were badly needed.[2] Happily one of her trustees, Eleanor Donnelley Erdman, had promised to leave the college over one million dollars. That autumn McBride asked another trustee, Eleanor Marquand Delanoy, how to choose an architect: should there be a competition, or should the college appoint one architect for all its buildings? Delanoy, who lived near Princeton, recommended the Princeton model, which was to hire a different architect for each building. She suggested it might be tactful to use an out-of-town architect, such as Richard Neutra or Marcel Breuer, rather than favoring one Philadelphian over another. But if McBride preferred a Philadelphian, Delanoy suggested Kahn, then building the Richard Medical Laboratory at the University of Pennsylvania.[3]

McBride preferred Neutra and arranged for an interview in April 1960, but when he postponed it she turned elsewhere. As it happened, Kahn had another fan among the trustees, who seemed to call the shots at Bryn Mawr: Phyllis Goodhart Gordan. Gordan's friend Vanna Venturi had a son, Robert, who had worked in Kahn's office.[4] Vanna Venturi's lobbying evidently won Kahn the job. At least Kahn must have thought so, since he immediately sent her a thank-you note when he got the news.[5]

Erdman had not finalized her million dollar gift when she died on December 30, 1959, which threw building plans into disarray.[6] McBride warned Kahn that funding was not certain. Nonetheless in May 1960 she sent him a building program for a dormitory to house 130 students in "a variety of size and shape of rooms."[7] The influence of the college's earlier dormitories is apparent. The five dormitories built between 1887 and 1904 by Cope & Stewardson were gems of the Collegiate Gothic, and with their rambling volumes, generous bay windows, and exquisitely lighted interiors, they were beloved (see fig. 22.1). McBride wanted a contemporary equivalent, and without the "excessive amount of glass" of recent college architecture. Like Cope & Stewardson's cozy rooms, those in the new dormitory were to have window seats and "concealed moldings for hanging photographs." And like its predecessors, Kahn's building was also to be self-sufficient, with its dining hall, living rooms, and a staff of live-in maids. Its social spaces would be the epitome of cheery domesticity: a "large reception room for teas," several smaller reception rooms, and "one large 'noisy' smoking room with a fireplace."

When McBride's program arrived, Kahn was at a design conference in Tokyo, but upon his return he went to work, although without great urgency.[8] A few of his early probing studies survive, none dated and some preserved only in photographs. These are divided into two groups: schematic studies which laid out the required number of rooms graphically (fig. 17.2) and more resolved sketch plans, which translated the parts of the program

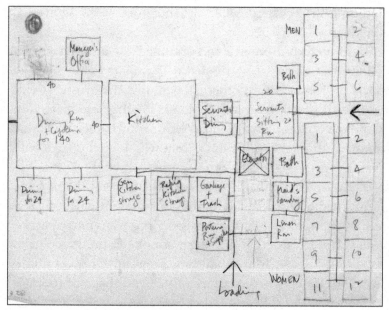

FIGURE 17.2 Kahn began his dormitory design, as the University of Pennsylvania had taught him forty years previously, by first drawing to scale the spaces required by the program. Not until these spaces were marked out could he begin finding meaningful relationships between them.

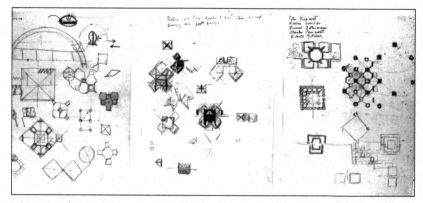

FIGURE 17.3 John Harbeson, one of Kahn's most influential teachers, told his students that at the beginning of a project "as many schemes of plan arrangement should be found as possible," before thinking about elevation and section. Kahn's early sketches for Bryn Mawr show him fighting against the linear corridor, the conventional solution for a dormitory.

into interconnected rectangular figures (fig. 17.3).[9] Kahn's principal interest in all of these was how to unite several large public spaces with the dormitory rooms themselves.

Without money to build, McBride did not press Kahn. Late that summer Robert M. Cooke, the college's insurance agent, went to check on Kahn's progress. He was told only that the building would be fireproof, with concrete floors and roof, and that the kitchen and service facilities would be "grouped in one general area." Cooke knew vamping when he heard it and reported to McBride that the dormitory plans were "not developed."[10] Only after she scheduled a meeting for November 25 to see Kahn's designs did things get serious.

For this first meeting, Kahn's long-time collaborator Anne Tyng prepared the main scheme and it was a prodigy of geometry (fig. 17.4). Throughout the 1950s, when their personal and professional relationship was at its most intimate, she had encouraged Kahn to study the formal possibilities of interlocking geo-

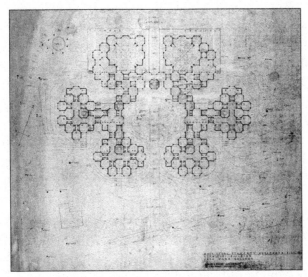

FIGURE 17.4 For Anne Tyng, the fundamental unit of the dormitory was the individual room. Having perfected its octangular form, she let its cellular geometry replicate itself as does DNA, the discovery of which had recently been announced.

metric units. During these experimental years, when he had not yet found his voice, abstract geometry briefly seemed to offer a solution. He explored it in his Philadelphia City Tower project (1952–53), which shows the influence of Buckminster Fuller, while his Trenton Jewish Community Center (1954–59) was more classical in its axial symmetry and order. But Tyng's Bryn Mawr design was the most furiously geometrical project ever to come out of Kahn's office. Two interlocking polygonal figures, a small square unit and a larger "octagon," created a module that could be repeated in interlocking fashion and extended indefinitely. The octagonal unit would represent the individual dorm room while the adjacent square would accommodate services. Tyng multiplied the modules freely until they sprawled into a massive six-lobed structure that was not quite building, not quite hive.

Kahn worried that Tyng's small-scale cellular structure, despite the ingenious dorm rooms, made for poor public spaces.[11] He now made an unusual move, and just before the November 25 presentation he dashed off an alternative design, an undistinguished scheme of two courtyards surrounded by ranges of simple rectangular rooms. The drawings were assigned to the newest man in the office, David Polk, who had joined just a week earlier.[12] Everything about the project suggests haste, and one senses that that it was not so much a design as a place holder, leaving Kahn an opening in which to work out other ideas.

McBride was baffled to confront two designs at the meeting, one wildly ambitious and the other a bland afterthought. She was taken with Tyng's complex geometry, which reminded her of the recent DNA research of James Watson and Francis Crick, and she dubbed this scheme "the molecular plan."[13] She was less taken with Kahn's project, especially its courtyard: "If you have ever heard young women shrieking across a courtyard on a warm spring day, you would know why you don't want one."[14]

At the same time, McBride must have sensed Kahn's ambivalence toward Tyng's design, for she diplomatically told him to develop both schemes.[15] This decision, or rather indecision, was

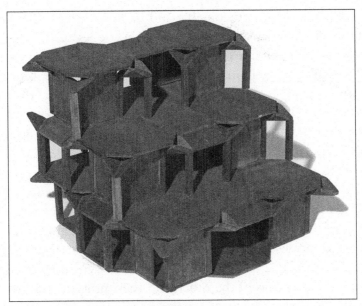

FIGURE 17.5 Tyng thought simultaneously in terms of space and structure, and she crafted exquisite study models in order to perfect their relationship. But while she struggled with the individual cell, Kahn brooded over the essential order of the whole.

fateful. Throughout the rest of the design process, the office would work concurrently on both projects—not the way Kahn usually treated a commission. Tyng continued to refine her octangular design in a more or less consistent line. Her challenge was to resolve structure and space within a single geometric order, which required her to make intricate study models (fig. 17.5). Kahn, on the other hand, was more restless and his successive projects showed sudden changes and abrupt deviations from preceding plans. He brooded over the large public places of the building, studying them repeatedly in section, while Tyng devoted herself to the smaller rooms which established the module for the building.[16] Behind the scenes personal tensions were at play. Behind Tyng's back, Kahn mocked her project, referring to its additive, cellular structure as "algae."[17]

At their second meeting in early April 1961 the architects returned with their revised plans. Tyng had not stopped think-

ing about interlocking geometry and had now prepared a fascinatingly intricate model, in which the six lobes of the original
scheme were now drawn together in an extended horizontal
block, each story stepping back to make a shape uncannily like
a honeycomb.[18] Kahn, having been preoccupied by the Salk
Institute and the First Unitarian Church at Rochester, had not
focused on the project as Tyng had. To McBride's astonishment
he showed a plan that was "almost completely different" from
that of November.[19] It seems to have left her cold for she told
Delanoy, her closest confidant, that she was "more interested"
in Tyng's project, and so was her committee. But once more she
refused to commit and told Kahn and Tyng to continue working.

Now a curious thing happened. At the time of their third presentation, on May 23, 1961, we see Kahn and Tyng each trying to
incorporate the ideas of the other into their projects. Inspired by
Tyng's idea that the dorm rooms should be interlocking modules,
Kahn proposed L-shaped rooms that would tuck neatly inside
one other (fig. 17.6). Polk, who drew up the project, came up
with the shape.[20] But Kahn was still more focused on the large
public spaces and he worked to emphasize their monumental

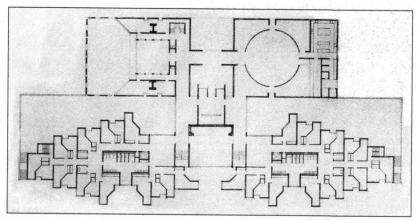

FIGURE 17.6 Kahn's plan of May 23, 1961, did not so much solve the
dormitory problem as state it: how to reconcile the intimate geometry
of the dorm's private rooms with its inspiring public spaces? Here they
refuse to integrate and draw apart, oil and vinegar.

nature. The dining hall was to be one large square space and the living room a circle, and each was inserted within a larger square. These two squares were to be independent units, standing free of the dormitory block, much as each of the blocks of the Richards Medical Laboratory was a discrete mass. It was an inspired idea to propose two entirely different sorts of geometry, one of simple elementary shapes for public life and one of interlocking modules for private space, and to emphasize their separateness.

Tyng, on the other hand, aimed for unity. Taking from Kahn the idea of placing the public functions in large, geometrically ordered spaces, she worked to integrate them with her octangular dorm rooms. While Kahn pushed his public spaces to one side, Tyng gathered them in the middle, wrapping the dorm rooms around the perimeter. She placed three large squares in a row and into each she inserted a form to serve one of its public functions: a square tilted diamond-fashion for the living room, a circle for the entrance lobby, and another inset square for the dining room. All was made clear in a delightfully compact study model (fig. 17.7). In it we see for the first time what would be

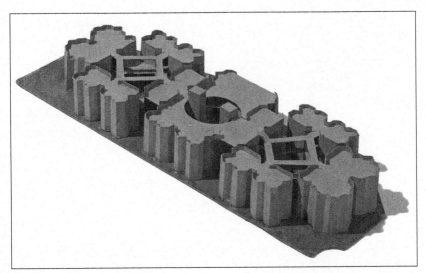

FIGURE 17.7 For the same May 23 meeting, Tyng made a model in which the large public spaces were encased within a mantle of dorm rooms.

Erdman's defining feature: the enclosure of monumentally-scaled public spaces within a mantle of smaller private spaces.

Favorably impressed, McBride described Tyng's project to her friend Delanoy in a way that showed she grasped its essence: the "octangular plan [was] reshaped in a long rectangle which is made up of several quadrangles, the inside of each being used for public rooms."[21] Although it needed "much more work," she much preferred it to Kahn's fragmented scheme of freestanding units, which did "not seem as promising . . . to my eye. Mr. Kahn maintains his interest in his set, however, and I think may work on it further." It is odd, given the subsequent evolution of the design, that Kahn overlooked for the moment the potential of Tyng's three squares. For the rest of the summer and early autumn of 1961 he continued to experiment restlessly while Tyng made variant after octangular variant of her geometric scheme.[22]

For the next meeting in October 1961, Kahn combined Polk's L-shaped rooms with Tyng's notion of wrapping smaller rooms around larger central spaces (fig. 17.8).[23] He liked the double-

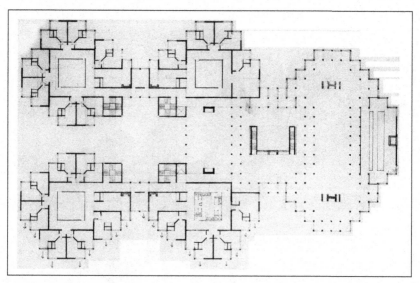

FIGURE 17.8 Kahn's plan of October 1961 took from Tyng the idea of wrapping the private rooms around the public spaces, but he struggled to draw its rambling parts into a unified whole.

shelled motif but was not sure exactly how to translate it into a resolved and balanced composition.[24] Still thinking additively, he grouped the rooms into four separate blocks, much like the detached towered masses of Richards Medical Laboratory, recently completed. He was not happy about it, however, as he confessed at a public lecture at Bryn Mawr on "Rule and Architecture" on October 23. Calling the Bryn Mawr dormitory one of the most difficult problems he had faced, he said he was struggling to find "the qualities which make a school great."[25] This, he told the students, was accomplished "through the use of space, architecture itself being a 'thoughtful making of spaces.'" The peculiar problem at Bryn Mawr was "to distinguish each space, each room as a single entity, not just a series of partitions." Evidently he was still thinking of the design as the union of many discrete entities, the repeated modules of Tyng's octagons or Polk's L-shapes. About the formal unity or monumentality of the building as a whole there was no discussion.

An event now occurred which drastically accelerated the pace of work. On November 8, 1961, the family of Eleanor Donnelley Erdman, who had died nearly two years before, announced they would make a bequest. Since her son Donnelley was studying architecture at Princeton, where Kahn was then giving seminars, a gift to the building fund seemed appropriate. Her husband, C. Pardee Erdman, wrote to Katharine McBride from Santa Barbara to say he was "very much interested in the possibility of giving a building to Bryn Mawr in memory of Eleanor. Perhaps you do not need another building, and perhaps there is no room for one . . . but will you please give this a little thought."[26] McBride fairly leapt at the offer. The only condition attached to the gift was that Donnelley might be able to attend the presentation meetings.

After more than eighteen months of false starts, the sense of urgency concentrated Kahn's mind. Within the next few weeks, and certainly before December 6, Kahn found his solution. On that date he flew to Pittsburgh to give three lectures in which he drew on the blackboard a plan that for the first time contained all of the essential elements of the Erdman dormitory: three tilted squares (or diamonds) joined at their corners, a large public space at the center of each, and an arrangement of interlocking rooms along the perimeter. He told his former assistant William S. Huff, who had invited him, that he had finally broken the mental block that had bedeviled him throughout the project: "All this time, I had been thinking *boys' dormitories.* That was the trouble. . . . Men accept a barracks mentality. They can live two and three in a room, but women can't."[27]

Here for the first time was a proposal which resolved many requirements in one simple formula, both the formal plan and the rich, monumental exterior. A week later, Kahn presented McBride with a plan dated December 14 (fig. 17.9).[28] He seems to have drawn no elevations, but on one drawing, now in the collection of the Museum of Modern Art, he dashed off a quick sketch, showing the three blocks in strong sunlight, with strong diagonal shadows highlighting the volumes of the three squares in vivid relief. Plan and elevation were unified, each showing the same association of the twin motifs of the square and diagonal. McBride, finally presented with a design which resolved the ideas of both Kahn and Tyng, gave it her endorsement.

The resemblance to Tyng's project of the previous May, with

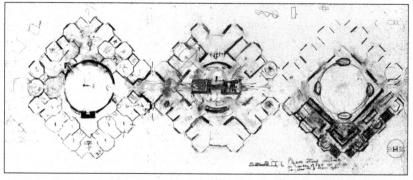

FIGURE 17.9 By December 14, 1961, Kahn had brought all the elements together: geometrically interlocking dorm rooms, public spaces of monumental character, and a succinct compositional order of three aligned cubes.

its tight scheme of three squares arrayed in a row, is clear. Ironically, she herself seems to have forgotten it, for she was still brooding over her octangular geometry. On December 12 she made one last effort to draw all the dorm rooms together into one bulky rectangular mass, relieved at regular intervals by projecting clusters of rooms.[29] But it was now too late. A few days later McBride wrote Erdman to acknowledge his one-million-dollar bequest, which was now definitively to go toward Kahn's building.[30]

This was only the schematic design and much needed to be resolved, particularly the character of the internal public spaces. These developed in rapid succession as the project was refined between January and May 1962.[31] At first these were little more than circles inserted within squares. The circles soon gave way to squares on the two ends of the building (January 26) and eventually in the middle as well (April 6).[32] As these spaces were refined, they took on a more public and monumental character, chiefly through the generous provision of natural light. On March 15, the central spaces were raised slightly to form a clerestory, light being admitted through narrow slit windows capped by lunettes; on April 6 the clerestories were raised in height and a single square tower rose above on one of the corners of the square, bringing in light indirectly from above.[33] This was a new theme in Kahn's work, recalling the light towers of the Rochester church or the light hoods of his Esherick House. By the time of the May 2 presentation, the clerestory had vanished and light now was channeled solely through towers at all four corners of the inner squares.[34] The arrangement of light towers was the last major plan issue to be resolved.

In the early proposals, much of the octangular modularity of Tyng's work survived, as in the bathrooms which were to be placed in the joints between the three squares. By April 6, when the revised design was submitted to McBride, the bathrooms were transferred to the corners of the central spaces, eliminating the knuckle joints between the cubes, which now touched at their edges. These changes occurred in tandem with the development of the public spaces. At last on May 10, 1962, Kahn wrote to McBride that the design of Erdman was "essentially settled." The working drawings were to be completed by the end of July.[35]

In fact, they were not completed until March 25, 1963. The preparation of the working drawings went much more slowly than foreseen and there was resistance to some of Kahn's ideas among members of the college administration. This was particularly true with respect to materials. In a memorandum to McBride dated August 1, 1962, a campus committee criticized some aspects of the design. Above all, the committee wrote, "we oppose exposed concrete anywhere."[36] But McBride supported Kahn stalwartly. Still, compromises were made, especially on the exterior, which was ultimately clad with a revetment of Pennsylvania slate.[37]

It took less time to build Erdman than to design it. Excavation began in July 1963, and the reinforced concrete structure was poured in stages throughout the autumn and into next summer.[38] It was completed structurally that autumn, although the college did not formally accept the building until May 1965.

Erdman, perhaps more that Kahn's Yale Art Gallery or his Richards Medical Laboratory, was his breakthrough building. Its most remarkable feature is the nature of its spaces, which are neither contemporary nor archaic, but rather timeless. With Erdman's vast but mournful living room, Kahn restored to architecture those two fundamental building blocks of form that modernism had effectively banished, the room and the solid wall (fig. 17.10). The room had fallen victim to modernism's insistence on flowing uninterrupted space, while the solid masonry wall gave way to the transparency of glass. After Erdman, Kahn's mature work continued to develop the idea of the solidly-walled room as a noble and beautiful thing, a creation of sculpture and space, and the dignified place of human action. Near the end of the project, when the dormitory was nearing completion, Kahn wrote proudly "the building committee like my building very much. . . . I had faith in it all the time."[39]

FIGURE 17.10 Revolution literally means "turning back," and by turning back to the lessons of his Beaux-Arts training Kahn revolutionized modern architecture. The chief lesson was that a building should have a spatial sequence with a satisfying culmination, ideally a space of great dignity and grandeur, such as the austere living room of Erdman.

Coda

When writing the first version of this essay, which was published in 1991, I refrained from any mention of Kahn's personal life. Although the years when he designed Erdman coincided with the end of his romantic relationship with Anne Tyng and the beginning of one with Harriet Pattison, this did not seem germane. I separated the personal from the professional, and concentrated only on the plans and their significance.

But this was one instance where the personal could not be kept out. A decade or more after the essay appeared, I ran into Anne at our local supermarket, and she did a double take when she saw me. Taking my arm, she told me that she had just read my essay, coincidentally, the night before. "I understand it now," she said, wistfully. "He was breaking up with me."

CHAPTER 18

Gehry at the Philadelphia Museum of Art

■ THE FALL OF 2018 gave us our first look at Frank Gehry's ambitious remodeling of the Philadelphia Museum of Art, on which the architect has been toiling for more than a decade. If intended to reassure skeptics that his work will be respectful and understated, his new museum restaurant could hardly have performed better. Called "Stir," it is a warm and handsome space with floors of red oak and walls of Douglas fir. The open lattice of curved wooden beams that hangs from the ceiling like a late-Gothic net vault imparts a cozy sense of enclosure to those who dine beneath it. This distinctive shape, the architect tells us, will be reprised in the new galleries he will add in the course of his renovations.

When it was announced in 2006 that Gehry, the designer of the extravagantly unbuttoned Guggenheim Bilbao, would be turned loose on Philadelphia's serene temple of art, there was excitement but also alarm. Gehry had never worked on a significant historic building. Conscious of this, the museum made a point of stressing that although his mandate was "to create dynamic

new spaces for art and visitors," he was to do so "without dis-
turbing the classic exterior of a building that is already a defining landmark in Philadelphia." And, in fact, his first intervention
was fairly restrained, though not as restrained as Atkins Olshin
Schade, the firm that gave the museum a 425-car parking garage
and tucked it out of sight, invisible except for the most discreet
of pavilions projecting above ground. Gehry's new loading dock
on the museum's south flank was more obtrusive but was seen as
an acceptable trade-off, one that made it possible to reopen the
long-closed public entrance to the north, which had been turned
into a makeshift loading dock.

The current round of alterations, for which ground was broken in 2017, are more consequential. In an effort to create a natural flow between the upper floors and the newer galleries below,
Gehry has reconfigured the entire entrance sequence. The eastern
and western entrance halls, originally conceived as distinct spaces,
are to be joined together and linked to a new grand hall or forum,
placed directly below the main stair. This, in turn, will lead to the
grand cross axis of the lower level, a 640-foot vaulted passage that
runs across the breadth of the building and that has been inacces-
sible to the public for decades. Here another 23,000 square feet
of exhibition space is to be created. This first building campaign,
budgeted at $196 million, is focused on the historic building and
has been called the "core project" to distinguish it from the next
phase, which will extend the building underground.

The breathless cheerleading with which Gehry's plans have
been sold to the public is not without incongruity. According to
Gail Harrity, the museum's COO, "This is about restoring, preserving, and at the same time reimagining the building for Philadelphia's future." But how exactly do you preserve something
that you imagine (i.e., wish) to be something else? For the most
part, these claims have been accepted uncritically by the press.
It is only when one looks closely at the plans and models (which
were exhibited in 2014) that one realizes that, beneath the bal-
lyhoo and fanfare, one of America's great buildings is quietly preparing itself for disfigurement.

FIGURE 18.1 The Philadelphia Museum of Art (1916–28) terminates the Benjamin Franklin Parkway with uncommon brilliance. Rather than bringing the axis to a full stop with a classical colossus, it suggests a relaxed ensemble of hilltop temples. Here the formal geometry of the City Beautiful begins to melt into the informal landscape of Fairmount Park.

CAN YOU ALTER a great building without knowing why it is great? The greatness of the Philadelphia Museum of Art is inseparable from its site (fig. 18.1). It stands alone among the world's museums in being situated upon its city's richest and most consequential parcel of real estate—which is itself ironic, since Philadelphia was not intended to have consequential real estate. Just as a Quaker meetinghouse has no presiding minister or pulpit, Philadelphia was to have no spatial hierarchy. The city that its Quaker founder William Penn laid out in 1682 was an uninflected grid, running from the Delaware River in the east to the Schuylkill River in the west. It had no notable topography apart from a lone hill to the northwest, just beyond the city limits, which he named "Faire Mount." This gave Philadelphia what no other American city has, certainly not in such compact and dramatic form: its own acropolis.

Beyond this hill, the topography changes. The prim Quaker grid abruptly gives way to a meandering landscape of picturesque hills and cliffs, stretching far upriver along the east bank of the Schuylkill. Fashionable Philadelphians, drawn by the attractive scenery and healthy elevation, built their summer seats here. But these estates became less desirable once textile mills upstream began to pour their effluvium into the Schuylkill, the river that provided most of the city's drinking water. Out of self-preservation, the city began acquiring upriver estates; in 1855 Fairmount Park was formed by city ordinance, and four years later J. C. Sidney began implementing its design. After it incorporated the Wissahickon, it encompassed 4,250 acres, making it one of the largest municipal parks in the world (that oft-heard boast is no longer true: we have fallen to 39th place).

It was sheer luck that Penn's Faire Mount was preserved for the art museum. Other cities have taken far more picturesque sites and squandered them. But for most of the nineteenth century, the hill was set aside as a water reservoir. Only in 1909, long after water from the "poisoned chalice" of the Schuylkill had become undrinkable, was it put out of commission. And so the site became available at the best possible moment, just as the City Beautiful Movement was carrying out its idealistic quest to embellish and refine America's cities by means of broad boulevards, gracious civic buildings, and inspiring monuments. The Faire Mount was made to order for that movement, fortuitously placed just where gridded Philadelphia touched picturesque Philadelphia; all that was needed was to draw a line connecting the two.

That connecting road had long been in the works. After the Civil War, when Philadelphia placed a new city hall on its central intersection, the logic of a grand boulevard connecting it to Fairmount Park became instantly clear. It took decades to secure the political backing for such an audacious move, slicing a bold diagonal right through Penn's Cartesian grid, and the first proposals involved only a new formal entrance to the park. But City Beautiful doctrine loved to terminate every axis with an eye-catching monument, and Philadelphia City Hall—a swaggering

Second Empire leviathan—demanded an equally swaggering pendant. So began the twenty-year campaign to design and build the Philadelphia Museum of Art, which advanced hand in hand with the construction of the diagonal boulevard, known today as Philadelphia's Benjamin Franklin Parkway.

Because of the project's complexity and urban component, it was assigned to a team of architects: Paul Cret, Horace Trumbauer, and the firm of Zantzinger, Borie & Medary. Cret, a prodigy of the École des Beaux-Arts, was the most gifted, but he chanced to be in his native France when World War I broke out, and he stayed to serve; he was absent during the critical years. Leadership defaulted to Trumbauer, more an impresario than an artist, who proved a capable administrator. The story is admirably told in David B. Brownlee's *Building the City Beautiful* (1989). Trumbauer wanted to terminate the parkway with one compact and mighty monument—a full stop, as it were. His collaborators preferred something more like the Acropolis in Athens, a loose collection of temples atop a sacred hill. Howell Lewis Shay, a young architect in Trumbauer's office, came up with the inspired solution to achieve the two desires. He made a plan in the form of an uppercase E, placing entrances at both sides of the cross bar. Each of the arms terminated in a pedimented temple front, eight in all, so that one could read the building as either a single object or a congeries of parts. This ambiguity was precisely the right note to strike in a building occupying a transitional site between city and park.

Shay's brainstorm came in June 1915, but construction had to wait for the end of the war. The project was overseen by the Fairmount Park Commission, the semi-independent agency responsible for the city's cultural and landscape patrimony, and it quickly proved that it knew its way around the corridors of City Hall. Fearing that the city might call a halt to construction once the museum's central block was finished, the commission started with the outer wings, correctly guessing that the city would never tolerate the public embarrassment of a building with a missing middle.

The orthodox solution for civic museums of the period was to build in pristine white marble, but this would have meant inserting civic formality into the park. Instead the architects opted for Mankato stone, a robustly grained dolomitic limestone from Minnesota that is resistant to erosion and is a tawny yellow color. The result is a museum at once ceremonial and picturesque, perched where the formal order of the city gives itself over to the irregularity of natural landscape, making the museum as splendidly contextual a work of art as one is likely to see.

Vibrant color, of course, was everywhere in the 1920s. The building's most startling chromatic passage can be seen in the North Wing's pediment, with its unified sculptural group of larger-than-life-size figures. The theme is "sacred and profane love in Western civilization," and it is depicted by statues of Greek gods and goddesses in electrically vivid color. It had been known for a century that the sculpture of the ancient world was in fact colored, but few modern sculptors dared to revive the practice, and rarely with the intensity of C. Paul Jennewein, who molded the statues, and Léon-Victor Solon, the accomplished colorist who chose the hues (and would go on to design the color scheme for Rockefeller Center). Perhaps only the tolerance for high-keyed color during the Art Deco age made the sculpture possible. A second sculptural group designed by John Gregory for the facing pediment was never installed; it remains unfinished, as do the other six temple porticos, all provisionally backed with blank brick walls. Nonetheless, Jennewein's sculpture is there in all its wanton chromatic glory, perturbing even those who know their archaeological history.

The museum's other essay in archaeological rectitude is not quite so shocking, since it is practically invisible, but it is far more radical. The museum was the first—and to this date the only—large-scale implementation of the so-called optical refinements of ancient Greek architecture. These were the series of subtle and as yet poorly understood departures from the orthogonality that distinguishes Greek temples. Among them are stylobate curvature, i.e., the nearly imperceptible rise and fall of the temple base across its length, and the slight inward tilt of the columns of the portico (those of the Philadelphia Museum of Art tilt so minutely that their axes converge two and a half miles above the earth). Just why the Greeks did this is an enigma. Was it to compensate for perspective distortion, and to make things appear straight that would otherwise seem to sag? Or to impart a sense of living elasticity to the stone? At any rate, the Philadelphia Museum gives us our one chance to experience the effect of these refinements at full scale in bright sunlight, which is the only way they can be appreciated.

AND SO THE Philadelphia Museum of Art is a bafflingly complex object: formal yet picturesque, superbly archaeological yet sparkling with Jazz Age pizzazz. It shows that curious 1920s sensibility that has been called "Greco Deco." To appreciate just how distinctively personal and local it is, one should follow up with a visit to a more properly "correct" museum of the age such as the National Gallery of Art in Washington, D.C., a museum that is equally impeccable but of purely formal civic character. Complete unto itself and visible from all sides, the Philadelphia Museum of Art defies enlargement. It has no rear facade, as the Metropolitan Museum of Art does, that can simply be pushed outward. And so until recently it has grown only by acquiring satellites on the Parkway. The great Paul Cret, back from the war in which he was three times gassed, added the peerless gem of the Rodin Museum in 1927; originally built for a private collector, it has been administered since 1939 by the PMA. In 2007 the museum acquired the nearby Perelman Building, an Art Deco insurance company office that now provides space for the costume and textile department and for exhibiting contemporary art. There should have been a third satellite: in 2001 Tadao Ando designed a characteristically graceful Calder Museum for the Parkway, but it came to grief when the sculptor's descendants and the museum could not agree on loan terms.

For these reasons, the Philadelphia Museum is intact in its original historical fabric to an extraordinary degree, perhaps more so than any other major American museum. Under the circumstances, Gehry made the correct decision to find space below ground, and, happily, there was space waiting. The long passage on the lower level—crowned by a handsome Guastavino vault and stretching more than twice the length of the Hall of Mirrors at Versailles—is the great hidden gem of the building. Whatever galleries Gehry might later burrow beneath the museum's terrace, they will be bound into this generous cross axis and thereby into the classical order of the building. Unfortunately, the logic of that classical order is emphatically upward. Both the glorious eastern stair hall and the lower western entrance were designed to lift and lead visitors up to the art. Gehry's task was to find a way of directing them downwards, which is always a challenge. His solution was to create a third grand hall, directly beneath the main stair, and to make it appealingly visible from the western entrance. This requires demolishing the stone wall between the original entrance halls and the elegantly detailed stairs that link them. Under the circumstances, it seems that Gehry could hardly have acted otherwise.

Or perhaps he might have, had his clients viewed the ceremonial spaces of the museum as valuable works of art in their own rights, which one would no more think of defacing than the Rogier van der Weyden *Crucifixion* (1460) upstairs. When Robert Venturi gave the western entrance its postmodern facelift, he made certain to leave the building fabric so that his emendations were easily reversible (as now proven by the ease with which his modifications are removed). Gehry is nowhere near as scrupulous. By demolishing the rear wall of the stair hall, he exchanges a spatial order of discrete rooms for one of flowing continuity. This is no trifling tweak. It turns back the clock on one of the most important architectural developments of the last half century. It was Louis I. Kahn, Cret's brilliant pupil, who restored to modernism an appreciation for the well-formed room as the fundamental unit of architecture. One can hardly imagine a space more important for Kahn's development than the entrance hall of the museum, which was built during his student years. Its mutilation is a loss to Philadelphia's architectural patrimony. (Gehry can leave nothing untouched: the doors of the western portico are to be enlarged until there is virtually no wall left at all but only stubby cylinders between the entrances.)

One has the unhappy sense that the officers of the museum and their architect have no particular reverence or even fondness for the building that has been entrusted to them. It is not as bad as at the Brooklyn Museum, whose stewards have long acted as if they loathed their own building, but one senses glimmers of frustration and resentment. Clearly there is no appreciation for the exquisite display of Greek optical refinements that make this building unique in modern architecture. To see the subtlety of stylobate curvature requires that one put his nose at the base of the building and look directly across its whole length. Gehry's renovations will make this impossible if, in the second phase of the project, he is permitted to affix circulation towers to the north and south ends of the museum. Those blank swaths of wall are one of the delights of the building, and to despoil them with what are in effect glorified fire towers is bad enough in its own right without also compromising the assiduous investigation of Greek architecture below.

Other violations are in store, such as the plan to poke out the blank pediments above the entrances and fill them with glass. The idea is that the glazed aperture at the center will grant a great axial view along the length of the Franklin Parkway all the way to City Hall. But that view already exists from the museum entrance, and in much more satisfying fashion. Here one can see neatly aligned Alexander Milne Calder's statue of William Penn (1892–94) atop City Hall, the *Swann Memorial Fountain* by his son Alexander Stirling Calder (1924), and—directly overhead in the stair hall—his grandson Alexander Calder's mobile *Ghost* (1964). (Philadelphia wags call this trinity "the Father, Son, and Holy Ghost.") The view from the punctured pediment is superfluous, and it comes at the cost of destroying the visual meaning of the classical portico, whose beauty comes from the balance between the tapered columns below and the mighty pediment above, weight and support exquisitely gauged to one another. Hollow out the pediment, and the portico becomes grotesquely bottom-heavy.

To expect appreciation for these niceties of form is asking too much from a man who, after all, made his name as a master of anti-form architecture, thrilling critics in the 1970s with his insouciant refusal to give order and resolution to his designs. He may be the right man, but Philadelphia is the wrong place. It would have made far more sense to have commissioned him to give the museum a second building, on the model of the Met Breuer.

A German prince-bishop of the eighteenth century who built himself an exorbitantly wanton palace was said to be *vom Bauwurmb befallen*: in the grip of the building bug (literally "building worm"). Today our building-mad prince-bishops are our museum directors and college presidents. But there is a difference. Those prince-bishops expected to remain in their palaces, unlike the modern administrator for whom a successful building is merely the most tangible of all résumé items. The incentive to build will always be stronger than the incentive to preserve and maintain. This is not to say that everyone is a restless careerist for whom there can be no rest until attaining the presidency of Yale or the directorship of the National Gallery, but the cultural pressures and incentives are the background noise of our day. In an age marked by careerism, it takes a powerful will to resist the lure of the Bauwurmb.

How was this slow-building shambles permitted to happen? One cannot blame Timothy Rub, the museum's director, and Gail Harrity for wanting more space. And it was not they who engaged Gehry (although Harrity had worked with him on his Bilbao project) but their predecessor, the splendid Anne d'Harnoncourt. But until recently there has always been a check on the ambitions of the museum's stewards. Since 1867, Philadelphia's cultural heritage was watched over by the Fairmount Park Commission, the semi-autonomous body that protected the city's cultural interests from political and commercial pressure.

It exercised enormous control over the design and construction of the Philadelphia Museum of Art, which does not own its site and which is a tenant of the city. In 2010 the city abolished the Fairmount Park Commission and turned its duties over to Philadelphia Parks & Recreation, an agency led by a commissioner appointed by the mayor. Any insulation between immediate political concerns and long-term cultural considerations has been removed. The result is a crude utilitarian calculus by which any increase in museum visitorship and tourist dollars justifies itself. Once the Philadelphia Museum of Art becomes merely a means to an end, then Gehry's interventions become not only logical but necessary.

CHAPTER 19

Trashing the President's House

■ TO THOSE OF US who can recall the year 1968, there is something both familiar and unfamiliar in the social unrest that convulsed America in the spring of 2020. One notable difference is that in 1968 no sudden wave of fury burst out against the monuments and symbols of the past. Contemporary issues were much more urgent: Vietnam, the draft, race relations. But in this year's turmoil, century-old statues have played a conspicuous part. The sculpture-smashing was at first aimed at Confederate war memorials but soon took in honored figures of American history, including Thomas Jefferson, Ulysses S. Grant, Theodore Roosevelt, Frederick Douglass, and even George Washington. How those luminaries could so swiftly become objects of hatred is a question that will preoccupy the historians and psychologists of the future. But perhaps it did not happen all that swiftly. Ten years ago Philadelphia witnessed a heated public battle over history that signaled the coming story. In retrospect, we can see that early battle over George Washington's house as a full-dress rehearsal for today's iconoclastic moment.

The brick townhouse that housed presidents Washington and Adams in the first years of the United States was built in 1768. When the United States capital moved to Philadelphia in 1790, President Washington leased it because of its size and proximity to Congress, which convened just a block away. The house's run as the executive mansion of the United States ended when the White House was completed in 1800. Thereafter, it languished and was unsentimentally demolished in 1832 to make room for a row of stores. They were demolished in turn a century later, and the entire block was cleared in the 1950s to create Independence Mall.

No reliable image of the house survived, nor was its location known with any exactitude. There was more agreement about the form of ancient Troy. And as with Troy, it took an amateur historian to find the real thing. Edward Lawler, Jr., by profession a singer, had a longstanding interest in the house. Not satisfied with any of the existing literature, he made his own study of the documents and deeds and was able to pinpoint the house's location and reconstruct its form. His groundbreaking 2002 article in the *Pennsylvania Magazine of History and Biography* was fortuitously timed, as the National Park Service was then in the process of redesigning Independence National Historic Park, on whose grounds the house had stood.[1] Lawler's most explosive revelation was that the area in which Washington housed his stable-hands, most of whom were slaves, stood only five feet from the entrance to the new Liberty Bell Center. Flustered, the National Park Service conducted an archaeological dig and promptly found the foundations of the President's House, enough of which remained to show its perimeter, interior divisions, and even the great bow window that Washington added to the Dining Room. The intact footprint of America's first White House was still there.

Not for generations had there been such an important archaeological find in the field of American history. Here was the very crucible of the American presidency, where the executive branch of the United States government first came into its own, and where an extraordinary Cabinet including Jefferson and Hamilton took positions on the key issues that still constitute the crux of American political life: the division of government powers, the role of the president in conducting diplomacy, the role of the states in a federal system, the mission and nature of a national bank. All these issues were mooted and acted upon, and with fateful consequences, from within this slender townhouse.

But one would not know this from a visit to the house today, which was opened to the public in 2011 as a commemorative site called the President's House: Freedom and Slavery in the Making of a New Nation. To call it revisionist would be an understatement. It is as if its makers sought singlehandedly to atone for two centuries of positive or idealistic shrines by making a national monument to the sins and failings of the Founding Fathers.

WHENEVER A BUILDING has completely vanished, or has been reduced to an archaeological excavation, there are two ways to make it speak to the general public. One is to make a facsimile, based on physical evidence, documentary records, and historic photographs. This is the approach used famously during the 1930s to recreate Colonial Williamsburg, and more recently (and more controversially) to recreate German monuments destroyed during World War II. Although popular with the public, this approach long ago fell into disfavor among professional historians, who like to point out that such recreations are at best pastiches, in which frail shards of evidence are eked out with conjecture and improvisation. The making of facsimiles is now considered taboo. Preservationists have come to insist on a clear distinction between the surviving elements of the original building (to be reverently preserved) and any new construction, which must be clearly legible as a modern intervention.

The boldest example of this approach was by the architect Robert Venturi, who restored Benjamin Franklin's house in Philadelphia in 1976. Apart from a few passages of foundation wall, nothing remained of the house, not a single image. Any reconstruction would be all guesswork. Instead, Venturi raised up a great metal lattice that recreated the house as a ghostly abstrac-

FIGURE 19.1 Venturi and Rauch's Franklin Court (1976) sketched a kind of ghost building in the sky, inviting the visitor to imagine Benjamin Franklin's house and printing shop, of which no image survives.

tion, staking out its basic dimensions the way a mime might suggest a box (fig. 19.1). Below this lattice he placed a slate floor, inscribing into it excerpts from Franklin's letters that referred precisely to the activities and furnishings in the very spaces in which the viewer was standing. Visiting this ghostly trellis required more than the passive theatrical experience of Williamsburg; one must bring an active imagination.

One can make a persuasive argument for either tactic, the literal facsimile or the abstract abstraction, but one has to choose. To combine them both in the same building is to undercut the virtues of each and to make a cartoon. Yet this is precisely what the firm of Kelly-Maiello, the architects for the National Park Service, have done. They have recreated the lower story of the President's House, complete with a quartet of carved marble fire-

FIGURE 19.2 The house that served as the executive mansion for George Washington and John Adams was demolished in 1832. Its foundations were rediscovered in 2000 and made visible in a contentious reconstruction by Kelly/Maiello Architects.

places, but only to waist height (fig. 19.2). Above this the house dies away into an array of abstract window frames. It is as if someone had begun to reproduce literally but then switched to abstraction when the money ran out.

Even more embarrassing, what purports to be a rigorous, scientific projection of the outline of the house is nothing of the sort. The proportions of the superstructure have been shrunk slightly so its rooms do not precisely align with the foundations below. Weirdly, the architects have played fast and loose with the only solid information we have about the house, which are its dimensions. It turns out there's actually something worse than a facsimile of a vanished building: a facsimile of an excavation.

But the real scandal of the President's House is not in its confused and inaccurate construction but rather in its didactic material. And therein lies a tale. Once concrete physical evidence of housing for slaves had been found on the site, the National Park

Service decided it had to work assiduously to ensure that the story of slavery was not left out of the interpretation of the site. To do this, and to draft the wall texts that would interpret the site to the public, the prominent historian Gary Nash was enlisted. This was the same Gary Nash who had been tasked by the National Endowment for the Humanities to draft new National Standards for the teaching of American history in 1994—and whose work on it was taken to task by Lynne Cheney, who was chair of NEH when Nash received his assignment. In a celebrated *Wall Street Journal* op-ed entitled "The End of History," Cheney showed that the new standards systematically presented American history in the worst light possible, consistently downplaying the achievements of constitutional government and free enterprise while placing America's sins front and center (she noted, for example, nineteen mentions of McCarthy and McCarthyism and none of Thomas Edison or the Wright Brothers).

A revised version of the standards in which some of the more flagrant omissions were corrected was published two years later, although Nash refused to concede any merit whatsoever in the criticism of the standards, blaming them on a cabal of Rush Limbaugh, Newt Gingrich, and the Republican Congress of 1994. In a sense, what has come to pass at the President's House might be thought of as Nash's revenge.

As HISTORICAL SITES GO, the President's House is uncommonly verbose. Nash has swathed its walls with numerous text panels, artist's renderings, and flat-screened video monitors that constantly stream re-enactments of life in the house. The only moment of visual rest is the granite wall near where the slave quarters stood and on which are inscribed the names of Washington's nine slaves. Visitors who approach from the east will first encounter this mournful slab, and most will find it deeply moving. It raises the specter of slavery in a vivid and appropriate way and, given the proximity to the Liberty Bell, in the most poignant of locations.

Indeed, slavery permeates every aspect of the President's House, every panel and every room, even the state dining room where Washington held his celebrated public levees. By bringing his slaves to Philadelphia, the prologue to the exhibition tells us, Washington "exposes the core contradiction at the founding of this nation: enshrinement of liberty and the institution of slavery." Nash uses "core contradiction" as a synonym for hypocrisy, which is his charge against the Founding Fathers.

No presidential actions are cited unless they pertain to race relations or reveal something shameful. Thus Washington's primary achievements shown here are the signing of the Fugitive Slave Act and a meeting with a delegation of American Indians, while John Adams is noted for meeting the Haitian envoy and for signing the Alien and Sedition Acts, those early tests of free speech and the right to argue against the government. (These mark the only appearances of Adams, who, as someone who owned no slaves, seems not to have been useful polemical fodder.)

To be fair, the panels contain much valuable historical information. For example, out-of-state slaves who were held in Pennsylvania could claim their freedom after a residency of six months, a law, one is disappointed to learn, that Washington circumvented by regularly rotating his slaves back to Virginia. (He seems to have done so furtively and with an evident sense of guilt; at any rate, he manumitted all his slaves upon his death.) This stress on slavery is not due to Nash alone. The National Park Service was intensively lobbied by a local activist group, the Avenging the Ancestors Coalition, which called for "a culturally-dignified, historically-complete, prominently-conspicuous, physically-dramatic, formally-official, and timely-installed commemoration on the grounds of the President's House to honor, primarily, the nine enslaved African descendants."[2]

With such a vocal pressure group pushing for a restoration that would serve "primarily" as a memorial to Washington's slaves, a revisionist historian with an ax to grind, intense secrecy surrounding the whole process, and no countervailing force in the form of traditional historians or an engaged public, one can easily see how what might have been a balanced interpretation turned into one-sided tendentiousness.

EVEN ON ITS own limited terms, however, the President's House fails to do what Nash intended it to do. His goal seems to have been to express the laminated complexity of its history, its different constituencies and variegated meanings. This is the attitude on display in his preamble to the exhibition, which begins by admonishing us that "History is not neat. It is complicated and messy." That thin gruel is merely a breezy version of the ideas put forth in a 1995 article in which Nash praised "the multi-layered, multi-faceted social history of the last generation that has transcended semi-official versions of this country's development." He contrasted this nuanced history, offering multiple voices and perspectives, with traditional curricula, which he dismissed variously as "self-congratulatory history" or "happy-face history." He might have been thinking of the hagiographic accounts of Washington, including Parson Weems's apocryphal fable (*"Father, I cannot tell a lie; I did cut down that cherry tree"*).

Nash's contempt for hagiography, however, extends only to the patriotic variety; other forms are apparently acceptable. One wall text, for example, informs us about Washington's cook Hercules, reputedly the finest chef in Philadelphia. Hercules, we learn, was "skilled, strong and determined," the sort of pious platitude familiar from inspirational juvenile literature. He may well have been all those things, but we will have to take Nash's word for it. As for Washington, whose own skill, strength, and determination are all copiously documented, he has nary a word.

In the end, the President's House's claim to offer up a "complicated and messy" history presents one as lucid and reductive as a medieval morality tale. But of all the voices excluded from the interpretation, the silence of the building in which they appear is most lamentable. For as garrulous as Nash's panels are, they say virtually nothing about the house itself. While they use it as their point of departure, they have nothing to offer about the specific meaning of its spaces and forms and seem oblivious to the peculiarly vivid lessons that physical objects can impart and that can be conveyed by no other means.

For example, by far the most interesting element is the bow window that Washington added to the south of the State Dining Room, a favorite neoclassical form that terminated the room in an elegant 180-degree arc. This ensured that when he entered the space for public receptions, he would have the sun at his back, a dramatic wall of light behind him. This was his principal alteration to the house, and with it he transformed his stylish merchant's house into a formal building of state. This was the origin and prototype for the Oval Office of the White House, which would be designed in a few years for Washington, D.C. But this pioneering feature goes unmentioned. Indeed, in a shocking gesture of indifference, the architects utterly disregarded it, building a bulky polygon with three *straight* sides above the foundations of the graceful *curved* semicircle below, as a visitor can easily confirm.

Washington's bow window is not merely an architectural footnote of interest only to the specialist. It is a richly expressive testimony of his serious effort to establish what the tone and character of the American presidency should be. It is part and parcel of his brooding over when and how he should present himself to the public, which centered on the State Dining Room. It was here that he instituted the practice of conducting weekly levees in which ordinary citizens might be introduced to him. His concern was to balance accessibility and dignity, and he cultivated the habit of holding papers in his right hand so that it would not be tactlessly grasped by an overeager supplicant. In other words, this room is the crucible in which the American president's peculiar identity as citizen executive, rather than sovereign ruler, was forged. To relegate it to a theater for showing an amateurish video of a Washington impersonator signing the Fugitive Slave Act is to throw away one of the great teaching opportunities of this spectacular archaeological find.

In the end, all these omissions and emphases tend to the same effect, which is to brand the American enterprise as something intrinsically flawed. It is not so much a memorial as an exposé. The issue of slavery deserves a prominent place at this site. But the President's House should not have become by default a national monument to it. If the slave quarters at the rear tell an important story, so does the executive mansion at the front. For that story is of how a military hero who conquered a continent and was universally acclaimed would voluntarily step down to become a citizen executive, situated not in a palace or building of state but a kind of private house. One should contrast that experience with Napoleon a decade later. And recall that the democracy whose establishment Washington oversaw, whatever its flaws, proved to be a self-correcting instrument.

When I wrote the original version of this essay a decade ago, I suggested that the President's House, honorable in its intention but misguided in execution and offensive in its omissions, had failed badly. An item of agitprop masquerading as a memorial, it would only cause ill-feeling and resentment, particularly among those whose sentiments it was meant to flatter. Little did I dream how deeply those currents of ill-feeling and resentment would run.

CHAPTER 20

The "New" Barnes

■ THERE CANNOT BE many architects who have refused a job
on moral grounds. I can only think of one, and whenever an
architect accepts a commission that is in some way odious or ob-
jectionable, I find myself thinking of him. In 1832, Julius Eugen
Ruhl, the municipal architect to the provincial German town of
Hanau, refused to design a scaffold for the public execution of a
notorious mass murderer. This was in direct contravention of his
professional duty to design whatever structure the town needed,
and even though a willing substitute was eventually found, Ruhl
was duly and severely fined.

But very few architects have the fortitude to be a Ruhl, and
the most we can ask of them is to design, as it were, the best scaffold possible, not to question its fundamental rightness. And so if
one has moral qualms about the new Barnes Foundation, which
opened in Philadelphia on May 18, 2012, one's real quarrel must
be with the clients—and, in this case, with the political-philan-
thropic axis that enabled them to break Barnes's will, to wrest his
great collection of Post-Impressionist and early modern art from

its home in suburban Merion, and to recreate it in downtown Philadelphia.

About their actions much has been said, and much will continue to be said, but for the moment it is fitting to consider the building itself, and on its own terms. If one does so, it is instantly clear that the architects, the husband-and-wife team of Tod Williams and Billie Tsien, have performed very well indeed. The project could have gone wrong in any number of ways. The instantly recognizable signature style of a celebrity architect would have overwhelmed the original Barnes, just as a cringing pastiche would have been overwhelmed, in turn, by the monumental scale of its new site on Philadelphia's Benjamin Franklin Parkway. But Tsien and Williams, who first came to fame with their American Folk Art Museum in New York, are unusual in not having a distinctive signature style. They are known instead for their spatial imagination and exquisite sensitivity in using materials, both of which are on display in their new building, which manages to respect the integrity of the original Barnes even as it presents a bold civic presence in its own right. Only in one respect do they falter, as we shall see, but given the nature of the problem any architect would have.

The fortune that financed Albert C. Barnes's impeccable art collection came from argyrol, the twentieth century's first wonder drug. A silver-protein compound, argyrol ended that tragic cycle by which an infected mother, at the instant of birth, might pass a disease to her own baby. A few drops of argyrol in the baby's eyes, the passage point of infection, could protect the child. It is the stuff of poetry that Barnes's fortune and the peculiar art foundation he established shared the same purpose, to bring health and clarity to the eyes.

To design his gallery, Barnes selected that gifted architectural prodigy Paul Cret. Cret was a product of the École des Beaux Arts, and he practiced an intelligent modern classicism, abstracting and simplifying his classical detail and applying it in the form of elegantly sculpted panels to steel-frame construction. Some of the most distinguished civic buildings of the era are his work,

including the Federal Reserve in Washington, D.C., the De-
troit Museum of Art, and Philadelphia's flawless Rodin Museum.
But Barnes's building, Cret recognized, was of a different order.
A private museum, attached by a passage to the owner's house,
could not be treated as a civic building, with an elaborate sequence of formal spaces. Instead, its character should suggest domestic informality, with rooms of intimate scale and a generous
use of warm wood.

As designed by Cret in 1924, Barnes's gallery was a tasteful
French *maison de plaisance*, two stories in height, built of limestone with a low tile roof (fig. 20.1). Only its jaunty cubist panels
by Jacques Lipchitz suggested the radical nature of its contents.
Within were some twenty-four rooms of varying sizes, although

FIGURE 20.1 Paul Cret and Albert Barnes gave much thought to the viewing
experience when making the original Barnes Foundation: "instead
of having the usual type of gloomy sky-lighted rooms as in most art
museums, they will be sidelighted rooms of limited area, which will
make for a feeling of intimacy."

none was large except for the double-height grand gallery at the center, with its three great lunettes that Matisse would fill with his painting *The Dance*.

Here Barnes installed his famously eccentric hanging scheme. There were none of the didactic devices of the contemporary art museum: no labels and wall texts, and no grouping of paintings according to style or chronology (a Franz Hals might sit companionably between a pair of Renoirs). Instead, each wall was organized as a visual unity, forming one of Barnes's symmetrical and highly idiosyncratic "wall pictures." Odder still was the way that Barnes hung examples of historic metalwork—hinges, ladles, lock faces—above and between the paintings, to propose subtle affinities in their compositions. Visually charged but verbally silent, the Barnes was not very good for teaching conventional art history but was very good indeed for looking at art.

And for Barnes, this was the point. As a German-trained scientist (and friend of the educational philosopher John Dewey), he found paintings to be as clear as molecules. He had no room for mumbo-jumbo or cant, or genteel aestheticism: the study of art was to be objective: a matter of line, color, and form. To put a sublime Cézanne bather beneath an equally languid iron hinge was not sacrilege but served to make the form clearer, purging it of preciousness or literary meaning.

Throughout his life, Barnes maintained the private character of his gallery. Having been publicly humiliated by the reviews that his first exhibition drew in Philadelphia's newspapers, he closed his collections to anyone but the students of his own art program and any curious tradesman or factory worker who happened to knock at his door (a certain number of whom were academics in mufti, art historians being categorically unwelcome at the Barnes). He continued to bait Philadelphia even in death: When he died in an automobile accident in 1951, his will was found to place his foundation under the control of Lincoln University, a historically black college that to patrician Philadelphia stood on the wrong side of every possible set of tracks. Barnes was advanced in his racial views (he invariably hired black workers, although he insisted on paying their wages to their wives) and believed that Lincoln would be more receptive to progressive views on art and education.

Such was the oyster of an institution that was gradually pried open by successive lawsuits, the latest of which came in 2004 when Lincoln's own trustees won the right to transform the Barnes into the one thing we can be certain that its founder did not wish it to be: a world-class public museum.

IN 2007 WILLIAMS AND TSIEN received their bracing mandate: the entire institution was to be uprooted bodily, transplanted to another site, and made to serve a vastly expanded program. The original museum would be augmented with additional galleries for changing exhibitions, library, auditorium, the obligatory restaurant and museum shop, and administrative offices, increasing its square footage by a factor of more than seven (from 13,000 to 93,000 square feet). All this must happen without any loss to the essential identity of the Barnes.

The architects correctly recognized that the original museum gallery and its new spaces were two different things, on the order of a gemstone and its setting, and that the gemstone should dominate. Accordingly, the gallery was given pride of place along the Parkway while the new functions, including the entrance lobby, were tucked to the rear in a second parallel wing, making a composition much like two train cars on adjoining tracks. The space between the two was roofed over to form a vast light court that is the spatial heart of the new Barnes and is surely its most spectacular feature.

Nothing is so coveted in the contemporary museum as a festive, hangar-sized courtyard; if museum brochures were honest, each would be prominently labeled as rental opportunity space. This one is unusually grand. It runs the full length of the building, extending well beyond it to the northwest as a roofed terrace. Atop it is a mighty "light canopy" that acts as a baffle to direct sunlight, softening and diffusing it, and giving the visitor the distinct sense of being outdoors (fig. 20.2). It is from here that

FIGURE 20.2 The greatest challenge faced by architects Tod Williams and Billie Tsien was that the north entrance of the celebrated Barnes plan, which they preserved, meant turning its rear to the Parkway.

one enters the museum gallery itself, as if it were a freestanding building, and in some sense it still is.

The light canopy is the only self-consciously architectural feature of the Barnes, and it rides atop the building as a translucent white block, thrusting deep into space at the northwest end. It is far larger and more prominent than it needed to be—more prominent, in fact, than the original gallery itself—but this must be seen as a concession to the new site of the Barnes. The domestically scaled original building did not have the commanding presence for its monumental setting on the Parkway, and the architects seem to have felt it required something of a grand gesture to hold its own among its haughty neoclassical neighbors, which include the Free Library of Philadelphia and Cret's Rodin Museum.

IF THERE IS a chronic failing of contemporary architecture, it is a certain schematic blockiness, the tendency to conceive of form in graphic terms—how they look in digital presentation—rather than in terms of actual tactile experience. But the great strength of Williams/Tsien is a scrupulous sensitivity to the tone and texture of materials, which the light court shows off in dazzling fashion. The walls are lined with panels of Israeli limestone, chiseled by hand to produce the finely scored surface that Williams jokingly calls "cuneiform." As one moves around the building, its treatment varies. In the light court, the chiseling is broad in effect, befitting the monumental space; in the museum gallery, it modulates to a more finely rendered scale and is organized into parallel horizontal channels. And where the museum walls emerge from the enclosed space of the light court into the open air the tooling ceases entirely and the color shifts from buff to gray, in deference to the traditional palette of the Parkway's neoclassical landscape.

Here, and throughout the building, there prevails an appealingly quiet sensuousness of materials—in the patterned mosaic flooring at the entrance, in the lush bronze vestibule opening onto the outdoor terrace, and even in the woven wool panels set among the limestone of the light court as a sound-absorbent material (and quite effectively, for voices can be heard quite clearly here). The Williams/Tsien aesthetic, strangely, is not so much architectonic as woven. It focuses less on the expression of weight and support, and the strenuous poetry of structure, as it does on the textile qualities of pattern and interval, texture and grain. At times, this can lapse into self-indulgence, especially when a more purely architectural expression is required. Along the exterior base of the building, for example, the stone projects to form vertical flanges, suggesting tiny parodies of buttresses. Similarly, bronze strips extend from the upper-story windows, scattered haphazardly across the wall. Here the delight in surface patterning does not serve them well, for the sort of whimsical touches that might be playful on the interior are too fussy to achieve architectural force on the exterior.

In the creation of the new spaces of the Barnes, Williams and Tsien were given carte blanche, but the recreation of Cret's 1924 building—now called the Collection Gallery—was a vastly more complicated operation. The guiding principle was that the original spaces and hanging scheme were to be maintained exactly as they were, with precisely the same proportions, dimensions, and sequential arrangements. Williams told me that he experimented with enlarging the scale of all the galleries by a certain amount, say 5 or 10 percent, to accommodate the larger crowds, but he abandoned the effort once they noticed that the increasing distance between the paintings threw off the careful balance of object and wall that makes the hanging scheme so memorable (and so weird).

Yet the new gallery is neither a recreation of the original Barnes nor a facsimile, but a simulacrum. It scrupulously preserves its empty spaces but not the solid masses that delimited those spaces. These are merely approximated. Moldings, cornices, window surrounds, parquet floors, and baseboards: everything has been simplified and pared down so as only to suggest the original detail. Characteristically, the materials are used well. Tsien has noted how the character of Cret's Barnes was a mixture of the civic and domestic, in which a display of warm woodwork figured largely. But like most modern firms, Williams/Tsien is somewhat ill at ease with the making of a molding and the art of finely calibrating their profiles to match the temperament of a room. Theirs seem bulky and roughly blocked out, without the sensitivity otherwise seen in their use of materials.

The point is that it is not Barnes's building but rather his installation that has been moved to the Parkway, and no attempt has been made to reproduce its facades. In place of Cret's richly sculptural walls, these are highly abstracted, slender planar objects, without projecting elements or cornices. Only the voids of the window openings, cut cleanly through the walls, evoke the ghostly outline of the original Barnes (fig. 20.3). These unrelieved blank walls, combined with the look-but-don't-touch landscaping and lack of welcoming gestures on the Parkway and

FIGURE 20.3 The modestly-scaled Barnes Foundation would have been lost among the neoclassical giants of the Franklin Parkway without some boldly monumental element.

Twenty-first Street sides of the building, give it the somewhat aloof and standoffish character of a compound, and, from certain angles, it can suggest an American embassy in one of those high-spirited countries where political donors do not ask to be made ambassador.

The problem is that in its original suburban context, the Barnes was entered from the north, which made this its formal public facade. But in being transposed to the Parkway, while maintaining its interior configuration, the building now turns its back to the public side. Laurie Olin, the architect who collaborated with Williams/Tsien on the landscaping of the building, worked diligently to overcome this. He has opened up a path that gently threads its way to the right of the building and behind it, leading the visitor alongside a reflecting pool to enter the building from the side opposite the Parkway. At the same time, he introduces several right turns into the path, which force the visitor to "slow down" from the tempo of the city.

Viewed purely as a design exercise, Olin's planting scheme is quite handsome. In one of his most inspired ideas, a tree court is sunken deep into the volume of the galleries, bringing natural light into the underground level where the library is housed. But the terraced landscaping and the row of trees that front the building on the Parkway are not successful. In contrast to the gardens that preface the nearby Rodin Museum, for example, which are delightfully welcoming because the visitor passes through them on the stroll to the entrance, the plantings of the Barnes are not meaningfully integrated into the experience of the building. They have the unfortunate disembodied quality common to the well-tended strips of landscaping before corporate office parks, which suggest affluence and respectability, but do not offer anything like a hearty welcome.

ALL THIS IS beside the main question, which is how the art looks. The answer, I am surprised and pleased to say, is that it looks terrific. Williams/Tsien have installed louvered skylights in some galleries that never previously had them, allowing for a generous but diffuse play of natural light. Juxtaposed against the well-chosen wall fabric—a straw color that closely reprises the neutral palette of the original building—the paintings have a fresh vibrancy. At times the improvement in lighting makes it seem that they have been cleaned (they have not been). When seeing how successfully this has been accomplished, one thinks regretfully of the Crystal Bridges Museum, which Moshe Safdie designed for natural light and which its directors unaccountably vetoed.

In one case, the improvement is startling. Matisse's great liberating work of 1906, *Le Bonheur de vivre*, had been previously lodged unhappily across from a stair, so it could only be seen obliquely from above or below. Now a slight change in the arrangement of the stairs has given it an intimate new gallery of its own, where it can be seen as never before. Had it been given more prominence over the years, one wonders if it might have had something of the reputation of Picasso's *Demoiselles d'Avignon*.

In some instances, alas, there is a loss. The large south-facing French windows of Cret's building were draped and curtained at two levels, so as to control the light, but in the new curtainless installation the paintings hung between these windows (including Matisse's chromatically pulsating *Le Rifain assis*) are lost in the light flooding in behind them. Presumably this can be corrected, and, even if not, one of the delights of a museum lighted naturally is that the art changes along with the light.

THE IMPROVED LIGHTING will have the inadvertent effect of calling attention to objects that have deteriorated because of too much prolonged exposure to light, such as works on paper. In particular, I was struck by how faded some of Demuth's elegant watercolors now seemed (they have been "loved to death," one curator told me). I am not sure how this can be remedied, given the mandate to preserve Barnes's installation. Lower the lighting to the threshold of visibility? Replace the object with a photographic surrogate? There is no easy answer, and it is the unavoidable consequence of the determination to embalm the Barnes, as it were, in perpetuity.

This is perhaps the ultimate paradox of the new Barnes, that it has worked so ardently to make its collection fresh and new and yet has come perilously close in the process to turning it into that deadest of things, a period room. It so happens that the nearby Philadelphia Museum of Art has the country's finest collection of period rooms, from its Chinese scholar's study to its Pennsylvania-German living hall to its Spanish romanesque cloister. These are gorgeously realized, and yet in the end they are disembodied effigies. They are not alive in the way that an actual house can be, even after its owner has died. One thinks of Frederic Church's Olana or Isabella Stewart Gardner's original museum, where one sometimes has the uncanny sensation that the owner has just stepped out for a minute and will be right back. One used to have this sense at the Barnes (not necessarily in a pleasant way), but one has it no longer.

A collection is a tangible thing, consisting of so many discrete physical objects, and valued at so many dollars. (The value of the Barnes collection, being subject to market fluctuation, can only be guessed at, but it has been put at between twenty-five and thirty billion dollars.) It is also an intangible thing, as any complex work of human intelligence is, and it cannot be reduced to a utilitarian calculus of visitors per year and tourist dollars spent. If this were the case, then one might simply move Stonehenge to the British Museum and be done with it. (And perhaps lower the Sistine Chapel ceiling as well so that we might get a better look.)

Of course, the moment that the blocks of Stonehenge are disassembled, they are no longer Stonehenge. In much the same way, once the Barnes is moved, it is no longer the Barnes. Each painting may still sit in its precise relationship to each of its neighbors, but it no longer sits in its precise relationship to the world. The genteel parlor-sized rooms of the Cret building were calibrated for its cloistered suburban location, with its distinctive microclimate and for close personal supervision. To take a building of a gently domestic nature and make it function as a civic monument is to put demands on it that it will not be able to meet. The spaces themselves are simply not large enough to accommodate crowds. One can scarcely cross a threshold without stepping too close to an object. If only to avoid theft and vandalism, one can expect a level of security that will be several shades more oppressive than Barnes's famous rudeness.

If this happens, it will be a pity, because Williams and Tsien have lavished more loving care and intelligence on their building than one usually sees today. I find myself wishing they had been chosen a decade ago to design the expanded Museum of Modern Art. A prediction: When the Barnes hoopla subsides, buoyed aloft by novelty and the fear of offending the cultural funders, there will be a recognition that a cultural crime has been perpetuated, an irrevocable crime on the order of the demolition of Pennsylvania Station, and right under the noses of the city's custodians. When that happens, there will be a widespread consensus that the move was a tragedy, even as everyone now knows to call it a triumph.

CHAPTER 21

A Museum That Overcomes
Its Correctness

■ Not so long ago the very idea of building a museum in Philadelphia to tell the story of the American Revolution would have been laughable, since Philadelphia itself is just such a museum. Here, within a few paces, are Carpenters Hall, where the Continental Congress first assembled; Independence Hall, where the Declaration of Independence was debated anxiously and then ratified; the Liberty Bell, with its thrilling injunction from Leviticus: "Proclaim Liberty thro' all the Land to all the Inhabitants thereof." These objects speak eloquently of the central event in American history—so long as one knows something of that history.

Those of us over 50 will remember when American history was taught as an instrument of citizenship. The Revolution that gave us our independence also gave us our system of government, and so to learn about the Revolution was to learn citizenship. Between the history lesson in the classroom and the Fourth of July parade there was a seamless continuity. But American history has since been purged of its civic content. Today's pupil is taught to look at it with the disinterested detachment of the professional historian, not as a participant with a stake in the outcome. Even the nominally traditional Common Core standards ask pupils to see the Revolution from all sides, and to write a broadside representing "the Loyalist perspective."

Such a widely inclusive approach broadens our understanding of the Revolution even as it diminishes its significance. If all history is simply the perpetual contention between individuals pursuing their naked self-interest, then any invocation of ideals or principles must be suspect. Pupils so trained are hardly likely to regard the American Revolution as a great step forward in human history. They need to be told why the events in Independence Hall were indeed unique—even exceptional—but they are unlikely to learn it from their teachers. At the very moment when a Museum of the American Revolution becomes necessary, it becomes unattainable.

For this reason the fact that there is a Museum of the American Revolution at all is something of a miracle. It certainly would not have happened had there not already been an embryonic one waiting in the wings. The embryo was the collection of W. Herbert Burk, an Episcopalian minister who in 1903 conceived the idea of building a national memorial at Valley Forge. He collected artifacts and relics, but after his death in 1933 the idea languished. In 2005, a philanthropist named H. F. (Gerry) Lenfest became interested in the project and bought land at Valley Forge to build the museum. But Lenfest ran up against intense local opposition and was forced in the end to swap his site with the National Park Service. In exchange he received a prime site in Philadelphia, a few blocks from Independence Hall. It is here, in its Robert A. M. Stern–designed neocolonial building, that the Museum of the American Revolution opened in April 2017 (fig. 21.1).

Stern clearly studied the surviving eighteenth-century buildings of the neighborhood, with their palette of red brick and white marble trim, and general air of restraint and sobriety. The

FIGURE 21.1 Like Ritter & Shay's United States Customs House (1932) looming above it, Robert A. M. Stern's Museum of the American Revolution is a freewheeling abstraction of the brick and marble Georgian architecture of its historic neighborhood.

same stately order continues into the interior, with its lucid sequence of space: a generous entrance lobby under a shallow dome, a broad passage leading to an elegant curved stair, and a lofty top-lighted public hall granting access to the exhibition galleries. Reviews have generally been unfavorable, and have ignored the dignity, logic, and good proportions of the interior; the *Philadelphia Inquirer* called the museum "a retro-monster." (Perhaps Stern was being punished for the crime of having designed George W. Bush's presidential library.)

If the building is refreshingly, even startlingly, traditional, so is the exhibition strategy. Recently it has become fashionable for museums to abjure an orderly system of knowledge. Any such system, according to those fed on Michel Foucault, is arbitrary and serves merely to project power. But the American Revolution was a contest of power, and the museum presents that contest in lucid chronological order in 18 major and minor spaces, arranged in linear sequence. One passes through the unruly pre-revolutionary 1760s, the first feints and skirmishes, the Declaration of Independence, and so forth, all the way to the ratifying of the Constitution. The story is told with a lively mixture of items, new and old.

The core is formed by Rev. Burk's venerable collection of wooden canteens, exquisitely carved powder horns, and an arsenal's worth of swords, rifles, and blunderbusses. These are supplemented with a variety of interactive computer displays, historical tableaux, a simulated battlefield theater, and even a full-size replica of a schooner. The visual and aural density is staggering. The interactive computer displays are to be expected, but not the historical tableaus. At one time these were the chief attraction of any local historical society—those mannequins in loose-fitting period clothes, settling into moth-eaten ruin. Most have long since been put out of their misery and replaced by video monitors, but they have now been out of fashion long enough to seem fresh and daring. The museum has seven of these tableaus in which life-size figures dramatize historic scenes. In one, an outraged mob drags New York's public statue of King George III from its pedestal; in another an exasperated George Washington breaks up a snowball fight among rowdy Continental soldiers. The figures are uncannily realistic, as well they should be, having been cast from life by "a specialty sculptural fabrication studio which has created performance pieces for Lady Gaga among other high-profile projects."

At times these crowd-pleasing but rather hokey tableaux distract from the quiet artifacts nearby that in their way are wonderful. A printed loyalty oath shows the citizens of Exeter, New Hampshire, renouncing their allegiance to King George III, and thereby risking their lives, in thirteen careful signatures. One recalls from youth the horrors of the intolerable Stamp Act, and here are actual documents, to which is affixed a surprisingly innocuous seal. And for readers of the naval novelist Patrick O'Brian, here is a display of bar and chain shot, those gruesome iron projectiles that were meant to spin like a whirligig and mangle both a ship's rigging and human limbs.

By far the most moving and unexpected display is of George Washington's own Battle Tent. Visitors enter a comfortably intimate theater to watch a film about the Continental Army's winter at Valley Forge. At first one thinks that the film itself is the point but then, wondrously, the screen lifts and one is looking at the real thing. Because the linen fabric is fragile and degrades under light, it can only be shown sparingly, and in subdued light, all of which only adds to the solemnity and reverence. This is precisely what a museum should do: show us objects in a way that helps us see them more clearly, and through them see history more clearly.

Any museum that displays real objects enjoys one great advantage over its digital competitors, and that is that it offers *physical reality*, not virtual reality. Real objects made of real materials, all showing the poignant marks of time and use, of neglect and care. These engage the viewer at a visceral level, and in a way that no pixilated object can ever do. But in order to do this a clear distinction must be drawn between the real and the pretend, and here the museum falters.

Committed to creating "immersive environments and interactive experiences that will bring to life the personal stories of the founding generation," the Museum of the American Revolution found itself limited by its traditional collection of revolutionary relics piously gathered a century ago. On the one hand, this has spared it from the political tendentiousness that has come to figure in a large way in history exhibitions during the past generation. There is none of the reductive emphasis on identity politics, for example, that disfigured the nearby recreation of Washington's house in Philadelphia (discussed elsewhere in this book). But such a collection of family keepsakes is ill-suited to presenting the broad social history to which the museum aspires, and so the curators have chosen to fill them out with a mass of prints and paintings. With a half dozen or so exceptions, all of these are facsimiles, photo-reproductions of works of art that hang elsewhere. This is acceptable museum practice only when the facsimiles are identified as such, and I counted only two instances where the image was clearly identified as a reproduction. Most egregious is the image that introduces the entire exhibition, Allan Ramsay's famous portrait of King George III from the National Portrait Gallery in London. This is not so much a facsimile as a parody; it bulges into our world, as if trying diligently to become sculpture and failing in the process.

The danger is not that a viewer might take these facsimiles for the genuine artifact but the other way round. The unacknowledged jumbling of the real and the imitation tends to downgrade all the objects into generic visual material, ultimately indistinguishable from the undifferentiated images that flicker across our computer screens. Here the museum squanders its one great chance to reach someone who has grown up in today's world of easily accessible, and therefore devalued, imagery.

As is now customary, a consistent effort is made to give voice to those excluded in traditional accounts of the revolution, particularly slaves, Indians, and women. There is one astonishingly blatant, almost comical, example of what might be called museological pay-to-play. To complete the underfunded building project, the Oneida Nation gave $10 million, for which reason the main public space is named Oneida Hall. As a further quid pro quo, the exhibition includes a gallery in which we see Oneida Indians debating whether or not they should ally themselves with the British or the Americans. Here is none of the spirit of skeptical revisionism that we see elsewhere in the museum, as in the analysis of the 1770 Boston Massacre engraving, which is dissected as a study in manipulative propaganda. Instead, the contribution of the Oneida Nation is celebrated without irony or cynicism. Such episodes of feel-good inclusiveness, some of them rather spurious, led Andrew Ferguson of the *Weekly Standard* to propose that what the museum displays "isn't really history at all."

It is true that the casual visitor will not leave the museum with anything like a truly coherent sense of the Revolutionary War, a sense of the convulsive dynamics of its strategic chessboard—the initial British policy of cutting the colonies in half by seizing control of the Hudson (which one must know in order to grasp the enormity of Benedict Arnold's treason) or the subsequent pivot to a "southern strategy," centered on the capture of Charleston and Savannah. Rather than focusing on decisions and their consequences, the military history on display here is impressionistic and episodic. Typical is the chamber in which the Battle of Brandywine is simulated, where visitors stand behind a low stone wall and face the British bayonet charge, advancing through billows of gunpowder smoke, wafting into the room at the key moment. This is designed to convey what historical events *felt* like, rather than what they *meant*.

And yet despite it all—despite the occasional intrusions of ideology, the hokey tableaus, and the cloyingly simplified language of the labels—the museum somehow works. The impressionistic sense it gives of the Revolutionary War is essentially true. The war was a long arduous slog that sprawled confusingly over land and sea; loyalties were tested and communities cruelly divided; the calculus of attrition and willpower came to count for more than strategic brilliance. The long linear sequence of galleries, experienced on foot, makes this physically palpable in a way that no book or film can.

Perhaps the Revolution will never again loom as large as it once did because of photography. The Civil War lives for us in the mournful faces photographed by Matthew Brady in a way that the stately heroes painted by John Trumbull never will. This is why Civil War films will continue to be made regularly, and Revolutionary War films infrequently. It is for this reason that the Museum of the American Revolution closes with one of the most brilliantly conceived codas imaginable—a gallery of photographs of those alive at the time of the Revolution. Fifty-six years separated the treaty that ended the war and the invention of photography, so all of the faces shown here are old and wizened. But we find ourselves in a room of people like us, and realize with a shock that up until now we have known the faces of the

American Revolution only as neoclassical platitudes. The exhibition could not possibly end on a more satisfying, more haunting note.

It is sometimes said that it is impossible to make a genuine anti-war movie if one shows scenes of battle. Battles are intrinsically gripping, and one is inevitably pulled into the cathartic excitement. And so while the Museum of the American Revolution may represent "an attempt to de-sacralize the Revolution," as Edward Rothstein of the *Wall Street Journal* put it, its sheer sweep and scope project a heroic significance that no niggling wall text can undermine. In the end, the kitsch and the political correctness cancel each other out, and the visitor who sits in darkness contemplating Washington's brave linen pavilion at Valley Forge will find the Revolution to be surprisingly, and movingly, re-sacralized.

CHAPTER 22

My Favorite Building

Pembroke, Bryn Mawr College

■ THERE ARE SO MANY counterfeits of Pembroke, the superb and stately dormitory that defines the Bryn Mawr College campus, that it is not easy to see it with fresh eyes. But one should try. It is the best of its kind, the very best of those turreted whimsies that make up the Collegiate Gothic movement. Its countless replicas always have an air of amiable preposterousness about them—crenellated and castellated against the pillagers who never come—but Pembroke is flawless (fig. 22.1). Like a great piece of music, it has an ineffable fitness and rightness to its parts that defies all analysis. I am no closer to understanding it than I was when I first saw it, over forty years ago.

In 2005 the *Chronicle of Higher Education* asked a few dozen college professors and administrators to write a short piece on "My Favorite Building." It is possible that I was the only respondent who answered honestly. For, by some remarkable coincidence, almost every one of the others decided that the newest building on their campus was their "favorite." But I chose one at Bryn Mawr College, which I did not attend, although two of my sisters did, and where I taught for a few years.

FIGURE 22.1 Pembroke Hall, according to Bryn Mawr's first president M. Carey Thomas, "brought the new Bryn Mawr Gothic to its perfect flower." She was proud of the "artistically uneven way in which the stones were built into the wall," many of them laid by the architects with their own hand. Pembroke stretches 475 feet and boasts the "first collegiate entrance tower" in America.

Pembroke is the work of Cope and Stewardson, America's finest college architects, who drew its plans in 1892. They later reprised its theme at the University of Pennsylvania, at Princeton, and at Washington University—but never so successfully or so simply. Perhaps the reason is light. The typical college dormitory is a barrack, camouflaged with a few sprigs of ivy: bedrooms and bathrooms wrapped around a stingy and badly lighted corridor. But Pembroke is as bright as a greenhouse. The wings that seem from the outside to meander aimlessly are in fact purposefully broken, and turn at right angles so that each run of corridor terminates in a bay window and a generous view. These wings stiffen and become more formal as they converge at the centerpiece of the building: a massive arched gateway that serves as the base for the lofty dining hall above, its corners graced by four octagonal towers. In the evening, the high mullioned windows of this dining hall catch the sunset, and for half an hour it is a shimmering cage of stone and light.

Alas, the building has suffered at the hands of its unkind ren-
ovators—who sliced up the gracious flow of the public spaces
and removed the transom lights above the doorways that once
drenched its halls with sunlight. But Pembroke is exquisite even
with its scars. And like every great building, it has a mystery at
its heart: how is it that a style that emerged in the monastery—
marked by introverted quadrangles and sheltered cloisters—
should serve so aptly and so splendidly as an image for the modern
woman of the progressive era?

Acknowledgments

I first realized that a building could be an interesting object when I began third grade at Mayfair Elementary School. My former school was a pre-World War I citadel, whose oak handrails were polished every September to greet returning pupils with the warm scent of beeswax. But Mayfair had no earthy fragrance; it was sleek and modern, and it had an endless corridor that meandered fascinatingly from classroom to auditorium to cafeteria. I explored its every nook with my new companions, Brian Mandel, Doris Hackl, and Victor Thompson; without even knowing it, they were the first to open up for me the architecture of Philadelphia. I thank them.

Three gifted teachers gave shape and order to my childhood fascination: David B. Brownlee, my loyal *Doktorvater*, who asked for the essay on the Bryn Mawr dormitory that is the oldest in this book; George E. Thomas, who led that first memorable walking tour; James F. O'Gorman, whose monograph on Furness I toted through Europe for a year. I thank you all.

Philadelphia's architectural mafia (may I use that phrase?) represents the best of the city, its generosity, unpretentiousness, and uncomplicated matter-of-factness. I am especially grateful to Jeffrey A. Cohen, Emily Cooperman, Nathaniel Kahn, Barbara Miller Lane, Elizabeth Milroy, Maria Thompson, and Aaron

FIGURE 23.1 Baader-Young-Schultze's Mayfair Elementary School (1949) brought International Style planning to Philadelphia's booming postwar Northeast. To the left are the cafeteria and gym, to the right are the classrooms, and between them the principal's offices gently curve so as to keep 600 or 700 pupils constantly in sight.

Wunsch. Two brilliant archivists, Bruce Laverty of the Athenaeum of Philadelphia and William Whitaker, of the Architectural Archives of the University of Pennsylvania, went far beyond the call of duty.

I also gratefully acknowledge the counsel, friendship, and selfless assistance of Hannah Bennett, David Brigham, Jack Coyne, Allen Crawford, David G. DeLong, James M. Duffin, Kenneth Finkel, Kathleen A. Foster, Theodore Green, Greta Greenberger, Harrison Haas, Katherine Haas, Kenneth Hafertepe, Wayne Hammond, Aaron Helfand, Sandy Isenstadt, Robert Jackall, A. Robert Jaeger, David Leatherbarrow, Daniel McCoubrey, Michael Merrill, Charles Savage, Mike Seneca, Sandra Tatman,

Michele Taillon Taylor, Nicola Tenaglia, Marianna Thomas, Radclyffe F. Thompson, and Sarah Weatherwax.

The essays in this book were summoned into existence by my cheerfully ruthless editors: William Ayres, Sarah Hardesty Bray, Eric Gibson, Kenneth Hafertepe, John Dixon Hunt, Roger Kimball, Neal Kozodoy, James Panero, John Podhoretz, Ian Quimby, and Warren Ashworth. Please accept my heartfelt thanks.

Finally, I owe a very special debt to Peter Conn, former director of the Athenaeum of Philadelphia, who graciously named me the Athenaeum's Writer in Residence, under the auspices of which I completed this book.

Notes

Chapter 1 ■ William Penn's Modest Utopia

1. Published in French translation as *De l'Esprit des villes: Nancy et l'Europe urbaine au siècle des Lumières 1720–1770* (Nancy: Musée des Beaux Arts, 2005), 295–97.

2. Michael J. Lewis, *City of Refuge* (Princeton: Princeton University Press, 2016).

3. David Hackett Fischer, *Albion's Seed* (New York: Oxford University Press, 1989), 417–603.

4. Walter Klinefelter, "Surveyor General Thomas Holme's 'Map of the Improved Part of the Province of Pennsilvania,'" *Winterthur Portfolio* 6 (1970): 41–74; Anthony N. B. Garvan, "Proprietary Philadelphia as Artifact," in *The Historian and the City*, ed. O. Handlin and J. Burchard (Cambridge, MA: Harvard University Press, 1963), 177–201.

5. Letter from William Penn to William Crispin, John Bezar, and Nathaniel Allen, dated September 30, 1681; see Edwin Wolf, *Philadelphia: Portrait of an American City* (Harrisburg: Stackpole Books, 1975).

6. Fischer, *Albion's Seed*, 537.

7. Benjamin Franklin, *Proposals Relating to the Education of Youth in Pensilvania* (Philadelphia, 1749).

8. Equally pragmatic were Franklin's recommendations on student health, and he gives us, although in capsule form, what must be America's first collegiate athletic program: "to keep them in Health, and to strengthen and render active their Bodies, they [should] be frequently exercis'd in Running, Leaping, Wrestling, and Swimming &c."

9. In order to establish priority over Princeton, the University of Pennsylvania claims (and on laughably spurious grounds) a founding date of 1740.

10. George B. Tatum, *Philadelphia Georgian* (Middletown, CT: Wesleyan University Press, 1976).

11. "To the Publisher of the Gazette," *Pennsylvania Gazette*, December 13, 1733, 1.

12. Bruce Laverty, Michele Taillon Taylor, and Michael J. Lewis, *Monument to Philanthropy: The Design and Building of Girard College* (Philadelphia: Girard College, 1998).

13. Richard J. Webster, *Philadelphia Preserved* (Philadelphia: Temple University Press, 1976). Norman B. Johnston, *Eastern State Penitentiary: Crucible of Good Intentions* (Philadelphia: Philadelphia Museum of Art, 1994).

14. Thomas S. Kirkbride, *On the Construction, Organization, and General Arrangement of Hospitals for the Insane* (Philadelphia: Lindsay & Blakiston, 1854).

15. Samuel Sloan, *The Model Architect*, vol. 1 (Philadelphia: E. S. Jones & Co., 1852), 73.

Chapter 2 ■ William Birch and the Culture of Architecture in Philadelphia

1. So important was the Bank of the United States to Birch's concept that he discarded his first engraving and redrew the building. Emily T. Cooperman and Lea Carson Sherk, *William Birch: Picturing the American Scene* (Philadelphia: University of Pennsylvania Press, 2011), 77.

2. One exception, which looks at the continued role of builder-architects in Philadelphia, is Donna Rilling, *Making Houses, Crafting Capitalism: Builders in Philadelphia, 1790–1850* (Philadelphia: University of Pennsylvania Press, 2001).

3. Such restrictions could not be enforced in a growing and increasingly cosmopolitan city, and in the Carpenters' Company celebrated rule book of 1786, its members lamented that "strangers from time to time arrived from other countries, where many elegancies were in use; thus such improvements were made in the mode of building, as made it necessary to alter the method of measuring." *The Rules of Work of the Carpenters' Company of the City and County of Philadelphia* (Philadelphia, 1786).

4. Charles E. Peterson, *Robert Smith: Architect, Builder, Patriot 1722–1777* (Philadelphia: Athenaeum of Philadelphia, 2000).

5. The assignment of the Bank of the United States to Samuel Blodgett is contested. See Matthew Baigell, "James Hoban and the First Bank of the United States," *Journal of the Society of Architectural Historians* 28, no. 2 (May 1969): 135–36.

6. "Theatre," *Dunlap's Daily American Advertiser*, May 6, 1793.

7. "Joseph Bowes, Architect," *General Advertiser*, October 16, 1794.

8. *Philadelphia Gazette and Universal Daily Advertiser*, November 24, 1795, 2 (also December 8, 1795, 2). One wishes for an example of his "descriptive drawing exhibiting grass, arable, and woodlands; hills, mountains, and the course of rivers; the whole expressed in species of perspective, called bird eye views."

9. *Pennsylvania Packet*, October 15, 1794.

10. *General Advertiser*, January 7, 1794 and April 19, 1794.

11. *General Advertiser*, October 20, 1794; *Federal Gazette*, May 22, 1795. Occasionally Falize was spelled Fallise (*General Advertiser*, April 28 and May 12, 1794).

12. *Pennsylvania Gazette and Universal Daily Advertiser*, November 24, 1795, 2. Birch would have known Repton's work, although his emigration kept him from seeing Repton's landscape at Kenwood, the estate of Lord Mansfield, Birch's important patron. See Emily T. Cooperman, introduction to *The Country Seats of the United States*, by William Russell Birch (Philadelphia: University of Pennsylvania Press, 2009), 7.

13. Beatrice B. Garvan, "Walnut Street Jail," in *Philadelphia: Three Centuries of American Art*, ed. Darrel Sewell (Philadelphia: Philadelphia Museum of Art, 1976), 123–25.

14. For an overview of the teaching of architectural drawing, see Jeffrey A. Cohen, "Early American Architectural Drawing and Philadelphia, 1730–1860," in *Drawing Toward Building: Philadelphia Architectural Graphics, 1732–1986*, ed. James F. O'Gorman (Philadelphia: University of Pennsylvania Press, 1986), 15–32.

15. *Pennsylvania Packet*, October 15, 1794. Bowes not only taught aspiring builders but addressed himself to "ladies and gentlemen who wish to study these noble Arts." Falize and Lacour had a more comprehensive curriculum: "Drawing, architecture, figures, landscapes, animals, flowers, ornaments, plans and charts." *General Advertiser*, April 19, 1794.

16. *Pennsylvania Packet*, December 21, 1796; *Aurora General Advertiser*, December 11, 1797. Hallet first taught "in the Academy, north Fourth, near Mulberry street," and in the second year moved to "Messrs. Demilliers & Delvanne's Drawing and Painting Academy," at 83 South Front Street. Who took his classes? We do not have a single name. Could he have taught John Dorsey, who emerged as a competent enough architect a few years later, and without any apparent education?

17. "Architectural Evening Drawing School," *Philadelphia Gazette and Universal Daily Advertiser*, November 21, 1797. Minifee's letter was dated 16 November.

18. Falize and Lacour's drawing academy was an exception.

19. *Aurora General Advertiser*, October 13, 1807. Hills's advertisement was unusual in not soliciting architectural but drafting commissions: "Gentlemen, builders and mechanics, that wish to have good and accurate drawings from their rough work, machinery or model, may have them executed by applying as above, at the N. W. corner of 8th and Walnut street."

20. Hills is known primarily as the maker of the great 1796 map of Philadelphia. See Peter J. Parker, "John Hills," in Sewell, *Philadelphia*, 215–17. He arrived in Philadelphia in 1785 as a "land surveyor, architect, and draftsman," having just made "a general survey of the forfeited estates in the southern district of the New-York government" for Aaron Burr. He claimed to possess "the works of the principal architects in English and French" (*Pennsylvania Evening Herald and the American Monitor*, July 29, 1786). During his first year in Philadelphia he formed the partnership of Messrs. Vancouver & Hills, who listed their skills as "Land surveying, architecture, drafting, leveling, and drawing sections of rivers, or of given tracts of country" (*Pennsylvania Mercury and Universal Advertiser*, September 2, 1785). Exactly who Vancouver was is unclear, although the *Pennsylvania Packet and Daily Advertiser* described him as "lately arrived from Europe" on January 11, 1785. No building by Hills has been identified, although his site plan and elevation of the Edward Burd house Ormiston (1798) suggests he may have been the architect.

21. *The Constitution of the Columbianum, or American Academy of the Fine Arts* (Philadelphia, 1795). William Birch's son Thomas made his public debut at the Columbian exhibition with a number of views of Philadelphia. See Richard Anthony Lewis, "Interesting Particulars and Melancholy Occurrences: Thomas Birch's Representation of the Shipping Trade, 1799–1850" (Diss., Northwestern University, 1994), 25–27, 49.

22. None of these drawings appear to have survived. The Columbianum itself was short-lived, and the plan for Joseph Bowes to give quarterly lectures on architecture seems not to have been realized.

23. *Philadelphia Gazette and Universal Daily Advertiser*, November 24, 1795; Dictionary of Irish Architects 1720–1940 (website), http://www.dia.ie.

24. *Philadelphia Gazette and Universal Daily Advertiser*, February 18, 1796.

25. "Joseph Bowes, Architect," *General Advertiser*, October 16, 1794. The advertisement placed by Bowes was a masterpiece of grammatical larceny. After referring to Adam, Bowes wrote that "in order to show in some measure the opportunities he has had in the service of this great man, he will here take the liberty of inserting a few of the most remarkable Designs made by him the last year," an ambitious sentence construction that leaves open whether the pronoun *him* refers to Bowes or Adam.

As it happened, the dozen buildings that are listed, including the Edinburgh University, the Trader's Hall in Glasgow, and "one Public Square in London, now building," were all by Adam, but a casual Philadelphia reader could easily draw the conclusion that these were works of Bowes.

26. *Pennsylvania Packet*, October 15, 1794; *Federal Gazette*, November 16, 1797.

27. *Pennsylvania Packet*, January 4, 1773. Williams's advertisement implies but does not state that he trained with the Adam brothers, although his account of their "new, bold, light and elegant taste" shows that he grasped its essence.

28. These were the competitions for the Library Company of Philadelphia (1789); the Philadelphia Dancing Assembly, the United States Capitol, and the President's House (all in 1792); and for an "elegant and convenient hotel or inn" to be built in the District of Columbia (1793). Little is known about this last competition, other than that Samuel Blodgett organized it—requesting elevation drawings, sections, and estimates, and offering a premium of $100 for the best design—and that James Hoban won it. See *General Advertiser*, March 1, 1793; *Dunlap's American Daily Advertiser*, March 4, 1793.

29. "To the gentlemen builders in Market-street," *Pennsylvania Evening Herald and the American Monitor*, May 17, 1786.

30. The three houses stood on the east side of Second Street, between Walnut and Spruce streets, and were built between 1768 and 1776 for Samuel Powel; they have long since been demolished and no image has been found. Peterson, *Robert Smith*, 107–12, 127–28.

31. There is no other architectural discussion in the *Pennsylvania Evening Herald* during these years that could shed light on the author. On the other hand, there are a good many advertisements by the architect and mapmaker John Hills, who would have known Bath (for he certainly boasted of his maps of Europe), but this is too slender to count as evidence.

32. Thomas Carstairs (ca. 1759–1830) was a Scottish "architect and House-carpenter" from Largo, County Fife, who came to Philadelphia in 1784, having recently worked in London. *Pennsylvania Packet*, February 5, 1784.

33. *Philadelphia Gazette and Universal Daily Advertiser*, December 25, 1797.

34. The review is one of the strongest bits of evidence that Blodgett was indeed the designer of the Bank, since it boasts that "The architect was an American and born in the state of Massachusetts" [actually New Hampshire, which was then part of Massachusetts]. Other candidates have been proposed, including Christopher Myers and James Hoban. See Baigell, "James Hoban," 135–36.

35. Especially awkward is the way that Birch cut the windows straight across his curved bays, rather than radiating outwards from the center of the curve so as to maximize the view. Cooperman and Sherk, *William Birch*, 80–82.

36. Manasseh Cutler to Mrs. [Mary Cutler] Torrey, 22 November 1803, in *Life, Journals and Correspondence of Rev. Manasseh Cutler, LL. D.*, vol. 2, ed. William Parker Cutler and Julia Perkins Cutler (Cincinnati: Robert Clarke and Company, 1888), 144.

37. So Hamilton's gardener, Bernard McMahon, wrote in the *American Gardener's Calendar* (1806).

38. Sterling Boyd's 1966 dissertation proposes the Adam Brothers as the authors of the design, largely on the basis of comparisons; Richard Betts rejects the Adamses and proposes young John Soane instead; Timothy Long rejects both of them, suggesting that John Plaw, who sent designs for the Bingham House on Third Street did so for Woodlands as well—which is plausible, as both Hamilton and Bingham were in England at the same time. But, as Roger Moss has noted, Bingham did not patronize Plaw exclusively, and he also solicited designs from the English architect Henry Ashley Keeble. See Roger W. Moss, *Historic Houses of Philadelphia* (Philadelphia: University of Pennsylvania Press, 1998), 78; and Birch, *Country Seats*, 68.

39. This is the suggestion of the Historic American Buildings Survey report on the house, PA-1125, as expanded in 2002.

40. C. Ford Peatross, ed., *Capital Drawings: Architectural Drawings for Washington, D.C., from the Library of Congress* (Baltimore: Johns Hopkins University Press, 2005), 66. Also see Saul K. Padover, ed., *Thomas Jefferson and the National Capital* (Washington: US GPO, 1946), 184–86.

41. Jeffrey A. Cohen, "Building a Discipline: Early Institutional Settings for Architectural Education in Philadelphia, 1804–1890," *Journal of the Society of Architectural Historians* 53, no. 2 (June 1994): 139–83.

Chapter 3 ■ The Author of Fairmount Park

1. The indispensable account is Elizabeth Milroy, *The Grid and the River: Philadelphia's Green Places, 1682–1876* (University Park: Penn State University Press, 2016). Also see Theo B. White, *Fairmount, Philadelphia's Park: A History* (Philadelphia: Art Alliance Press, 1975).

2. George B. Tatum, *Penn's Great Town* (Philadelphia: University of Pennsylvania Press, 1961), 88, 183. Also see Tatum, "The Origins of Fairmount Park," *Antiques* 82 (November 1962): 502–7.

3. Richard Webster, "Fairmount Park, Philadelphia," in *Philadelphia: Three Centuries of American Art*, ed. Darrel Sewell (Philadelphia: Philadelphia Museum of Art, 1976), 363.

4. White, *Fairmount Park*, 16–19.

5. David Schuyler, *The New Urban Landscape: The Redefinition of City Form in Nineteenth-Century America* (Baltimore: Johns Hopkins University Press, 1986), 105.

6. Charles S. Keyser, *Fairmount Park: Sketches of Its Scenery, Waters, and History* (Philadelphia, 1871).

7. See Frederick Graff, Jr., *Plan of Lemon Hill and Sedgley Park, Fair Mount and Adjoining Property*, lithograph by L. N. Rosenthal (Philadelphia, 1851).

8. The purchase of Sedgeley was secured partly by private funds, in which James H. Castle played a crucial organizing role. See James H. Castle correspondence, 1854–58, Society Small Collection, Historical Society of Pennsylvania.

9. The competition for "Plans for the Improvement of Fair Mount Park" was organized by the Committee on Public Property. Announcements were published in late 1858 in the major Philadelphia papers. See, e.g., *Philadelphia Press*, November 27, 1858.

10. "I visited Lemon Hill with Messrs. Keyser and Castle last tu[e]sday . . . I never saw any ground with half the advantages for a park—None of the London Parks can compare with it. . . . Hunting Park is tame—tame—No expense can ever make it like Lemon Hill as it is now—" William Saunders to J. J. Smith, n.d, James H. Castle correspondence, 1854–58. For Saunders, see the biographical entry in *Pioneers of American Landscape Design*, ed. Charles A. Birnbaum and Robin S. Karson (New York: McGraw Hill, 2000).

11. "The New Fairmount Park, Philadelphia, and Its History," *Gardener's Monthly* 1 (1859): 57–58.

12. Aaron Wunsch, "Sidney, James C.," in *Pioneers of American Landscape Design*, 360–63.

13. These include *Map of the Circuit of Ten Miles around the City of Philadelphia* (Philadelphia, 1847); *Map of the City of Philadelphia* (Philadelphia, 1849); *Sidney's Map of Twelve Miles around New-York* (Philadelphia, 1849); *Map of Dutchess County, New-York, from Original Surveys* (Philadelphia, 1850); *Map of Westchester County, New York* (White Plains, NY, and Philadelphia, 1851); and *Map of the Vicinity of Albany and Troy* (1851).

14. See Wunsch, "Sidney, James C.," 360–63. Sidney maintained his connections to New York, where he designed the Evergreen Cemetery in Salem (1859) and Woodlawn Cemetery in the Bronx (1863)

15. Sidney typically worked in partnership. From 1850 to 1855 he had worked with one James P. Neff; after Adams (1858–60) came Frederick C. Merry (1860–65), and then in 1875, a Mr. Kirby (probably Henry P. Kirby). Sidney's important works include the Episcopal Church of the Covenant, Philadelphia (1861, demolished), Wyoming Valley House in Wilkes-Barre, Pennsylvania (1863, demolished), the Germantown Savings Bank (1868). He was admitted to the Philadelphia Chapter of the American Institute of Architects on May 9, 1870.

16. J. C. Sidney, *American Cottage and Villa Architecture* (New York, 1850).

17. This was the Hollingsworth School on Broad Street, and its ventilation system was developed further by Frank Furness and George Hewitt in their 1875 addition to the Deaf and Dumb Asylum. See "Model School Edifice," *Evening Telegraph*, November 3, 1866, 3. Also see Edward Shippen, "Improvements in the Plans and Construction of Public School-Houses in Philadelphia," in *Report of the Commissioner of Education, with Circulars and Documents, United States*. Department of Education (Washington, DC, Government Printing Office, 1868), 601–11.

18. These women were trained at the School of Industrial Design for Women. "Our Working Women," *Philadelphia Times*, March 15, 1875, 3.

19. Sidney & Adams, *Description of Plan for the Improvement of Fairmount Park* (Philadelphia, 1859), 3, 6.

20. "The New Fairmount Park," *Gardener's Monthly*, 58.

21. Sidney & Adams, *Improvement of Fairmount Park*, 4.

22. J. C. Sidney, "Thatch," *Gardener's Monthly* 1 (1859): 35–36.

23. "The road along the river's edge will be a beautiful feature, and will be tunnelled through two large rocks and pass under the Girard Avenue Bridge. A piece of ground is set apart for the Zoological Society, which has just been formed." Ibid. It seems as if the excavation through the rocks was not undertaken until about 1870, although most of the other work was completed several years earlier. Perhaps it was difficult to procure the necessary explosives during the Civil War.

24. Of course rhetoric and reality often diverge, and it has been suggested that Central Park was far more exclusive than Olmsted's democratic language implied. For a revisionist interpretation of Central Park, see Roy Rosenzweig and Elizabeth Blackmar, *The Park and the People: A History of Central Park* (Ithaca, NY: Cornell University Press, 1992).

25. Sidney & Adams estimated that landscaping and road-building work would cost fifty-eight thousand dollars, earning them nearly three thousand dollars. Sidney & Adams, *Improvement of Fairmount Park*, 22; *Fourth Annual Message of Alexander Henry, Mayor of the City of Philadelphia* (Philadelphia, 1862), 84.

26. Sidney & Adams, *Improvement of Fairmount Park*; "The New Fairmount Park," *Gardener's Monthly*, 57; *Philadelphia Daily Evening Bulletin*, April 9, 1859. It is also reproduced in Schuyler, *New Urban Landscape*, 104.

27. Strickland Kneass, the Philadelphia engineer, was also involved; see George Francis Train, *Observations on Street Railways*, 2nd edition (London: Sampson Low, Son, & co., 1860), 43–44. George Francis Train, *Report of the Banquet, Given . . . to Inaugurate the Opening of the First Street Railway in Europe* (Liverpool: Lee, Nightingale, & co., 1860) 46, 89. While in Philadelphia, Palles was associated with architect John Fraser, with whom he worked on the Gray's Ferry Street Railroad in 1858; in 1860 he returned to Britain. See "Palles, Andrew Christopher," Dictionary of Irish Architects 1720–1940 (website), http://www.dia.ie.

28. Webster, "Fairmount Park, Philadelphia," 363.

29. "Improvement of Fairmount Park," *Public Ledger*, November 21, 1859, 1.

30. "Fairmount Park, Philadelphia," *Gardener's Monthly* 2 (1860): 278.

31. The boathouse served a public function and was equipped with a surgeon's room "with a galvanic battery . . . for restoring animation" to drowning victims. "The Philadelphia Skating Club and Humane Society," *Public Ledger*, November 24, 1860, 1. Also see Thomas Beischer, "Control and Competition: The Architecture of Boathouse Row," *Pennsylvania Magazine of History and Biography* 130 (2006): 299–329.

32. *Fourth Annual Message of Alexander Henry*, 84.

33. Sidney George Fisher, *A Philadelphia Perspective: The Diary of Sidney George Fisher Covering the Years 1834–1871*, ed. Nicholas Wainwright (Philadelphia: Historical Society of Pennsylvania, 1967), 409.

34. Sidney & Merry received a fee of twenty-five dollars for their work in 1861, that is, 5 percent of five hundred dollars. *Ordinances and Joint Resolutions of the Select and Common Councils, of the Consolidated City of Philadelphia* (Philadelphia, 1854–75), 1862, no. 51, items 8, 38 (March 17, 1862), 73, 76.

35. *Ordinances and Joint Resolutions*, 1862, no. 51, item 8 (March 17, 1862), 73.

36. *Fifth Annual Message of Alexander Henry, Mayor of the City of Philadelphia* (Philadelphia, 1863), 93–94.

37. *Journal of Select Council, 1863*, vol. 2 (Philadelphia, 1864), Appendix, 20–21.

38. *Journal of Select Council, 1863*, vol. 2, 35; *Ordinances and Joint Resolutions*, 1863, no. 261 (September 18, 1863), 269; Sidney & Adams, *Improvement of Fairmount Park*, 3; quoted in Schuyler, *New Urban Landscape*, 103.

39. *Journal of Select Council*, vol. 2 (Philadelphia 1865), Appendix, Ordinance no. 168, 282.

40. *Appendix to the Journal of City Council, 1866*, vol. 1 (Philadelphia, 1866), 458–63.

41. For the membership of the original commission, see the appendix in White, *Fairmount Park*, 123.

42. *Annual Report of the Chief Engineer of the Water Department of the City of Philadelphia* (Philadelphia, 1867), 36. One of these rustic shelters is illustrated in George E. Thomas, Michael J. Lewis, and Jeffrey A. Cohen, *Frank Furness: The Complete Works* (New York: Princeton Architectural Press, 1991), 148.

43. Frederick Law Olmsted to the Chairman of the Committee on Plans of the Park Commission of Philadelphia, December 4, 1867, in *The Papers of Frederick Law Olmsted*, vol. 6, *The Years of Olmsted, Vaux & Company, 1865–1874*, ed. David Schuyler and Jane Turner Censer (Baltimore: Johns Hopkins University Press, 1992), 233. The commission also consulted landscape architect R. Morris Copeland.

44. Philadelphia's Quaker founders, not requiring university-educated clergymen, were late in founding institutions of higher learning and concentrated instead on the practical and useful arts; this is the insight of David Hackett Fischer, *Albion's Seed: Four British Folkways in America* (New York: Oxford University Press, 1989).

45. Olmsted letter (December 4, 1867), quoted in White, *Fairmount Park*, 40.

46. Ibid.

47. White, *Fairmount Park*, 43.

48. Schwarzmann (1846–91) was a Bavarian architect, son of the decorative painter Joseph Anton Schwarzmann. He attended military school, then studied architecture, perhaps at the royal academy in Munich (although this remains unclear). He emigrated to Philadelphia at the age of twenty-two, and spent most of the next decade connected with Fairmount Park. His principal work was the design of the 1876 Centennial Exhibition grounds and many of the important pavilions. In 1878 he left Philadelphia for New York where he retired in 1886, already unable to work from the syphilis that killed him in 1891. It was an ignominious end after such a promising start. See John Maass, *The Glorious Enterprise: The Centennial Exhibition of 1876 and H. J. Schwarzmann, Architect-in-Chief* (Watkins Glen, NY: American Life Foundation, 1973).

49. White, *Fairmount Park*, 43.

50. Sidney reflected this tradition. An especially adept horticulturalist, he was chosen by the city of Philadelphia in 1860 to select those species of trees to be planted. Assessing such variables as durability, susceptibility to

pests, and amount of foliage, he recommended different types of trees for public streets and for squares. For public streets he advocated horse chestnut, English sycamore, sugar maple, Norway maple, red maple, American linden, tulip poplar, etc.; for public squares it was horse chestnut, sugar maple, tulip poplar, Kentucky coffeetree, *Magnolia acuminata*, *M. conspicua*, *M. tripetala*, deciduous cypress, European beech, American beech, purple beech, white birch, sassafras, dogwood, red maple, European ash, five types of oak, and so forth. See "Shade Trees in Cities," *Gardener's Monthly* 2 (1860): 348.

Chapter 4 ■ "Facts and Things, Not Words and Signs": The Idea of Girard College

1. Thomas Cope, *Diary of Thomas Cope*; entry dated July 19, 1843, 394.

2. *Hazard's Register of Pennsylvania*, June 23, 1832, 394.

3. *Hazard's Register of Pennsylvania*, January 12, 1833, 27; also see Agnes Addison Gilchrist, "List of Competition Drawings," *Journal of the Society of Architectural Historians* 14, no. 2 (May 1955): 26.

4. Five competitors had recently submitted designs for the 1829 competition for the New York State House: Ithiel Town, Isaiah Rogers, Edward Shaw, John Kutts, and Robert Higham. See Mary Raddant Tomlan, ed., *A Neat Plain Modern Stile: Philip Hooker and his Contemporaries, 1796–1836*, catalogue of an exhibition at Hamilton College (Amherst, MA: University of Massachusetts Press, 1993), 264.

5. *National Gazette*, February 13, 1833, 2.

6. *Journal of the Forty-fourth House of Representatives of the Commonwealth of Pennsylvania*, vol. 2 (1833–34), 439. The subsequent premiums paid are taken from this volume.

7. The Free Library of Philadelphia owns an undated German-language manuscript by Egelmann: "Commonplace Book of Formulas Along with Notes on Sundry Mechanical and Scientific Topics," item no. frkm098000.

8. Israel's design was prepared with "others," as his letter indicated. He himself enjoyed close Philadelphia contacts, as the nephew of the wealthy local merchant Lewis Waln, with whom he was in touch. Israel sent Waln detailed accounts of the new factories at Lowell, which suggests just how rapidly the industrial advances in America were already being disseminated, in an age still without telegraph or any real railroads. See Israel's submission letter in the Thomas U. Walter papers, Athenaeum of Philadelphia.

9. St. Michael's stood only eleven years, falling victim to the anti-Catholic riots of May 1844. Sadly, we know virtually nothing about Crisp, whose Philadelphia office was at Fourth and Tamany Streets.

10. The key source is the Pennsylvania state legislature's 1842 investigation into whether or not the city of Philadelphia had violated Girard's

will by authorizing T. U. Walter's design. *Journal of the Fifty-second House of Representatives of the Commonwealth of Pennsylvania*, vol. 2 (1842), part 2, pp. 652–96; for Stewart see 677.

11. When testifying in February 1842, Stewart said he had been practicing as an architect for "five or six years." Among his important works were St. Luke's Church, Philadelphia (1839–40), and St. Paul's Church, Richmond, Virginia (1843–45), both fluent Greek Revival essays.

12. Stewart's contribution lay in the subdivision of one ground story room, two on the second story, and also the insertion of a system of ventilation shafts. *Twelfth Annual Report of the Board of Directors of the Girard College for Orphans* (Philadelphia, 1860), 10.

13. His later projects included a house for President John Tyler and alterations to the wall of Christ Church's burying ground cemetery so that the public could see the grave of Benjamin Franklin. See "Presidents and Poor People," *Council Grove Republican*, August 3, 1844, 3; and "Unveiling the Tomb of Franklin—the Work Commenced," *Fort Scott Bulletin*, October 14, 1858, 3.

14. David S. Rotenstein, "John Skirving: From Bricklayer to Men of Progress" (2010), https://blog.historian4hire.net/2010/09/12/skirving/ #_edn5

15. "George Strickland," *National Gazette*, March 19, 1833, 2.

16. James F. O'Gorman, *Edward Shaw of Boston: Antebellum Architect and Author—An Introduction* (Philadelphia: American Philosophical Society Press, 2016).

17. Shaw gives a disarming account of his education: "In answer to many inquiries respecting my practical knowledge as a Carpenter and Joiner, I would say, that I served in that capacity twenty years,—fourteen of which as a contractor and builder, drawing all of my own plans and designs for private and public dwellings costing from five hundred to forty thousand dollars each; since which time I have spent fifteen years in the theoretical practice and science of Architectural Drawings and Plans, both ancient and modern." See Edward Shaw, *The Modern Architect: or, Every Carpenter his Own Master* (Boston: Dayton & Wentworth, 1855), 3.

18. Ibid., 60.

19. Other than an address at 63 South 2nd Street, Philadelphia, where he stayed only briefly, nothing is known of Chaumer's career.

20. "Obituary," *Cambria Freeman* (Ebensburg, PA), December 12, 1867, 4.

21. Rodrigue subsequently moved to New York where he designed several Catholic churches and served as partner to James Renwick on the design of St. Patrick's. See Jeffrey A. Cohen, "William Rodrigue, Design for Wills Hospital, Philadelphia," in *Drawing Toward Building*, ed. James F. O'Gorman (Philadelphia: University of Pennsylvania Press, 1986), 75–76.

22. "John Kutts, Architect," *Public Ledger,* December 5, 1849, 2.

23. After spending six years in New York working with Richard Upjohn and Minard Lafever, Kutts moved to Philadelphia in 1841 in order to offer "lessons in drawing, adapted to practical builders"; "John Kutts, Architect," *Public Ledger,* November 23, 1841, 3. He was later associated with Philadelphia architect William L. Johnston, upon whose death in 1849, Kutts went into business on his own "as a theatrical architect, which comprises composition, order, harmony and good taste, and as a practical Architect in design of construction and execution, and as a general Draughtsman in the various branches, including machinery." See "John Kutts, Architect," *Public Ledger,* December 5, 1849, 2.

24. Cyrus Wetherill (or Wetherell) practiced from about 1814 to ca. 1835 in Orleans County, New York. Robert Higham is known from his entry in the Albany State House competition in 1829. See Talbot Hamlin, *Greek Revival Architecture in America* (New York: Oxford University Press, 1944), 270; also see Tomlan, *Philip Hooker,* 264.

25. James H. Dakin was only briefly in the partnership. See Amelia Peck, ed., *Alexander Jackson Davis, American Architect, 1803–1892,* catalogue of an exhibition at the Metropolitan Museum of Art (New York: Rizzoli, 1992), 127.

26. Isaac Holden, submission letter, Girard college competition, Thomas U. Walter papers, Athenaeum of Philadelphia.

27. Around 1838 Holden returned to England and established an office with his brother in Manchester.

28. Agnes Addison Gilchrist, *William Strickland, Architect and Engineer, 1788–1854* (New York: Da Capo, 1969).

29. "I made a tour through the Eastern States, and visited the various Colleges that are located in that section of country;—I then visited the University of Virginia, a seminary of great reputation, located near Charlottesville. After a thorough examination of these Colleges, and all the departments of learning connected therewith; I applied myself to the formation of the design . . ." Specifications submitted by T. U. Walter (December 31, 1831), Athenaeum of Philadelphia. There is no independent corroboration of Walter's trip, but there is also no reason to doubt him.

30. *Journal of the Fifty-second House of Representatives of the Commonwealth of Pennsylvania,* vol. 2 (1842), part 2, p. 671.

31. John Cresson Trautwine (1810–83) was with Strickland from 1828 to 1830. Although he occasionally worked as an architect, he was primarily an engineer; he is the author of the *Civil Engineer's Pocket Book* (1871). Michele Taillon Taylor, "Building for Democracy: Girard College, Educational and Architectural Ideology" (Diss., University of Pennsylvania, 1997).

32. The history and date of Strickland's second design remains unclear. The drawings themselves are undated, and it is not certain if they represent an alternative proposal submitted in January, 1833, during the judging, or in the subsequent two months. But because of its similarity to Walter's own revised design, with its full peristyle, it seems likely that it dates from the period between April 5 and 23, during which time Biddle worked with Walter on the revision of his drawings.

Chapter 5 ■ The Strange Germanness of the Academy of Music

1. The principal history of the Academy of Music is John Francis Marion, *Within These Walls: A History of the Academy of Music* (Philadelphia: The Academy of Music, 1984). Also see Richard Webster, "American Academy of Music," in *Philadelphia: Three Centuries of American Art,* ed. Darrel Sewell (Philadelphia: Philadelphia Museum of Art, 1976), 347–49.

2. Steve Cohen, "Unfairly Maligned: The Glory Years and Beyond for Philadelphia's Academy of Music" (2003), *Totaltheater.com.*

3. In addition to the seven competitors listed above, three other names are known: John T. Mahoney and John Carver, both of Philadelphia, and John M. Trimble, the New York architect of Laura Keene's Theatre (1856). At least two Baltimore architects and two other New Yorkers are known to have competed.

4. The three most important are the Morris L. Hallowell Stores, Market Street below Fourth, and Drexel's Banking House, 22 South Third Street, both of 1853; and Bailey's Jewelry Store, 817 Chestnut Street, of 1858.

5. *Mitteilungen des Deutschen Pionier-Vereins von Philadelphia*, vol. 3 (Philadelphia: Deutscher Pionier-Verein, 1907), 29.

6. Ibid.

7. The project is described in LeBrun and Runge, "To the Building Committee and Directors of the American Academy of Music" (Philadelphia, December 15, 1854), copy in the Archives of the Academy of Music.

8. "Directors' Minutes, June 20, 1853–June 2, 1871," vol. 1, March 9, 1855, 27; July 5, 1855, 32–34. Archives of the Academy of Music.

9. "History and Description of the Opera House, or American Academy of Music in Philadelphia" (Philadelphia, G. Andre & Co, [1857?]), copy at the Archives of the Academy of Music.

10. Nicholas B. Wainwright, ed., *A Philadelphia Perspective: The Diary of Sidney George Fisher Covering the Years 1834–1871* (Philadelphia: Historical Society of Pennsylvania, 1967), 268.

11. Aber was soll mir Geistes- und Körperkraft.
Was das Wissen, die Künstlermeisterschaft,
Wenn die Zimmerleut' und die Maurerpoliere
Die Architekten hier sind und die Ingeniere.

Was soll mein Geschmack unter Hottentotten,
Die den Krautsalat lieben of Mister Button,
Der die Fastenprezel wohl gar am End'
Noch einführt als kunstgerecht Ornament.

Mitteilungen des Deutschen Pionier-Vereins (1907), 31.

Chapter 6 ■ "Silent, Weird, Beautiful": The Making of Philadelphia City Hall

1. "Local Affairs. Proceedings in Councils," *Public Ledger*, October 21, 1859, 1; also see the revival of the project in "Local Affairs. Proceedings in Councils," *Public Ledger*, October 12, 1860, 1.

2. The committee included Mayor Alexander M. Henry, judges George Stroud, Joseph Allison, Oswald Thompson, and James Ludlow, and councilmen Theodore Cuyler and Charles B. Trego. It was bipartisan and included both Republican and Democrat party members.

3. Strickland Kneass, the city engineer, would inspect the drawings but presumably from only a technical point of view.

4. Lea's furious campaign against the Penn Square site is documented in the Henry Charles Lea papers; Van Pelt rare books; University of Pennsylvania, MS. 111; Box 164. An uncollated set of notes, presumably by a member of the building committee, is in the collection of the Historical Society of Pennsylvania.

5. "The Commissioners for the erection of New County Buildings," *Public Ledger*, July 7, 1860, 1.

6. "Meeting of the Commissioners of Public Buildings," *Public Ledger*, September 22, 1860, 1.

7. Besides John McArthur, the bidders were John Ketcham, Richard Dobbins, Henry Phillipi, Edwin Bender, and Killigore & Hudder. "The Public Buildings—Meeting of the Commissioners," *Public Ledger*, September 20, 1860, 1.

8. "Competition for the Public Building," *Public Ledger* (September 20, 1860), 1.

9. *Ketcham vs. City, Affidavits & c., Common Council Documents* (Philadelphia: King and Baird, 1860); Lea papers, Box 164, Folder 2081. Ketcham filed his suit on October 1, 1860; one week later a second suit was filed by Henry Phillipi, another defeated bidder.

10. "A New Truss Girder," *Journal of the Franklin Institute* (January 1849): 16–17.

11. This helps to explain why the city's architects decided at last to call a truce and organize in order to regulate competition and to promote fraternal relations. On February 8, 1861, twenty architects met in the office of John Notman and formed the Pennsylvania Institute of Architects, which did not survive the dislocations of the Civil War, in which two of its members were killed.

12. "Mr. Neal's Remarks on the Public Buildings Legislation," *Public Ledger,* October 11, 1860, 1; "Local Affairs. Proceedings in Councils," *Public Ledger,* October 12, 1860, 1.

13. Henry Charles Lea reiterated this point several months later in "The Public Buildings—their Cost," *Public Ledger,* February 13, 1861. He showed how Philadelphia's most prominent builder, John Rice, habitually underestimated costs to win a contract and then indulged freely in over-runs. Among his examples: the U. S. Capitol extension; the city's four market houses upon consolidation, where Rice received a five percent commission, giving him a motive to inflate costs. He also cited his faulty estimates as president of the Continental Hotel Company, for which McArthur served as architect.

14. *Journal of Select Council,* December 20, 1866, 341.

15. "City Intelligence," *Philadelphia Inquirer,* February 19, 1869, 2.

16. Richard Morris Hunt asked for a copy of the competition program but did not submit. One newspaper listed James H. Windrim as a competitor but this seems a mistake.

17. LeBrun learned to value German professionalism while designing the Academy of Music in partnership with Gustav Runge. When Paul Schulze emigrated to New York, he first worked for Charles Gildemeister, a childhood friend of Runge. Presumably Runge put them in touch.

18. The letter to John Rice, the builder of the Capitol extension, is cryptic but the meaning is unmistakable: "Your favor of yesterday is rec'd. I note what you say about LeBrun and the city buildings. I hope he will not succeed in his contemptible effort at detraction—it is an old trick of his." Letter, T. U. Walter to John Rice, September 26, 1860, Walter Papers, Athenaeum of Philadelphia.

19. "The Public Buildings," *Evening Telegraph,* September 7, 1869, 8.

20. T. U. Walter diary, January 1, 1870. Athenaeum of Philadelphia.

21. Edward Sculley Bradley, *Henry Charles Lea* (Philadelphia: University of Pennsylvania Press, 1931), 184–85.

22. Letter, Matthew Carey Lea, April 5, 1869 (Pennsylvania State Archives).

23. Lea's petition also argued that the Independence Square site offered "opportunities for architectural effect." Perhaps this is why his signers included a number of Philadelphia's leading architects, including the firm of Fraser, Furness and Hewitt (signed in Fraser's hand), James P. Sims, and T. Roney Williamson (Pennsylvania State Archives).

24. Minutes, Pennsylvania Academy of Natural Sciences, May 10, 1867; November 8, 1867. William Ruschenberger and Samuel Vaughn Merrick discussed the possibility of producing the site in May; the Committee to Procure Plans, which included Ruschenberger, William L. Vaux, Jeanes, Robert Bridges and Frederick Graff, was formally charged with procuring a site on Penn Square. Also see Michael P. McCarthy, "Traditions in Conflict: The Philadelphia City Hall Site Controversy," *Pennsylvania History* 57, no. 4 (October 1990): 309–10.

25. The petition from the Academy of Natural Sciences to the state legislature, asking for the northwest corner of the Penn Square site, was submitted on February 4, 1869; it survives in the Pennsylvania State Archives, Harrisburg. Second Annual Report, Academy of Natural Sciences (Philadelphia, 1869).

26. Henry M. Phillips was born in Philadelphia and in 1856 was elected to congress from Pennsylvania as a Democrat; he served one term. Mr. Phillips was a trustee of Jefferson medical college, a member of the board of park commissioners, and a director of the Philadelphia Academy of Music. See *Appleton's Encyclopedia.*

27. *Obituary Record of Graduates of Yale University Deceased during the Academical year ending in June, 1904* (New Haven, 1904), 311–12. Perkins was a lifelong Presbyterian and Freemason.

28. T. U. Walter diaries. Athenaeum of Philadelphia.

29. Minutes, Philadelphia Chapter of the A.I.A. Athenaeum of Philadelphia.

30. "The Intersection," *Philadelphia Inquirer*, March 1, 1871, 4.

31. "The Public Buildings," *Philadelphia Inquirer*, March 4, 1871, 3.

32. The crucial document is Lea's personal copy of *Broad Street, Penn Square and the Park* (1871), with annotations by Thomas Webster describing the history of the movement to abolish the Public Buildings Commission. There charges that the legislative committee solicited a $3,000 bribe (later reduced to $1,500) to eliminate the commission. Webster argued that this was the first intra-party reform movement in Philadelphia, and that it was the origin of political reform movement in Philadelphia in general. MS. 111 (Lea Papers); Box 164, Folder 2101.

33. Lea Papers, Box 164, Folder 2098. "Mass Meeting," *Philadelphia Inquirer*, March 18, 1872, 2.

34. *Public Ledger*, March 8, 1870. NB: can this be 1871?

35. "Penn Squares," *Philadelphia Inquirer*, August 19, 1871, 3.

36. "The Public Buildings," *Philadelphia Inquirer*, April 18, 1872, 2.

37. "At Last!," *Philadelphia Inquirer*, April 18, 1872, 4.

38. See McArthur's obituary in *Building* 7, no 15 (October 8, 1887): 118.

39. Walt Whitman, *Specimen Days & Collect* (New York: Dover, 1995), 138.

40. "Kipling in This City," *Philadelphia Times*, July 8, 1890, 3.

Chapter 7 ▪ The Carpenter: Owen Biddle

1. Owen Biddle, *The Young Carpenter's Assistant; or, A System of Architecture, Adapted to the Style of Building in the United States* (Philadelphia, 1805), 3. Biddle does not mention Asher Benjamin in his book, and seems to have been completely unaware of him: "Nothing on Architecture has heretofore appeared in this country, where the field for improvement in every useful art and science is, perhaps, more extensive, than in any other. Why there has not, appears to me [a] matter of surprise, whilst we have amoung us men of talents, fully acquainted with the subject, some of whom are also men of leisure: perhaps they have not viewed the subject in the same light, or given to it the same degree of importance that I have."

2. The house stood on what is today the 500 block of Delancey Street. See "Will be Sold at Public Vendue," *Aurora General Advertiser*, October 20, 1801. For Biddle's real estate ventures, see Conor Lucey, "Owen Biddle and Philadelphia's Real Estate Market, 1798–1806," *Journal of the Society of Architectural Historians* 75, no. 1 (March 2016): 25–47.

3. Jeffrey A. Cohen, "Arch Street Meeting House," in *Drawing Toward Building*, ed. James F. O'Gorman (Philadelphia: University of Pennsylvania Press, 1986), 49–50.

4. Ibid.

5. *Statistical Account of the Schuylkill Permanent Bridge* (Philadelphia: privately printed, 1807), 22.

6. Ibid., 30. Peters also noted that the roof of the cover required 110,000 shingles, each 3 ½ feet long.

7. Ibid., 44. Biddle published the bridge in the *Literary Magazine and American Register* (October, 1805); see George B. Tatum, *Penn's Great Town* (Philadelphia: University of Pennsylvania Press, 1961), 164–65.

8. "Pennsylvania Academy of the Fine Arts," *Portfolio* 1, no. 6 (June 1809): 461–64; Cohen, "John Dorsey," *Drawing Toward Building*, 39–41.

9. Biddle is generally credited with designing the cover but Peters' account makes it clear it was a collaborative process. Traquair "assisted to

delineate" the cover while Biddle "made additions to the design." *Statistical Account*, 24.

10. Peters provides detailed instructions for the making and applying of the paint in the *Statistical Account*, 30–33.

11. Tatum, *Penn's Great Town*, 56.

12. Cited in Jeffrey A. Cohen, "Building a Discipline: Early Institutional Settings for Architectural Education in Philadelphia, 1804–1890," *Journal of the Society of Architectural Historians* 53, no. 2 (June 1994): 140.

13. "Proposals for Printing by Subscription, *The Young Carpenter's Assistant*," *Aurora General Advertiser*, February 8, 1805, 4.

14. Biddle, *Young Carpenter's Assistant*, 3.

15. Ibid., 27.

16. Ibid., 34.

17. Ibid., 28.

18. Also offered was "A new carpenter's workshop and benches, situated on a lot of ground in Orange street, running from Seventh to Eighth streets, between Walnut and Spruce streets." See "Sales of Furniture," *Aurora General Advertiser*, June 16, 1806, 3.

19. For example, the roof trusses shown on Biddle's plate 24 closely match those on plates 6 and 7 of the Carpenters' Company book.

20. One must say first *original* architectural book, since a version of Abraham Swan's *The British Architect* was already published in Philadelphia in 1775. When a revised edition of the rulebook was published in 1805, Biddle himself drew some of the new plates.

21. Plate 22, for example, a design for "a fine open newel stairway," comes from William Halfpenny's *The Art of Sound Building* (1725).

22. Cohen, "Building a Discipline," 141.

23. Biddle, *Young Carpenter's Assistant*, 56.

24. Ibid., 54–55.

25. On the other hand, Biddle argued that his overcrowded facade was intended to provide a complicated drawing assignment for his students: "In these plans it has been more my object to throw as great a variety into a small compass as was readily practicable than to give eligible plans for the builder, thereby aiming at instruction for the student, which indeed has been my object throughout this work."

26. In 1806 Asher Benjamin brought out his second book and it clearly shows the influence of Biddle. This was *The American Builder's Companion; or, a New System of Architecture particularly adapted to the present style of Building in the United States of America*, whose subtitle is a clear paraphrase of Biddle's *A System of Architecture, Adapted to the Style of Building in the United States*. His preface even cribs from Biddle. Compare Benjamin's remark that "The American Mechanic is, therefore, in purchasing Euro-

pean publications, under the necessity of paying two thirds the value of his purchase for what is of no real use to him," with Biddle's "the American student of Architecture has been taxed with the purchase of books, two thirds of the contents of which were, to him, unnecessary."

27. John Haviland, *The Builder's Assistant, containing the five orders of architecture . . . for the use of builders, carpenters, masons, plasterers, cabinet makers, and carvers* (Philadelphia: John Bioren, 1818, 1819, 1821).

28. Cohen, "Building a Discipline," 145.

29. "Hudson and Goodwin," *Hartford Courant*, February 5, 1806, 5.

Chapter 8 ■ The Namesake: Peter Angelo Nicholson

1. Peter Nicholson, *The Carpenter's New Guide* (Philadelphia: Lippincott, 1871). This was the sixteenth printing of Lippincott's 1853 edition, which was augmented with "original designs for roofs, domes, etc." by Samuel Sloan.

2. John Notman (1810–65) was born in Edinburgh and emigrated to Philadelphia in 1831. Our only source for his association with Michael Angelo Nicholson is P. A. Nicholson, who told this in late life to Notman's grandniece. Constance Greiff, *John Notman, Architect* (Philadelphia: Athenaeum of Philadelphia, 1979), 17.

3. "To Architectural Draftsmen," *Public Ledger*, March 28, 1845, 3.

4. R. A. Smith, *Philadelphia As It Is In 1852* (Philadelphia: Lindsay and Blakiston, 1852), 197.

5. "Departure of the City of Glasgow," *Public Ledger*, March 17, 1851, 2. For the rest of his life Nicholson stayed in contact with his family in Glasgow. Over half a century after his emigration, he was still vivid enough for his grandniece (the granddaughter of his sister and Alexander Thomson) to paste his obituary into the family memoir. That he exchanged architectural ideas and gossip with his brother-in-law, as Gavin Stamp and Andor Gomme have suggested, seems likely.

6. "Architectural Drawing Academy," *Public Ledger*, October 29, 1850, 1. Wadskier's presence seems to have elevated the image of Sloan's school; a year earlier it had a humbler name: see "Drawing Academy for Mechanics," *Public Ledger*, September 4, 1849, 1.

7. Without Wadskier, Sloan taught a much-reduced program of three hours instead of the original fifteen hours weekly; "Sloan's Architectural Drawing Academy," *Public Ledger*, November 3, 1851, 4.

8. T. Wadskier, "Cottage and Villa Architecture," *Sartain's Union Magazine of Literature and Art* 9, no. 6 (December 1851): 484–485; 10, no. 1 (January 1852): 78–79; 10, no. 2 (February 1852): 178–79; 10, no. 3

(March 1852): 258–59; 10, no. 4 (April 1852): 338–39; 10, no. 5 (May 1852): 420–21; 10, no. 6 (June 1852): 498–99.

9. Oliver Bradbury, *Sir John Soane's Influence on Architecture from 1791: A Continuing Legacy* (Burlington, VT: Ashgate, 2015).

10. "Architecture," *Public Ledger*, June 12, 1852, 1.

11. "Personal," *Public Ledger*, December 7, 1853, 3.

12. *Fourth Annual Review of the Commerce, Railroads, and Manufactures of Chicago*, vol. 4 (Chicago: Democratic Press Steam Heating House, 1856), 56.

13. Henry Ericsson, *Sixty Years a Builder* (Chicago: A. Kroch and Son, 1942), 125.

14. According to the *Galena Gazette* of December 25, 1857 the drawings of the Jones House were made by "Messrs. Nicholson and Wadskier," perhaps the last reference to the firm's existence.

15. "P. A. Nicholson, Architect and Superintendent," *Cairo Evening Times*, September 7, 1865, 2; also "Public Improvements," *Cairo Evening Times*, November 22, 1865, 1.

16. "Fire Escapes," *Philadelphia Inquirer*, November 2, 1881, 3; "A Fire Escape," *Proceedings of the Engineers' Club of Philadelphia* 3, no. 1 (March 1882): 50.

Chapter 9 ■ The Impresario: Edwin Forrest Durang

1. I am grateful to Bob Jaeger who in 1992 first encouraged me to write about the work of E. F. Durang.

2. Sandra L. Tatman and Roger W. Moss, *Biographical Dictionary of Philadelphia Architects, 1700–1930* (Boston, G. K. Hall, 1985), 229–34. Also see Durang's privately printed resume of his work: *Architectural Album of Edwin F. Durang & Son*. The book is undated but the buildings listed suggest 1903 or thereabouts.

3. Durang's opera houses include Simmons & Slocum's Opera House, Philadelphia (1870); Misher's Opera House, Reading (1873); The Pittston Opera house (1874); the Columbia Opera House, near Lancaster (1875); and the York Opera House (1881).

4. Practicing with Peter E. Abel, he issued at least seven lithographs under the firm name of Abel and Durang.

5. It had the novelty of being "the only Panorama ever painted which shows both sides of the River at once." "Great National Work," *Louisville Daily Courier*, June 12, 1849, 2; "Great National Work," *Daily Republic* (Washington, DC), April 11, 1850, 3.

6. "Durang, Edwin F.," in Mary Sayre Haverstock, Jeannette Mahoney Vance, and Brian L. Meggitt, eds., *Artists in Ohio, 1787–1900: A*

Biographical Dictionary (Kent, OH: Kent State University Press, 2000), 248; Joseph Earl Arrington, "Henry Lewis' Moving Panorama of the Mississippi River," *Louisiana History* 6, no. 3 (Summer 1965): 239–72.

7. "The Mirror of Our Country," *Public Ledger*, January 18, 1851, 4; "For Sale," *Baltimore Sun*, August 29, 1851, 2.

8. Durang was still in the office in 1853 when Carver drew the plans of St. John's Episcopal Church in Lancaster, Pennsylvania. See J. M. W. Geist, *A Parochial History of St. John's Episcopal Church, Lancaster, Pa.*, second edition (Lancaster, Pa. 1901), pp. 71–72.

9. Jeffrey A. Cohen, "Building a Discipline: Early Institutional Settings for Architectural Education in Philadelphia, 1804–1890," *Journal of the Society of Architectural Historians* 53, no. 2 (June 1994): 162. William Watts Hart Davis, *The History of Bucks County, Pennsylvania* (Doylestown: privately printed, 1876), 412. Davis gives Carver's birth year as 1809, not 1803 as frequently cited.

10. "J. E. Carver," *Lancaster Intelligencer*, February 27, 1849, 3.

11. John Carver and William Johnston (the same team that taught drawing at the Franklin Institute in 1838) verified the soundness of Barnum's Museum in a way that suggests they were responsible for the remodeling. "An Old Woman's Story Refuted," *Public Ledger*, June 16, 1849, 2; "Local Affairs, Another Disastrous Fire," *Public Ledger*, December 31, 1851, 2.

12. "Local Affairs," *Public Ledger*, September 5, 1857, 1.

13. For John Ellicott Carver, see Jeffrey A. Cohen, "John E. Carver," in *Drawing Toward Building*, ed. James F. O'Gorman (Philadelphia: University of Pennsylvania Press, 1986), 95–97.

14. Henry A. Sims diary, September 16, 1867. For the full context, see the article on Sims elsewhere in this book.

15. The principal sources are in the Athenaeum of Philadelphia, including the office ledger from 1859/1860 and a selection of drawings. Durang's early projects include St. Patrick's Rectory, South 21st Street; the Moravian Church, Nazareth; a house for Clement Letourneau; the Sharpless house in Chelton Hills, and rowhouses on Spruce Street and Nectarine Street. Several of his early school designs erected during the Civil War are published in Franklin D. Edmunds, *The Public Schools of the City of Philadelphia*, vol. 3, 1853–1868 (Philadelphia, 1917). His Curwen House in Villanova (1864) was published in Gertrude Z. Thomas, "Living With Antiques: Walnut Hill," *Antiques* 86 (December 1964): 707–11.

16. For John T. Mahoney (ca. 1820–64), see the list of nineteen projects in *Metropolitan Catholic Almanac and Laity's Directory, for the United*, New Series, no. 2 (Baltimore: John Murphy, 1860), 30. It is possible that Carver and Durang had already established some connections with LeB-

run and his Catholic clients before the Civil War, for Carver for a time served as superintending architect for the cathedral. See Cohen, "John E. Carver," 95.

17. He was not the only one: Joseph D. Koecker (ca. 1820–89), also Catholic, executed several projects for churches.

18. Cohen, "John E. Carver," 95.

19. "Among the Architects," *Philadelphia Inquirer,* July 17, 1872.

20. *Philadelphia Inquirer,* November 22, 1875. Police recovered the watch.

21. James F. O'Gorman, *Some Architects' Portraits in Nineteenth-Century America: Personifying the Evolving Profession* (Philadelphia: American Philosophical Society Press, 2013). Scattaglia "studied in Venice," according to the *Harrisburg Daily Independent* (August 27, 1883). He also painted, among others, the interiors of St. Charles Borromeo, the Gesu, and St. James.

22. St. Anne's replaced a small Gothic church by LeBrun; *Evening Telegraph,* July 30, 1866.

23. "Our Lady of Visitation," *Philadelphia Inquirer,* October 23, 1876, 2. The cost was $100,000.

24. "A Fine Church for Fairmount," *Philadelphia Inquirer,* October 8, 1894, 5.

25. "The New Church at Bryn Mawr," *Philadelphia Inquirer,* November 20, 1897, 10. Unlike Philadelphia's working-class parishes, which lovingly cared for their Durang interiors, this church on Philadelphia's fashionable Main Line was evidently embarrassed by it. Its interior, which was still intact into the 1980s, has been stripped ruthlessly of its original detail, leaving a blindingly white shell.

26. In order "to give better proportionate lines to spire and tower," Durang heightened the original 230-foot tower. "Repairs to St. Peter's," *Philadelphia Times,* June 2, 1895, 3

27. "Laying of the Corner-stone of the Church of St. Anne," *Evening Telegraph,* July 30, 1866, p. 3.

28. "The Italian Church," *Philadelphia Inquirer* (June 29, 1891), p. 4.

29. The blocky proportions of Napoleon LeBrun's earlier church of 1842–47 can still be detected beneath Durang's cladding of Indiana limestone. "Repairs to St. Peter's," *Philadelphia Times,* 3.

30. "E. F. Durang Dead, Daughter Weds," *Philadelphia Inquirer,* June 13, 1911, 1, 6. The newspaper incorrectly gives his age as eighty-six. The practice did not end with Durang's death; it was continued by F. Ferdinand Durang (1884–1966), who had been made a partner in Edwin F. Durang & Son in 1909.

31. If Homer could interrupt the narrative of the *Iliad* with his famous Catalogue of Ships, I can end this essay with a personal Catalogue of

Buildings by Durang. My grandmother was baptized in one (St. Mary's, Wilkes-Barre); my mother taught at one (St. John's, Pittston); her sister studied at one (Misericordia College); I attended one in college (Our Mother of Good Counsel, Bryn Mawr), graduate school (SS. James and Agatha, Philadelphia), and today (St. Patrick's, Philadelphia—its rectory and parish house); and my nephew graduated from one (St. Joseph's Prep). All were by Durang or his son.

Chapter 10 ■ Incognito at Haverford: George Senneff

1. My gratitude goes to those colleagues who shared their Senneff finds with me. Donna Rilling found the reference in the William Eyre diaries; Jeffrey A. Cohen discovered the little house on Fawn Street. Aaron Wunsch also contributed his insights on the architecture of Quaker philanthropy.

2. The Senneff family produced several house carpenters. Jacob Senneff built and sold houses in Philadelphia in the late 1790s, as Isaac Senneff did later during the 1830s. The family relationship remains to be explored.

3. This was recalled by fellow pupil William Eyre on the occasion of Senneff's death. See William Eyre diary, January 14, 1872; Eyre Family Papers, 1840–1912, RG5/179, Friends Historical Library of Swarthmore College. Series 3: William Eyre Diaries, 1840–1880.

4. Deeds show that Senneff bought the parcel in 1823 and sold it with the completed house in 1834.

5. For Senneff's wayward apprentice, see "Master and Apprentice," *Hazard's Register of Pennsylvania*, February 4, 1832, 78.

6. "Obituary.—George Senneff—one of Philadelphia's Oldest Architects and Builders," *Philadelphia Inquirer*, January 15, 1872, 5. In 1829 Senneff was made an officer of the Carpenters' Company. We do not know when he taught architecture there. He is not mentioned in the principal source for the Carpenters' Company drawing school, Jeffrey A. Cohen, "Building a Discipline: Early Institutional Settings for Architectural Education in Philadelphia, 1804–1890," *Journal of the Society of Architectural Historians* 53, no. 2 (1994).

7. At Wills Eye Hospital, Senneff again competed against Philadelphia's leading architects: John Haviland, Thomas Ustick Walter, John C. Trautwine, and William Rodrigue. *Hazard's Register of Pennsylvania*, January 7, 1832, 4. He received a premium of $25.

8. It was decided that "all of the general jobbing work required previous to the commencement of the new buildings be given to George

Senneff, under the direction of the architect." Charles Lawrence, *History of the Philadelphia Almshouses and Hospitals* (Philadelphia: privately printed, 1905), 86, 111.

9. HCA.003.001, Haverford College Board of Managers minutes, vol. 1, 1833–37.

10. The members were John G. Hoskins, John Paul, Daniel B. Smith, Thomas Kimber, and Isaac Davis.

11. In fact, it cost $19,251.40. Construction began almost immediately. On April 28, 1832, the board of managers reported that it had "made the requisite contracts."

12. The image reproduced here is an engraving, not a lithograph, but this is perhaps what the college finally authorized. The artist was Oscar A. Lawson, whose original drawing is in the collection of the Academy of Natural Sciences.

13. The receipt is dated March 22, 1832 and made out to Thomas Kimber, Treasurer. Haverford College Archives, Receipt Book, 1832–34.

14. Lawrence, *Almshouses and Hospitals*, 84; Haverford Alumni Association, *A History of Haverford College for the First Sixty Years of Its Existence* (Philadelphia: Porter & Coates, 1892), 73. Cope's papers are at the Historical Society of Pennsylvania and Haverford College.

15. Within a few years, the third story was also divided into student rooms.

16. *History of Haverford College*, 106.

17. "Miscellaneous," *Hazard's Register of Pennsylvania*, July 20, 1833, 48.

18. "Obituary," *Philadelphia Inquirer*, January 15, 1872, 5. Wetherill, an influential member of Philadelphia's city council, was also on the building committee of Girard College.

19. "To Rent," *Public Ledger*, March 15, 1841, 3.

20. "Obituary," *Philadelphia Inquirer*.

21. These were the library (1863–64) by Samuel Sloan and R. Morris Smith, and Barclay Dormitory (1876–77), by Addison Hutton.

22. Among them were the Lloyd dormitories (1899–1926) and Roberts Hall (1903), both by Cope & Stewardson; Union Hall (1909), by Walter F. Price; and the Hall Chemistry Laboratory (1909–11), Morris Infirmary (1912), and Sharpless Hall (1917–18), all by Baily & Bassett.

23. These were Gummere Hall (1960–64), by Vincent Kling, and the trio of buildings known as the North Dorms (1966–68), by H2L2. I have a vivid sense of their inadequately lighted and ventilated bathrooms, of the sort which only the student worker who has cleaned them weekly could possibly know.

Chapter 11 ■ The Bibliophile: Henry A. Sims

1. Inventory of the library of Henry A. Sims, 1875, collection of author.

2. The library of T. P. Chandler is recorded in the collection of the Athenaeum of Philadelphia. For Windrim, see *Books on Architecture and the Fine Arts, including works on sculpture, paintings, furniture, decoration, iron and metal work and gardens; the library of the late John T. Windrim, Phila., Pa., to be dispersed at public sale, Nov. 6, by order of the administrators* (New York, American Art Association, Anderson Galleries, Inc., 1935); a copy is at the Library of Congress. Although many of the books listed were owned by the son of James H. Windrim, those published before about 1890 can be presumed to belong to the elder Windrim. An inventory of the library of Joseph Koecker is at the Houghton Library, Harvard University. This is the most conservative of the three, and reflects his training in the office of Thomas U. Walter.

3. "Books on Architecture," *Philadelphia Times*, November 23, 1875, 4.

4. "Local Summary," *Philadelphia Inquirer*, November 25, 1875, 5.

5. The papers of Henry A. Sims are on deposit at the National Archives of Canada, M-5480, MG, -29-B-36. These include two diaries (1863–64; 1866–68), two notebooks (1871 and 1875), and miscellaneous correspondence. A microfilm of the collection is available under RG-11, microfilm C-12801. Also see Barbara Humphries and Stephen Otto, "Henry Augustus Sims, 1832–1875," *Society for the Study of Architecture in Canada. Selected Papers* 5 (1982): 41–47; and George E. Thomas, "Henry A. Sims," in *Drawing Toward Building*, ed. James F. O'Gorman (Philadelphia: University of Pennsylvania Press, 1986); Sandra L. Tatman and Roger W. Moss, *Biographical Dictionary of Philadelphia Architects, 1730 to 1930* (Boston: G. K. Hall, 1985).

6. Even in Philadelphia, Sims continued to work in Canada and with Canadian architects. In 1869 he entered the competition for Philadelphia City Hall together with Thomas Fuller and Augustus Laver, the principal designers of the Canadian Parliament Buildings.

7. Henry A. Sims, "Gothic Architecture," a public lecture delivered in 1860. The manuscript is in the Sims papers. Quoted in Humphries and Otto, "Henry Augustus Sims," 43.

8. Sims diary, January 20, 1867.

9. H. A. Sims, "Report of the Philadelphia Chapter," *American Institute of Architects. Proceedings of the Fourth Annual Convention* (American Institute of Architects, 1871), 28–29.

10. "The Aesthetic Club," *Philadelphia Inquirer*, June 5, 1873, 2.

11. It was originally the Second Presbyterian Church; a subsequent merger produced the current name.

12. Calder carved some of the interior capitals but did not work on the exterior. He was assisted by John William Kitson, a recent English émigré.

13. Michael J. Lewis, *Frank Furness: Architecture and the Violent Mind* (New York: W. W. Norton, 2001), 93–94; Michael J. Lewis, "The Pennsylvania Academy of the Fine Arts as Building and as Idea," in *The Pennsylvania Academy of the Fine Arts: 200 Years of Excellence, 1805–2005* (Philadelphia: Pennsylvania Academy of the Fine Arts, 2005), 63–73.

14. The design was made in collaboration with his brother James Peacock Sims (1849–82), with whom he formed the partnership of H. A. & J. P. Sims in early 1872. The partnership dissolved for reasons unknown in 1874.

15. "The Centennial Buildings," *Philadelphia Inquirer*, November 4, 1873, 2.

16. "Independence Day," *Philadelphia Inquirer*, July 4, 1874, 2.

17. Henry A. Sims, Notebook, 1871. Sims Papers.

18. The church was designed in collaboration with James Peacock Sims, who seems to have been the principal designer for the adjoining school.

19. The cause of death was erysipelas. "Died," *Philadelphia Inquirer*, July 12, 1875, 5; *Intelligencer Journal* (Lancaster, PA), July 12, 1875, 1. His final year was tragic. An eight-year-old son died, causing him to withdraw from professional obligations; he apologized to the A.I.A. that he had to cut back his duties as Secretary because of "a private affliction of a very heavy character" that limited his correspondence as well as his architectural practice. *Proceedings of the Eighth Annual Convention of the American Institute of Architects, Held in New York October 14 and 15, 1874.* Report of the Secretary for Foreign Correspondence, 35–37, 39.

20. The obituary is laconic: "This partnership was dissolved not long ago, each of the brothers starting business on his own account." See "Obituary," *Philadelphia Inquirer*, July 13, 1875, 4.

21. "Bought a lot of books and drawings which an English architect named Edmunson left with him for his board." Sims diary, April 22, 1866. Edmunson is unidentified; the context implies that he had left the books as security with the landlord of Sims's boarding house in Ottawa.

22. It is possible that he designed the first wing of the Haverford country house of A. J. Cassatt, with whom Sims consulted repeatedly in 1871. After the death of Sims, the house was repeatedly worked on by Frank Furness.

23. [Henry A. Sims], "The American Institute of Architects," *Penn Monthly* 4 (1873): 499–505.

24. The minutes of the Philadelphia Chapter of the American Institute of Architects are on deposit at the Athenaeum of Philadelphia.

25. American owners of the *Architektonisches Skizzenbuch* includes Richard Morris Hunt, P. B. Wight, E. T. Potter, Henry Austin, Addison Hutton, T. P. Chandler, and Frederick Graff, Jr.

26. Sims was not the only Philadelphia architect to own volumes by Ungewitter. T. P. Chandler owned the *Vorlegeblätter für Holzarbeiten* (1860) as well as the *Lehrbuch der gotischen Konstruktionen* (1890–92). Collection of the Athenaeum of Philadelphia. For Ungewitter see Karen David-Sirocko, *Georg Gottlob Ungewitter und die malerische Neugotik* (Petersberg, 1997).

27. E. W. Godwin, *A Handbook of Floral Decoration for Churches* (1865; purchased January 31, 1868), Bruce J. Talbert, *Gothic Forms Applied to Furniture* (1867; August 31, 1868), and Maw & Company's catalogue (August 31, 1868). Among titles he borrowed were John Ruskin, *Lectures on Architecture and Painting* (1854; December 20, 1863), Ruskin, *The Two Paths* (1859; September 23, 1867), and Edward Peacock, *English Church Furniture* (1866; September 23, 1867). In January 1864 he read Edward Lacy Garbett, *Rudimentary Treatise on the Principles of Design in Architecture* (1850), although it is uncertain if he borrowed or bought it.

28. Henry A. Sims, "Architectural Fashions," *Penn Monthly* 7, no. 9 (September 1876): 700–711.

29. This photograph, along with several others from the Sims estate, was purchased and glued into an album that was donated to the University of Pennsylvania Architectural Archives by John Harbeson. It has been suggested that the photographs were purchased at the auction by T. U. Walter.

30. Sims, "Architectural Fashions."

31. Sims diary, November 4, 1867.

32. Sims diary, February 1, 1868.

33. The divided shield ("impaled") indicates that Sims was married; the tabbed bar running across the top of the shield is the brisure used by an eldest son; and the helm turned to the side indicates a commoner. I am grateful to Allen Crawford for sharing his encyclopedic knowledge of heraldry.

Appendix: The Architectural Library of H. A. Sims

Because the auction catalogue usually does not specify which edition of a book Sims owned, it has not been possible to list them in complete chronological order. They are listed here in approximate order, although for ease of comparison, works by the same author are grouped together.

ANTIQUARIAN BOOKS

Andrei Putei, *Perspectiva Pictorum et architectorum Andrea Putei e Societate Jesu.* (Rome, 1693) Bound with Leon Battista Alberti, *della Pittura, della Statua*

Domenico de Rossi, *Studio d'Architettura Civile, &c.* (Rome, 1721)

Le Fabbriche e i disegni di Andrea Palladio (Vicenza, 1796)

Andrea Palladio, *Le Terme dei Romani* (Vicenza, 1797)

Dell' architettura di M. Vitruvio Pollione (Perugia, 1802)

Francesco Milizia, *The Lives of Celebrated Architects, Ancient and Modern* (London)

ENGLISH BOOKS

Batty Langley, *Builder's Jewel* (Dublin, 1768)

George Saunders, *A Treatise on Theaters* (London, 1790)

Archibald Alison, *Essay on the Nature and Principles of Taste*

Humphrey Repton, *Landscape Gardening*

James Hall, *On Gothic Architecture* (London, 1813)

M. H. Bloxam, *Principles of Gothic Architecture*

Thomas Rickman, John Henry Parker, ed., *Gothic Architecture* (London)

John Henry Parker, *Introduction to the Study of Gothic Architecture* (London)

John Henry Parker, *Architectural Guide to the Neighborhood of Oxford* (London)

John Henry Parker, *Glossary of Architecture*, 3 vols. (Oxford)

[William Butterfield], *Instrumenta Ecclesiastica*, Ecclesiological Society (London)

Henry E. Kendall, Jr. *Designs for Schools and School Houses, Parochial and National* (London)

John Ruskin, *The Seven Lamps of Architecture*

John Ruskin, *The Stones of Venice*

John Ruskin, *The Political Economy of Art*

John Ruskin, *The Crown of Wild Olive; Work, Traffic, and War*

R. and J. A. Brandon, *Open Timber Roofs of the Middle Ages* (London)

R. and J. A. Brandon, *Analysis of Gothic Architecture* (London)

F. A. Paley, *A Manual of Gothic Architecture* (London)

F. A. Paley, *A Manual of Gothic Moldings* (London)

A. J. B. Beresford Hope, *The English Cathedral of the XIX Century* (London)

Thomas Morris, *A House for the Suburbs* (London)

Robert Kerr, *The Gentleman's House* (London, 1864)

C. J. Richardson, *The Englishman's House* (London)

Thomas H. King, *The Study-Book of Medieval Architecture and Art; being a Series of Working Drawings of the Principal Monuments of the Middle Ages* (London, 1868)

Owen Jones, *702 Monograms* (London, 1864)

J. Gwilt, *Encyclopedia of Architecture* (London, 1867)

Benjamin Ferrey, *Recollections of A. N. Welby Pugin*

W. Eden Nesfield, *Specimens of Medieval Architecture*

Richard Norman Shaw, *Architectural Sketches from the Continent* (1858)

C. L. Eastlake, *Hints on Household Taste* (London, 1868)

George Gilbert Scott, *Church Restorations*

George Gilbert Scott, *Remarks on Secular and Domestic Architecture, Present and Future* (London)

George Gilbert Scott, *Executed Examples by Sir Geo. Gilbert Scott and others*, 26 plates (London)

William Burges, *Architectural Drawings* (London, 1870)

M. A. Racinet, *Polychromatic Ornament. One hundred Plates . . .* (London, 1873)

William Fairbairn, *Cast and Wrought Iron*

ENGLISH PERIODICALS

Building News (1864–75)

The Builder (1850–1875)

The Architect. A Journal of Art, Civil Engineering, and Building (1869–75)

J. C. Loudon, *Architectural Magazine*, 5 vols. (London [1834–38])

AMERICAN BOOKS

Asher Benjamin, *Elements of Architecture*

A. J. Downing, *Country Houses*

A. J. Downing, *Landscape Gardening and Rural Architecture*

A. J. Downing, *Cottage Residences*

A. J. Downing, *Rural Essays*

Downing and Vaux, *Villas and Cottages*

Richard Upjohn, *Rural Architecture. Designs, working drawings, and specifications for a Wooden Church, and other rural structures*

O. S. Fowler, *A Home for all, or the . . . Octagon Mode of Building*

Robert Dale Owen, *Hints on Public Architecture*

Martin Field, *City Architecture*

John Bullock, *The American Cottage Builder*

Gervase Wheeler, *Homes for the People*

Gervase Wheeler, *Rural Homes*

R. G. Hatfield, *American House Carpenter*

A. J. Bicknell & Co., *Wooden and Brick Buildings, with Details, containing 160 plates*

Henry Barnard, *School Architecture*

Frank J. Scott, *The Art of Beautifying Suburban Home Grounds of Small Extent* (New York, 1870)

The New York Sketch Book of Architecture (1874)

Philadelphia Sketch Club Portfolio (1874)

GERMAN BOOKS

Byzantine Capitals, 3 6 plates (Munich)

Georg Gottlob Ungewitter, *Vorlegeblätter für Ziegel und Steinarbeiten*

L. [Ludwig] Degen, *Der Ziegel-Rohbau*

The Workshop, in 4 numbers (Hanover, Germany

Chapter 12 ■ "He was not a connoisseur": Willis Hale and the Widener Mansion

1. George E. Thomas, "Peter A. B. Widener Mansion," in *Philadelphia: Three Centuries of American Art*, ed. Darrel Sewell (Philadelphia: Philadelphia Museum of Art, 1976), 421–22.

2. Frederic A. Godcharles, ed., *Encyclopedia of Pennsylvania Biography*, 24 (New York: Lewis Historical Publishing Co., 1941), 1–5.

3. Charles R. Deacon, ed., *Biographical Album of Prominent Pennsylvanians* (Philadelphia: Biographical Publishing Co., 1890), 362–63.

4. It was Hale's misfortune that his years in Wilkes-Barre coincided with the presence of the immensely talented Bruce Price, who had married into wealthy Wilkes-Barre society and had his pick of the plum commissions. This may have prompted the disastrous farewell concert that ended Hale's musical ambitions. "Mr. Hale's Concert," *Scranton Republican*, August 27, 1875, 4.

5. *Philadelphia Inquirer*, January 29 and March 6, 1892; *Philadelphia Times*, August 20, 1896 and February 21, 1897. The *Philadelphia Record*, whose owner Hale served loyally, has not yet been digitized and yielded up what I expect will prove a great trove of puff pieces.

6. *Philadelphia Press*, September 21, 1871; Mark C. Luellen, "The Decorative Work of George Herzog, 1851–1920" (M.S. thesis, University of Pennsylvania, 1992).

7. Widener's source would have been *Artistic Houses* (New York: Appleton, 1883–84), reprinted as Arnold Lewis, James Turner, and Steven

McQuillin, *The Opulent Interiors of the Gilded Age* (Mineola, NY: Dover, 1987).

8. Earl Shinn [i.e. Edward Strahan], *Mr. Vanderbilt's House and Collection* (New York, 1883–84); "Mr. Widener's Palace," *Philadelphia Times,* August 1, 1886; "Costly Residences," *Philadelphia Record,* June 13, 1886.

9. William Taylor Blake Roberts "erected great numbers of the dwellings which have been added so profusely within recent years to the northern section of the city . . . Large numbers of these have been erected for Messrs. Widener and Elkins, the leading members of the Traction street railway syndicate, these gentlemen having purchased large tracts of land in the section of the city reached by their northward stretching lines of railway, and covered these with comfortable dwellings. The entire management of the erection of these buildings was given by them to Mr. Roberts, whose work has been so satisfactorily performed that his wealthy patrons entrusted to him the building of their palatial private residences." Charles Morris, *Makers of Philadelphia, an Historical Work Giving Sketches of the Most Eminent Citizen of Philadelphia from the Time of William Penn to the Present Day* (Philadelphia: L. R. Hamersley, 1894), 306.

10. Undated clipping from the *Philadelphia Times* (ca. late 1887–88), Herzog scrapbook. The Athenaeum of Philadelphia.

11. Undated clipping from the *Philadelphia Times,* Herzog scrapbook.

12. "Some Handsome Houses," *Philadelphia Inquirer,* September 5, 1887; "A Quaint Corner," *Philadelphia Inquirer,* November 12, 1887. The friezes were modeled by Cuthbert Studios, run by George Frank Stephens and Jesse Godley.

13. *Philadelphia Inquirer,* January 28, 1888; *Philadelphia Times,* January 29, 1888.

14. "Philadelphia in 1987," *Philadelphia Inquirer,* September 15, 1887.

15. Undated clipping from the *Philadelphia Times,* Herzog scrapbook.

16. *Catalogue of Paintings Forming the Private Collection of P. A. B. Widener, Ashbourne—Near Philadelphia 1885–1900* (Privately published, 1900; plates engraved by Goupil & Co., Paris).

17. Godcharles, *Encyclopedia of Pennsylvania Biography,* 1–5.

18. James Henry Duveen, *Collections and Recollections* (London: Jarrolds, 1937), 120.

19. "New Bank Building," *Philadelphia Times,* March 6, 1887, 4.

Chapter 14 ■ Frank Furness at Thirty: The Armory of the First City Troop

1. James F. O'Gorman, *The Architecture of Frank Furness* (Philadelphia: Philadelphia Museum of Art, 1973), 41, 94–95.

2. John Thomas Scharf and Thompson Westcott, *History of Philadelphia* (Philadelphia, 1884), 1016–17.

3. Edgar F. Smith, *Biographical Memoir of Fairman Rogers, 1833–1900* (Washington, DC: National Academy of Sciences, 1906).

4. *The Manual of Coaching* (Philadelphia: Lippincott, 1900) was edited by Horace Howard Furness, Fairman Rogers' brother-in-law and the editor of the landmark Shakespeare *Variorum*, which helps explain its unusually high literary quality.

5. So was Furness, a great lover of horses. In 1869 he built a "highly ornamented" drinking fountain for horses in Germantown at the behest of the Society for the Prevention of Cruelty to Animals. "Drinking Water Fountains," *Philadelphia Inquirer*, August 28, 1869, 2.

6. Robert McClure, *Gentleman's Stable Guide* (Philadelphia: Porter & Coates, 1870).

7. No architect is named for the parade shed in the records of the Troop, although Fairman's cousin Edward did serve on the building committee. First City Troop, Minute Book, November 6, 1862.

8. Michael J. Lewis, *Frank Furness: Architecture and the Violent Mind* (New York: W. W. Norton, 2001), 64–74.

9. The specifications required pointing "equal in quality to that in St. James' Church, Twenty-second and Walnut street," which was designed by the New York architect Emlen Littell, who used George W. Hewitt as his local superintendent. The church and the armory would use the same builders: Arthur Williams & George McNichol.

10. Five firms submitted bids on July 6, 1870; Williams & McNichol were the low bidders. Harrison T. DeSilver died on September 10, bequeathing another $10,000 to the Troop, but this was delayed by a life interest; he was among the principal benefactors, making this disastrous to the project.

11. The builders had to provide two estimates, one for the building as built and another for an all-stone front of bluestone, serpentine, and Ohio stone. Evidently the Troopers had second thoughts about a purple, green, and yellow armory (the *Philadelphia Inquirer* mistakenly describes the building in these terms on November 17, 1874, evidently working from an outdated description).

12. *Philadelphia Inquirer*, November 17, 1874.

13. So delighted, in fact, that one Trooper immediately commissioned Furness to build a house very similar to the armory. This is the Thomas Hockley House at the corner of South Twenty-first and Chancellor streets.

14. "Building in Philadelphia," *American Architect and Building News* (October 14, 1876), 335.

15. Robert M. Fogelson suggests that the national fad for medieval armories was a reaction to the labor strife of 1877 and that New York's Seventh Regiment Armory of 1879 was the first important example. See his *America's Armories: Architecture, Society and Public Order* (Cambridge, MA: Harvard University Press, 1989).

16. Lewis, *Frank Furness*, 69.

17. Ibid., 12.

18. Letter, William Henry Furness, Jr. to William Henry Furness, Sr., May 22, 1853. Private collection.

19. Letter, William Henry Furness, Jr. to William Henry Furness, Sr., May 29, 1853. Private collection.

Chapter 15 ■ Louis Kahn at Thirty: The Lenin Memorial in Leningrad

For their kind suggestions and comments I am indebted to Linda Gerstein of Haverford College, Danilo Udovički-Selb of the University of Texas at Austin, and most especially William Whitaker of the Architectural Archives of the University of Pennsylvania.

1. The project was first discussed in Michael J. Lewis, "What Louis Kahn Built," *Commentary* 93, no. 3 (March 1992): 39–43; and in *Drawn from the Source: The Travel Drawings of Louis I. Kahn*, ed. Eugene J. Johnson and Michael J. Lewis (Cambridge, MA: MIT Press, 1996), 16–18. A typed draft description of the Lenin project was found among the papers pertaining to Kahn's early life that his daughter Sue Ann Kahn donated to the University of Pennsylvania in 2000. Sue Ann Kahn Collection, The Architectural Archives, University of Pennsylvania (hereafter cited as AAUP), call no. 330 I.B.8.

2. The photograph of the lost perspective was found in a lot of periodicals recently acquired by a dealer in Russia, according to Ars Libri Ltd., Boston, which offered it for sale in 2006. *Ars Libri*, cat. 137 (2006), 34.

3. *Louis I. Kahn: In the Realm of Architecture*, ed. David B. Brownlee and David G. De Long (New York: Rizzoli, 1991).

4. Although the papers of Kahn's firm were given to the University of Pennsylvania following his death, his personal files relating to the ARG remained in the collection of his widow, Esther Kahn. Following her death in 1996, they were donated to Penn by their daughter Sue Ann Kahn. They include an undated draft of the ARG's founding manifesto as well as a comprehensive list of its projects, dated December 19, 1933. AAUP, call no. 330 I.B.

5. "Outline of the Principles of the Society for the Advancement of Architecture," n.d. AAUP, call no. 330.I.B.8. This rough draft, with its

corrections and marginalia, seems to have been the work of Kahn. Certainly its portentous opening suggests his later metaphysical language: "Architecture should be the visual resultant of the manifold cooperations of thought, social relations, biological activities, and cosmic backgrounds of a civilization." (The line was subsequently marked for deletion.)

6. An undated list names fourteen ARG members besides Kahn, many of them former graduates of the University of Pennsylvania's School of Architecture: Dominique Berninger, Urban Anthony Bowman ('32), J. Robert Buffler ('25), Willis Humphrey Church ('28), George R. Copeland, Hyman Cunin ('24), Leon Gould, Milton Bennett Medary III, Howell B. Pennell, Herman Polss, Joseph Rovner ('25), Henry Bryan Stevens ('31), and Anthony J. Schreiber. AAUP, call no. 330 I.B.8. Also see *Book of the School, Department of Architecture, University of Pennsylvania, 1874–1934* (Philadelphia: University of Pennsylvania Press, 1934).

7. "Competition for Lenin Mounment [sic] Announced," *Economic Review of the Soviet Union* 7, no. 9 (May 1932): 216.

8. Brownlee and De Long, *Louis I. Kahn*, 25ff.

9. Only one Soviet entry has so far come to light: Kazimir Malevich's ensemble of Suprematist skyscrapers, surmounted by a statue of Lenin. See Danilo Udovički-Selb, "Between Modernism and Socialist Realism: Soviet Architectural Culture under Stalin's Revolution from Above, 1928–1938," *Journal of the Society of Architectural Historians* 68, no. 4 (December 2009): 466–95.

10. A study of Zorach's design is in the collection of the Smithsonian American Art Museum (1970.65.206).

11. "Lenin Memorial," *Architectural Forum* 61, no. 6 (December 1934), sup. 35.

12. Cunin, a childhood friend of Kahn, was an eager follower of German events and brought the ARG Bauhaus publications, which he translated for them. Esther Kahn, interview with author, September 29, 1995.

13. This was conventional reinforced concrete beam and slab construction for the raised arms, while the tower was a structural steel frame, for which six hundred tons of steel were estimated.

14. Sabatini (1898–1985) studied at the Pennsylvania Academy of the Fine Arts, and his work includes the doors of the N. W. Ayer Building on Washington Square.

15. The typescript is addressed in pencil to the "Leningrad C.P.A. Secretary." AAUP, call no. 330 I.B. 10.

16. Kahn visited his childhood friend Norman Rice, who was the first American to work in Le Corbusier's office. Rice maintained that Kahn had no great interest in Le Corbusier's work at the time. Norman Rice, interview with author, March 21, 1983.

17. Dietrich Neumann, *The Architecture of the Night: The Illuminated Building* (Munich: Prestel, 2002).

18. Robert Reiss, "Air Castles Rise in 'Clinic,'" *Philadelphia Record*, May 14, 1934, sect. 2, p. 1.

19. Amy Knight, *Who Killed Kirov?* (New York: Hill and Wang, 1999).

20. See "Lenin Memorial." The competition entries, though unpremiated, do not seem to have been ignored. Zorach charged that Boris Iofan's winning design for the Palace of the Soviets plagiarized his Lenin project. See "Sculptor Charges Soviet Stole Idea," *New York Times*, March 8, 1934, Books, 21; also see "Art: Soviet Palace," *Time*, March 19, 1934.

21. Kahn might have seen the project by George S. Koyl, who returned to teach at the University of Pennsylvania in 1932. Michael J. Lewis, "George S. Koyl," in *Drawing Toward Building*, ed. James F. O'Gorman (Philadelphia: University of Pennsylvania Press, 1986), 184–85. Waterfront memorials were quite popular during the 1910s, including the 1910 Fulton Memorial competition, won by Harold Van Buren Magonigle, and the 1913 Paris Prize competition for the tip of Manhattan, won by the Philadelphia architect Grant Simon. See John F. Harbeson, *The Study of Architectural Design: With Special Reference to the Program of the Beaux-Arts Institute of Design* (New York: Pencil Points Press Inc., 1926), figs. 170, 171, 288, 364.

22. Louis I. Kahn, "Monumentality," in *New Architecture and City Planning*, ed. Paul Zucker (New York: Philosophical Library, 1944), 577–88.

23. *Coming to Light: The Louis I. Kahn Monument to Franklin D. Roosevelt in New York City* (New York: Cooper Union School of Architecture, 2005).

24. Peter S. Reed, "Philadelphia Urban Design," in Brownlee and De Long, *Louis I. Kahn*, 304–13.

Chapter 16 ■ Frank Furness, Perpetual Motion, and "The Captain's Trousers"

1. This essay was inspired by James F. O'Gorman, Hyman Myers, and George E. Thomas, who began the great and still ongoing hunt for a photograph of the Bloomfield Moore house forty-six years ago.

2. Louis H. Sullivan, *Autobiography of an Idea* (New York: American Institute of Architects, 1924), 190–91.

3. Albert Kelsey, an architect who knew both Furness and Sullivan, confirmed in 1924 that the Bloomfield Moore house was indeed the "flower by the roadside." "Men and Things," *Philadelphia Evening Bulletin*, April 18, 1924, 8.

4. "The present front of Ohio freestone is to be removed and a new front of Indiana limestone substituted." The new owner was Francis T. S. Darley. See "Among the Builders," *Philadelphia Inquirer*, July 1, 1895, 4.

5. "Johnson Art Moved," *Philadelphia Inquirer*, June 17, 1933.

6. These photographs also served as the basis for the set of *Ball of Fire*, the classic Gary Cooper–Barbara Stanwyck movie.

7. "Mr. Moore's Library," *Wilmington News Journal* (Delaware), July 24, 1878, 4.

8. "Moore, Mrs. Clara Jessup," in Frances E. Willard and Mary A. Livermore, eds., *A Woman of the Century . . . Leading American Women in All Walks of Life* (Buffalo, Chicago, and New York: Charles Wells Moulton, 1893), 515–16.

9. "Keely of Motor Fame is Dead," *Philadelphia Times*, November 19, 1898, 1–2.

10. "Mrs. Moore's Son Says She's Insane," *Philadelphia Times*, December 15, 1895, 12.

11. "New Publications. Mrs. Bloomfield Moore's Social Ethics and Social Duties," *Philadelphia Inquirer*, November 28, 1892, 5.

12. Mrs. H. O. Ward, *Social Ethics and Society Duties: Thorough Education of Girls for Wives and Mothers and for Professions* (Boston: Estes and Lauriat, 1892), 240–42.

13. The firm of Fraser, Furness & Hewitt dissolved on September 1, 1871 and by December of that year Furness had already secured the Bloomfield Moore commission. It appears in a list of projects in hand in a Furness sketchbook, where it is annotated as costing $40,000 and earning a fee of $2,000.

14. Letter of recommendation by General S. V. Benét in support of John Fraser's application to serve as Supervising Architect of the Treasury, March 7, 1877. Benét's letter is one of several by prominent Philadelphians in support of Fraser, all speaking highly of his practical skills. National Archives, Record Group 56, Series 209, Box 12, Recommendations of Division of Appointments, Application for Appointments, Heads of Treasury Offices, 1830–1910.

15. *Exercises at the Meeting of the First Congregational Unitarian Society, January 12, 1875: Together with the Discourse Delivered by Rev. W. H. Furness, Sunday, Jan. 10, 1875, on the Occasion of the Fiftieth Anniversary of his Ordination, January 12, 1825* (Philadelphia: Sherman & Co., 1875), 4–6.

16. The house of Robert and Lucy H. Hooper, previously unknown to Furness scholars, stood at 1502 Locust Street. The architects were Fraser, Furness & Hewitt but when the house was sold some three years later, the sales advertisements made a point of mentioning both the architectural firm as well as the specific contribution of Furness in decorating the

interior. "For Sale, No. 1502 Locust Street," *Philadelphia Inquirer*, March 7, 1873, 8; "Important Sale," *Philadelphia Inquirer*, March 24, 1873, 3.

17. For a reconstruction of the floor plan, see George E. Thomas, Jeffrey A. Cohen, and Michael J. Lewis, *Frank Furness: The Complete Works* (New York: Princeton Architectural Press, 1991), 168–69.

18. Like Brimmer's house, the facade of Moore's house involved detailed stone-cutting. Furness's masons were Atkinson & Mylhertz, the same expert stone carvers who created the facade of the Pennsylvania Academy of the Fine Arts. See letter, Atkinson & Mylhertz to Fairman Rogers, April 18, 1878, archives of PAFA.

19. This makes all the more prophetic Jeffrey A. Cohen's stress on the Brimmer house as an early source for Furness. See his "Styles and Motives in the Architecture of Frank Furness," in *Frank Furness: The Complete Works*, 99–100.

20. Montgomery Schuyler, "The Works of the Late Richard M. Hunt," *Architectural Record* 5, no. 2 (October–December, 1895): 104. Schuyler suggested that Hunt's "staccato style" first announced itself in Boston in 1870, "and a very startling announcement it seemed."

Chapter 17 ■ Breakthrough at Bryn Mawr: Louis Kahn's Erdman Dormitory

1. *Louis I. Kahn: In the Realm of Architecture*, ed. David B. Brownlee and David G. De Long (New York: Rizzoli, 2001), 100–102.

2. Cornelia Meigs, *What Makes a College?* (New York: McMillan, 1956), 179ff.

3. Letter, Delanoy to McBride, October 24 [1959]; letter, Delanoy to McBride, September 28 [1959], Katharine McBride Papers, Bryn Mawr College. All subsequent correspondence, unless otherwise noted, is from the McBride Papers.

4. Letter, Robert Venturi to author, March 21, 1990.

5. Letter, Kahn to Venturi, April 13, 1960, Box LIK-9, Louis I. Kahn Collection, University of Pennsylvania and Pennsylvania Historic and Museum Commission (hereafter cited as Kahn Collection). Ironically, this is the earliest reference in Kahn's surviving papers to his work at Bryn Mawr.

6. C. Pardee Erdman to McBride, January 15, 1960.

7. "Plans for new residence hall," Katharine McBride Papers, 14A. Also see copy of cover letter, McBride to Kahn, May 24, 1960.

8. Letter, Kahn to McBride, May 31, 1960, "Bryn Mawr Dormitory," Box LIK-9, Kahn Collection.

9. The schematic room studies include 565.2 through 565.11, "Bryn Mawr Dormitory," Kahn Collection. The early idea sketches can only be

approximately dated by comparing them with the dated drawings beginning in November 1960. The earliest of these probably include Drawings
385.67 and 386.67 at the Metropolitan Museum of Art; and three drawings in the collection of Donnelley Erdman (numbers 1, 4, and 5).

10. Letter, Robert M. Cooke, Philadelphia Manufacturers' Mutual
Insurance Company, to Horace Smedley, Superintendent of Buildings,
August 29, 1960.

11. Several studies in Kahn's hand for the octagonal scheme are known:
two drawings in the collection of Donnelley Erdman (numbers 2 and 5) and
a now lost drawing reproduced as Figure 3 in Lynn Scholz, "Architecture
Alive on Campus," *Bryn Mawr Alumnae Bulletin* 47, no. 1 (Fall 1965): 2–9.

12. David Polk, interview with author, December 15, 1989. Polk was
in Kahn's office in 1960–61, 1962–63 and 1965–68.

13. Anne Tyng, interview with author, December 12, 1989. Tyng
enjoyed a good rapport with McBride, who had been dean when Tyng
attended Radcliffe.

14. Letter, William S. Huff to David B. Brownlee, David G. De Long,
et al [Michael J. Lewis], December 30, 1991. Huff recalls Kahn regaling
his office with comments made by McBride during a dinner "after Kahn's
first visit to Bryn Mawr." The timing seems off. Huff left Kahn's office in
June 1960, and so he could not be recalling the aftermath of the November presentation. But if McBride had said this earlier, why would Kahn
have submitted a design centered about a courtyard? My best guess is that
when Huff returned to the office in the summer of 1961, he heard about
McBride's dislike of courtyards and misremembered the timing.

15. No minutes for this first meeting survives. Those invited included
John Price, J. Edgar Rhoads, and Venturi's friend Phyllis Gordan, who
did not attend. See letters, McBride to Building Committee (Delanoy
and Gordan), May 25, 1961. Also see the memo to members of the building committee, dated November 11, 1960.

16. Drawings in the collection of Donnelley Erdman (numbers 11
and 12), dated March 20, 1961.

17. Polk interview. William Huff recalled that Kahn critiqued Tyng's
design "from time to time, in a manner he would have critted his university students—excepting that these crits often became exceedingly quar-
relsome."

18. Four undated plans in the Bryn Mawr College Archives are presumably the drawings from the April 1961 meeting, representing a transitional stage between the set from November 25, 1960 and that of May
23, 1961.

19. Letter, McBride to Delanoy, April 5, 1961. Kahn's submission at
this presentation has not been identified.

20. According to both Polk and Tyng, the idea of the L-shaped rooms in the May 23 plan were Polk's idea.

21. Letter, McBride to Eleanor Delanoy and Phyllis Gordan, May 25, 1961.

22. For example, a drawing in the Bryn Mawr College Archives dated June 21, 1961 shows Tyng reimagining her plan of November 1960, replacing two of its lobes with three interlocking diamonds to house the public spaces.

23. See the drawing dated October 1961, Bryn Mawr College Archives. Also see the undated drawing in the collection of Donnelley Erdman, previously cited (RP 1287).

24. This plan is reproduced and discussed in Alexandra Tyng, *Beginnings: Louis I. Kahn's Philosophy of Architecture* (New York: John Wiley & Sons, 1984), 44–46.

25. "Kahn Asserts Architects Duty is to make Institutions Great," *The College News* 47, no. 5 (October 25, 1961): 1.

26. Letter, C. Pardee Erdman to McBride, November 8, 1961.

27. Huff letter, December 30, 1991.

28. The earliest drawings for the three-diamond scheme are dated December 14, 1961 and provisionally catalogued as drawings B-61-71 and B-61-72, College Archives, Bryn Mawr College. The rendering of the foliage and the heavy overlay of explanatory pencil sketches both appear to be in Kahn's hand, suggesting that these are the drawings with which the architect first presented the three-diamond scheme to McBride.

29. Anne Tyng, interview with author, December 12, 1989; David Polk, interview with author, December 15, 1990.

30. Letter, McBride to C. Pardee Erdman, December 16, 1961.

31. Polk interview. By this point he and Tyng were assisted by David Rothstein, another recent addition to the office.

32. See the submission sets of drawings dated January 26 and April 6, 1962, College Archives, Bryn Mawr College. Duplicate submission sets of these (and of the following drawings) are also preserved in the Kahn collection, although the Bryn Mawr drawings are insightful for the pencil emendations and jottings made in the course of the job meetings.

33. Submission set of drawings, March 15, 1962; April 6, 1962.

34. Submission set of drawings, May 2, 1962. The final working drawings took even longer. Full sets of floor plans were not completed until May 21, 1963, while the section drawings and many construction details are dated January 10, 1964. Full sets survive in both the Kahn Collection and in the College Archives, Bryn Mawr College.

35. Letter, Kahn to McBride, May 10, 1962.

36. Memorandum from "Mrs. Marshall, Mr. Smedley, and Miss Howe," August 1, 1962. Horace Smedley was Bryn Mawr's superintendent of buildings.

37. Letter, Harlyn E. Thompson, a member of the committee, to McBride, June 11, 1963,

38. Nason & Cullen were the contractors. Bids were opened on March 29, 1963, and they were notified of their successful bid on May 7.

39. Letter, Kahn to Gertrude Ely, July, 1964, Kahn Collection.

Chapter 19 ■ Trashing the President's House

1. Edward Lawler, Jr., "The President's House in Philadelphia: The Rediscovery of a Lost Landmark," *Pennsylvania Magazine of History and Biography* 126, no. 1 (January 2002): 5–95.

2. Michael Coard, "The 'Black' Eye on George Washington's 'White' House," *Pennsylvania Magazine of History and Biography* 129, no. 4 (October 2005): 461–71.

Illustration Credits

Chapter 1 ■ William Penn's Modest Utopia

1.1 Thomas Holme, *Plan of Philadelphia*, 1682. Library Company of Philadelphia.

1.2 Peter Cooper, *The Southeast Prospect of the City of Philadelphia*, ca. 1720. Library Company of Philadelphia.

1.3 Nicholas Garrison and James Hulett, *A View of the House of Employment, Almshouse, Pennsylvania Hospital and Part of the City of Philadelphia*, ca. 1767. New York Public Library.

1.4 John Haviland, Plan of Eastern State Penitentiary. C. G. Childs, *A View and Description of the Eastern Penitentiary of Pennsylvania* (Philadelphia, 1830).

1.5 Samuel Sloan, Plans of School House, "Design XVII," *The Model Architect*, vol. 1 (Philadelphia: E. S. Jones & Co., 1852).

Chapter 2 ■ William Birch and the Culture of Architecture in Philadelphia

2.1 William Birch, "Bank of the United States, in Third Street," 1799.

2.2 William Birch, "Bank of Pennsylvania, South Second Street," 1800.

2.3 William Birch, "View in Third Street," ca. 1800.

2.4 Pierre Charles L'Enfant, "View of the Federal Edifice," engraving by Peter Lacour, *Massachusetts Magazine* (June 1789).

2.5 William Birch, "An Unfinished House, in Chestnut Street" [i.e. house of Robert Morris], from *The City of Philadelphia* (1800).

2.6 Joseph Bowes, "Plan and Elevation of the Jail at Philadelphia," *Philadelphia Monthly Magazine* 1, no. 2 (February 1798).

2.7 William Birch, "Arch Street, with the Second Presbyterian Church," 1799.

2.8 William Birch, "High Street, from Ninth Street," 1799.

2.9 Thomas Carstairs, "The Plan and Elevation of the South Buildings in Sansom Street," ca. 1800. Library Company of Philadelphia.

2.10 "Woodlands," William Hamilton estate, West Philadelphia. Photograph by Andrew Pinkham.

2.11 Plan of the Woodlands, redrawn from HABS measured drawing.

2.12 James Paine, Mansion House, Doncaster, England (1746–48), *The Mansion House and New Betting Room*, Doncaster (London, 1829).

2.13 Plan of Mansion House, Doncaster, from William Hamilton's signed copy of James Paine, *Plans, Elevations and Sections of the Mansion House of Doncaster*, 1751. Wagner Free Institute of Science.

2.14 William Birch, "South East Corner of Third, and Market Streets," 1799.

2.15 View, from left to right, of Congress Hall, State House, American Philosophical Society Hall, Hall of the Library Company of Philadelphia, and Carpenters' Hall. Anonymous engraving, *Columbian Magazine* (September 1790).

2.16 William Birch, "Philadelphia Bank," 1828.

Chapter 3 ■ The Author of Fairmount Park

3.1 Sidney & Adams, *Plan of Fairmount Park*, Philadelphia, 1859. Historical Society of Pennsylvania.

3.2 Andrew Palles. *Plan of Fairmount Park . . . with the Proposed Addition of the West Bank of the River Schuylkill*. Chromolithograph. Philadelphia: L. N. Rosenthal Lith., 1859. Library Company of Philadelphia.

Chapter 4 ■ "Facts and Things, Not Words and Signs": The Idea of Girard College

4.1 Robert Waln Israel, competition entry for Girard College, 1832. Courtesy of Girard College.

4.2 Somerville Stewart, competition entry for Girard College, 1832. Courtesy of Girard College.

4.3 John Skirving, competition entry for Girard College, 1832. Courtesy of Girard College.

4.4 George Strickland, competition entry for Girard College, 1832. Courtesy of Girard College.

4.5 Edward Shaw, competition entry for Girard College, 1832. Courtesy of Girard College.

4.6 Michel de Chaumer, competition entry for Girard College, 1832. Courtesy of Girard College.

4.7 William Rodrigue, "Perspective of the Girard Orphan College," August 1832. Courtesy of Girard College.

4.8 John Kutts, competition entry for Girard College, December 28, 1832. Courtesy of Girard College.

4.9 Higham & Wetherill, competition entry for Girard College, 1832. Courtesy of Girard College.

4.10 Town, Davis & Dakin, competition entry for Girard College, 1833. Courtesy of Girard College.

4.11 John Haviland, bird's eye perspective, competition entry for Girard College, December 31, 1832. Courtesy of Girard College.

4.12 Isaiah Rogers, competition entry for Girard College, 1832. Courtesy of Girard College.

4.13 William Strickland, Flank Elevation, first design for Girard College, 1832. Courtesy of Girard College.

4.14 William Strickland, Perspective of classroom, showing construction, 1832. Courtesy of Girard College.

4.15 Thomas U. Walter, first design for Girard College, 1832. Courtesy of the Athenaeum of Philadelphia.

4.16 William Strickland, revised design for Girard College, undated (probably early 1833). Courtesy of Girard College.

4.17 Thomas U. Walter, Girard College, 1835. Courtesy of the Athenaeum of Philadelphia.

Chapter 5 ■ The Strange Germanness of the Academy of Music

5.1 Philadelphia Academy of Music, 1855–57. Photograph by Andrew Pinkham.

5.2 John Notman, competition entry for the Academy of Music, 1854. Courtesy of the Athenaeum of Philadelphia.

5.3 Stephen Button, competition entry for the Academy of Music, 1854. Courtesy of the Historical Society of Pennsylvania.

5.4 Edwin Forrest Durang, competition entry for the Academy of Music, 1854. Courtesy of the Athenaeum of Philadelphia.

5.5 Collins & Autenrieth, competition entry for the Academy of Music, 1854. Courtesy of the University of Delaware.

5.6 Napoleon LeBrun and Gustav Runge, original competition entry for the Academy of Music, 1854. George B. Tatum, *Penn's Great Town* (Philadelphia, 1961).

5.7 LeBrun & Runge, second design for the Academy of Music, 1855 (in *Rundbogenstil,* or "round-arched style"). Courtesy of the Historical Society of Pennsylvania.

Chapter 6 ■ "Silent, Weird, Beautiful": The Making of Philadelphia City Hall

6.1 John McArthur, Jr. Philadelphia City Hall, 1874–1901. Photograph by Andrew Pinkham.

6.2 Samuel Sloan, project for City Hall, additions to Independence Hall, 1859. Library Company of Philadelphia.

6.3 John McArthur, Jr., project for City Hall on Center Square, Philadelphia, 1860. American Philosophical Society.

6.4 John McArthur, Jr. project for Courthouse on Center Square, Philadelphia, 1860. American Philosophical Society.

6.5 John McArthur, Jr., revised version of winning competition project, for Independence Square. *American Architect and Builders' Monthly* (March 1870).

6.6 Stereo photograph of model of City Hall, surrounding Independence Hall, December 1869. Library Company of Philadelphia.

6.7 John McArthur, Jr., Philadelphia City Hall, as revised for Penn Square. Historical Society of Pennsylvania.

6.8 Philadelphia City Hall, Details of Stone Work, North Entrance. *American Architect and Building News,* 1877.

6.9 James P. Kelly, *Alexander Milne Calder and Assistants at Work on Sculpture for City Hall, Philadelphia,* ca. 1890. Woodmere Art Museum.

6.10 Base of Tower, showing allegorical figures of the Four Continents. Photograph by Andrew Pinkham.

6.11 Plan of first floor, Philadelphia City Hall, 1880. Historical Society of Pennsylvania.

Chapter 7 ■ The Carpenter: Owen Biddle

7.1 Owen Biddle, Arch Street Meeting House, Philadelphia, 1803–5, 1810–11. Photograph by Andrew Pinkham.

7.2 Arch Street Meeting House, perspective, detail of presentation drawing, 1803. Athenaeum of Philadelphia.

7.3 "The Schuylkill Permanent Bridge," Castner Scrapbook Collection, vol. 6, p. 21 (Free Library of Philadelphia).

7.4 John Dorsey, "The Pennsylvania Academy of the Fine Arts," 1806. *The Port Folio Magazine,* June 1809.

7.5 Owen Biddle, design for three roof trusses. *The Young Carpenters' Assistant,* 1805, plate 24.

7.6 Owen Biddle, plan and elevation of a townhouse. *The Young Carpenters' Assistant*, plate 37.

7.7 Owen Biddle, plan and section of a townhouse. *The Young Carpenters' Assistant*, plate 38.

Chapter 8 ■ The Namesake: Peter Angelo Nicholson

8.1 *Athenaeum of Philadelphia*, drawn by John Notman; lithograph by Peter Angelo Nicholson, 1847; printed by Thomas S. Sinclair. Library Company of Philadelphia.

8.2 Theodore V. Wadskier, "A Villa in the Italian Style," *Sartain's Union Magazine of Literature and Art* 10, no. 6 (June 1852): 498.

Chapter 9 ■ The Impresario: Edwin Forrest Durang

9.1 *Edwin F. Durang*, Lorenzo Scattaglia. Athenaeum of Philadelphia.

9.2 Henry Lewis, New Orleans, from his Moving Panorama of the Mississippi, from *Das illustrirte Mississippithal* (1854–57).

9.3 Edwin F. Durang, National Guards Armory, Race Street, 1857. Historic American Buildings Survey (HABS).

9.4 National Guards Armory, during demolition, 1959. HABS.

9.5 Edwin F. Durang, "Church of St. Charles Borromeo," 1868–71. Philadelphia Archdiocesan Historical Research Center, Graphics Collection.

9.6 Edwin F. Durang, Church of the Nativity of the Blessed Virgin Mary, 1890. View of interior. Courtesy of Nativity BVM Roman Catholic Church, Port Richmond, Philadelphia.

9.7 "St. Mary Magdalen de Pazzi, Philadelphia," *Architectural Album of Edwin Forrest Durang & Son*, Philadelphia, ca. 1904.

9.8 "St. Joachim's Church, Frankford, Philadelphia," *Architectural Album of Edwin Forrest Durang & Son*.

9.9 Edwin F. Durang, south facade, Church of the Gesú, 1879–88. Photograph by Andrew Pinkham.

Chapter 10 ■ Incognito at Haverford: George Senneff

10.1 Alms House, Philadelphia. Lithograph by John Casper Wild, 1838. Courtesy of Yale University Art Gallery.

10.2 Founders Hall, Haverford College, 1832, drawn and engraved by Oscar A. Lawson.

10.3 Plan of Founders Hall, Haverford College, 1832.

10.4 Founders Hall, Haverford College. Photograph by Andrew Pinkham.

Chapter 11 ■ The Bibliophile: Henry A. Sims

11.1 Henry A. Sims, John McArthur, Jr., and Thomas U. Walter. Athenaeum of Philadelphia.

11.2 Henry A. Sims, Second Presbyterian Church, 21st and Walnut Streets, 1868–72; tower added by Frank Furness, 1900. Photograph by Andrew Pinkham.

11.3 Henry A. Sims and James P. Sims, Proposal for the Centennial Exhibition hall, 1873. Historical Society of Pennsylvania.

11.4 Girard Avenue Bridge in 1897, from *Philadelphia, Photographs Album*, British Library, HMNTS 010410.c.46.

11.5 Henry A. Sims and James P. Sims, Holy Trinity Chapel, 1874–75. Photograph by Andrew Pinkham.

11.6 Henry Hobson Richardson, Grace Church, Medford, Massachusetts, 1868. Architectural Archives, University of Pennsylvania.

11.7 Eugène Emmanuel Viollet-le-Duc, Duc de Morny Monument, Père Lachaise Cemetery, Paris, 1865–66. Architectural Archives, University of Pennsylvania.

11.8 Henry A. Sims, bookplate. University of British Columbia Library, Special Collections; BP MUR SL P S567.

Chapter 12 ■ "He was not a connoisseur": Willis Hale and the Widener Mansion

12.1 Willis G. Hale, Peter A. B. Widener House, Broad and Girard Streets, 1886–87 (rear gallery added 1892), demolished. Free Library of Philadelphia.

12.2 Willis G. Hale, Record Building, 1881–82, demolished. "Architectural Aberrations," *Architectural Record* 1 (January–March, 1892): 261–64.

12.3 Widener House, plan, drawn by Daniel McCoubrey. Courtesy Marianna Thomas.

12.4 Widener House, stair hall. Photograph by George E. Thomas.

12.5 Widener House, banquet hall. Photograph by George E. Thomas.

12.6 George Herzog, decorator, study for the picture gallery, Widener House, ca. 1892. Heinz Architectural Center, Carnegie Museum, Pittsburgh.

12.7 Keystone National Bank (later the Hale Building), Chestnut and Juniper Streets, 1887. *Architectural Record* 9 (1893): 207.

Chapter 13 ■ The Last Quaker: Robert Venturi

13.1 Robert Venturi. Architectural Archives, University of Pennsylvania.

Chapter 14 ■ Frank Furness at Thirty: The Armory of the First City Troop

14.1 and 14.2 Above is Fraser, Furness & Hewitt's original 1870 design for the facade of the First City Troop Armory, below the revised design of 1874. Collection First City Troop.

14.3 First City Troop, parade shed, 1863, demolished. Lithograph by James Queen (P. S. Duval, 1863). Collection First City Troop.

14.4 Furness & Hewitt, The Armory of the First City Troop, 1874, demolished. Collection First City Troop.

14.5 Fraser, Furness & Hewitt, Rodeph Shalom Synagogue, 1868–70. Library Company of Philadelphia.

Chapter 15 ■ Louis Kahn at Thirty: The Lenin Memorial in Leningrad

15.1 Louis I. Kahn, Proposal for a Lenin Memorial in Leningrad, 1932, photograph of a lost drawing. Architectural Archives, University of Pennsylvania.

15.2 Albert Kastner and Oscar Stonorov, Proposal for the Palace of the Soviets. *Architectural Forum* 56, no. 1 (March 1932): sup. A-4.

15.3 Michael J. DeAngelis, Lenin Memorial, 1932, photograph of a lost model. *Architectural Forum* 61, no. 6 (December 1934): sup. 35.

Chapter 16 ■ Frank Furness, Perpetual Motion, and "The Captain's Trousers"

16.1 Bloomfield H. Moore house, after alterations of 1895. *King's Views of Philadelphia* (New York, 1900).

16.2 Bloomfield Moore house, view from dining room into picture gallery. George William Sheldon, *Artistic Houses*, 1883.

16.3 Bloomfield Moore house, library. George William Sheldon, *Artistic Houses*, 1883.

16.4 Bloomfield Moore house, stair hall. George William Sheldon, *Artistic Houses*, 1883.

16.5 Richard M. Hunt, architect, Martin Brimmer House, Boston, 1869–70.

16.6 Furness & Hewitt, Rudulph Ellis House, Philadelphia, 1873. Photograph by Andrew Pinkham.

Chapter 17 ■ Breakthrough at Bryn Mawr: Louis Kahn's Erdman Dormitory

17.1 Louis I. Kahn, Erdman Hall, Bryn Mawr College. Architectural Archives of the University of Pennsylvania (AAUP).

17.2 Louis I. Kahn program study, probably summer 1960. AAUP.

17.3 Louis I. Kahn sketches, ca. May–November 1960. AAUP.

17.4 Anne Tyng, design for meeting of November 25, 1960. AAUP.

17.5 Anne Tyng, study model, winter 1960–61. AAUP.

17.6 Louis I. Kahn, project for Bryn Mawr dormitory, May 23, 1961. AAUP.

17.7 Anne Tyng, study model, May 23, 1961. AAUP.

17.8 Louis I. Kahn, project for Bryn Mawr dormitory, October 1961. AAUP.

17.9 Louis I. Kahn, project for Bryn Mawr dormitory, December 1961. AAUP.

17.10 Living Room, Erdman Dormitory, Bryn Mawr College. AAUP.

Chapter 18 ■ Gehry at the Philadelphia Museum of Art

18.1 Philadelphia Museum of Art. Photograph by Andrew Pinkham.

Chapter 19 ■ Trashing the President's House

19.1 Venturi Rauch, Franklin Court, Philadelphia, 1976. AAUP.

19.2 Kelly/Maiello Architects, President's House, Independence Mall. Photograph by Andrew Pinkham.

Chapter 20 ■ The "New" Barnes

20.1 Paul Cret, Barnes Foundation, Lower Merion, Pennsylvania, 1924–25. Athenaeum of Philadelphia.

20.2 Tod Williams Billie Tsien Architects, Barnes Foundation, Philadelphia. Photograph by Andrew Pinkham.

20.3 Tod Williams Billie Tsien Architects, Barnes Foundation. Photograph by Andrew Pinkham.

Chapter 21 ■ A Museum that Overcomes Its Correctness

21.1 Robert A. M. Stern Architects, Museum of the American Revolution, 2017. Photograph by Andrew Pinkham.

Chapter 22 ■ My Favorite Building: Pembroke, Bryn Mawr College

22.1 Cope & Stewardson, Pembroke Hall, Bryn Mawr College, 1892–94. Photograph by Andrew Pinkham.

Acknowledgments

23.1 Baader-Young–Schultze, Mayfair Elementary School, 1949; model as published in the *T-Square Journal*, 1950. Athenaeum of Philadelphia.

Original Publication Information

1. "Philadelphie, l'utopie modest de William Penn," in *De l'Esprit des villes: Nancy et l'Europe urbaine au siècle des Lumières 1720–1770* (Nancy: Musée des Beaux Arts, 2005), 295–97.
2. "William Birch and the Culture of Architecture in Philadelphia," *Studies in the History of Gardens & Designed Landscapes* 32, no. 1 (2012): 35–49.
3. "The First Design for Fairmount Park," *Pennsylvania Magazine of History and Biography* 130, no. 3 (July 2006): 283–97.
4. "The Architectural Competition for Girard College," in *Monument to Philanthropy: The Design and Building of Girard College, 1832–1848*, Bruce Laverty, Michael J. Lewis, and Michele Taillon Taylor, eds. (Philadelphia: Girard College, 1998), 24–48.
5. "The Architectural Competition for the Philadelphia Academy of Music," *Nineteenth Century* 16, no. 2 (Spring 1997): 3–10.
6. "'Silent, Weird, Beautiful': Philadelphia City Hall," *Nineteenth Century* 11, nos. 3 and 4 (1992): 13–21.
7. "Owen Biddle and the *Young Carpenter's Assistant*," in *American Architects and Their Books to 1848*, Kenneth Hafertepe and James F. O'Gorman, eds. (Amherst: University of Massachusetts Press, 2001), 149–63.
8. "A Nicholson in America," *Alexander Thomson Society Newsletter*, no. 33 (May 2003): 6–9, 17.
9. Previously unpublished.
10. Previously unpublished.
11. "The Architectural Library of Henry A. Sims," in *American Architects and Their Books, 1840–1915*, Kenneth Hafertepe and James F. O'Gorman, eds. (Amherst: University of Massachusetts Press, 2007), 173–93.
12. "*He was not a Connoisseur*: Peter Widener and his House," *Nineteenth Century* 12, nos. 3 and 4 (1993): 27–36.
13. "Robert Venturi, 1925–2018," *New Criterion* 37, no. 3 (November 2018): 78–80.

14. "Frank Furness at Thirty: The Armory of the First City Troop," *Nineteenth Century* 28, no. 2 (Fall 2008): 2–7.

15. "Louis I. Kahn's Lenin Memorial," *Journal of the Society of Architectural Historians* 69, no. 1 (March 2010): 7–11.

16. "Frank Furness, Perpetual Motion, and 'the Captain's Trousers'," *Nineteenth Century* 37, no. 1 (Spring 2017): 10–15.

17. "Eleanor Donnelley Erdman Hall," in *Louis I. Kahn: In the Realm of Architecture*, David B. Brownlee and David De Long, eds. (New York: Rizzoli, 1991), 352–57.

18. "Gehry in Philly," *New Criterion* 37, no. 6 (February 2019): 20–24.

19. "Trashing the President's House," *Commentary* 131, no. 4 (April 2011): 59–63.

20. "The 'New' Barnes," *New Criterion* 30, no. 10 (June 2012): 24–29.

21. "A Museum that Overcomes its Correctness," *Commentary* 144, no. 1 (July-August 2017): 39–42.

22. "My Favorite Building," *Chronicle of Higher Education* (25 March 2005).